Michael Baumgardt

Adobe Photoshop 5.5 Web Design

with ImageReady 2 and GoLive 4

Adobe Photoshop 5.5 Web Design
Michael Baumgardt

Copyright © 2000 Adobe Press
This Adobe Press book is published by Peachpit Press

For information on Adobe Press books, contact

Peachpit Press
1249 Eighth Street
Berkeley, CA 94710
800-283-9444
510-524-2178
510-524-2221 (fax)
http://www.peachpit.com

Peachpit Press is a division of Addison Wesley Longman

For the latest on Adobe Press books, go to http://www.adobe.com/adobepress

ISBN 0-201-70012-3
9 8 7 6 5 4 3 2 1

Printed and bound in the United States of America

Design by Mito Media, Inc.

FOR MY PARENTS

*You are the bows from which your children as living
arrows are sent forth. The archer sees the mark upon
the path of the infinite, and He bends you with His
might that His arrows may go swift and far.*

From Khalil Gibran, The Prophet.

Web design is currently, without a doubt, the most exciting and interesting field for designers. As in the mid-1980s, when desktop publishing was on the rise, designers are now faced with a field that is constantly changing, a field torn between exploring the possibilities of the medium on one hand, while at the same time trying to establish standards.

The way Web designers work today best reflects the changes going on in the field. In the beginning, many developed their sites directly in an HTML authoring tool simply because it resembled the familiar desktop publishing world, where everyone worked with a layout program. Also, browser limitations and lack of experience with HTML made it easier and safer for them to test their design in browsers before presenting them. But as Web designers became more HTML-savvy, most turned to Photoshop as their main design tool. Today most designers work entirely in Photoshop; it's only after the design is final that a Web site is sliced into its individual elements and brought back together with Go-Live. Adobe's strategic decision to include ImageReady with Photoshop means that this process will only become more common.

This book provides all the information that you need to create a professional Web site with these programs. From slicing to rollover buttons, from GIF animation to the Lossy command and optimizing a color table, all the new features of Photoshop 5.5 are explained. This book is not just a slightly updated version of a Photoshop 5.0 book, like many others on the market. I've tried to go beyond where other Web design books go and to answer some questions that never really have been answered before, questions I ran up against when learning these processes. For example:

- How does blurring affect the compression of JPEG and are there alternatives to Gaussian Blur?
- What are the options for really effective navigation tools?
- How does the LZW algorithm really work?
- How important are JPEG's 8 x 8-pixel compression blocks?
- What techniques are professional Web designers using?

This book also examines old and new tricks like how to save 75% in file size by using scaling, how to create multiple levels of transparency with GIFs, and how to custom-design a color table. Finally, the chapter on GoLive will show you how to use stationaries and components to recreate your design in GoLive easily and efficiently.

All in all, I believe that this book is one of the most comprehensive guides available for Web design with Photoshop. I hope you will find it useful and enjoyable. If you have any unanswered questions or if you just want to send me your comments, mail me at

MBaumgardt@mitomedia.com

How to Work Best with this Book

Part I, Basics: This book is divided in four parts. The first section focuses on the design aspects of Web design and are inteded for readers with no prior Web design experience. Anyone making the leap from Desktop Publishing to Web Design should read this.

Part II, Photoshop: The second part of this book features the essential Photoshop commands and techniques that are important for Web designers. It should help all Photoshop novices.

Part III, Optimizing Images: Compressing and optimizing the file size of images is one of the most important tasks in Web design and the third part in this books deals with this aspect. Many tests and studies on how to improve the file size and compression of an image have been done and these chapters offer new information even to pros.

Part IV, GoLive: The last part will show you how to bring the Photoshop design and elements into GoLive and make a fully functional Web Site. Even for those with prior GoLive experience, this guide will have some tips on how to set up your site in GoLive more efficiently.

The following people I want to thank for their help and support.

You'll find the Web sites and agencies mentioned in this book at the following URLs:

Jolene Woo, Jill Merlin, Grace Abbett

Adobe ● Mark Patton NetObjects

● Matt Cupal S-Vision ● Lori Iz-abelle, John Geyer Terran Interactive

● Bonnie Mitchell Casady Greene ●

Tim Nilson, Run Media New York, NY

● Christopher Stashuk Aristotle

Little Rock, Arkansas ● Debra

Boulanger, Nicholson NY New York

● Barbara Tempelton Studio Arche-type San Francisco, CA ● Mikko

Linnamaki HexMac Software Sys-tems Leinfelden ● Paul Ehrenreich

Blickpunkt Fotostudio Munich

Aristotle www.aristotle.net
www.amod.org
www.aristotle.net/july4th
www.arkansas.com
www.baldor.com
www.datsdigital.com
www.decc.org
www.geriatrics.uams.edu
www.vinosbrewpub.com

Razorfish www.razorfish.com
www.carnegiehall.org

Nicholson NY www.nny.com
www.viagra.com
www.sony.com/professional
www.ibm.com

N2K www.n2k.com
www.classicalinsites.com
www.musicblvd.com
www.jazzcentralstation.com
www.rocktropolis.com

Studio Archetype
www.studioarchetype.com

A very special thanks goes to the people at Peachpit Press. In particular Becky Morgan who did an incredible job editing this book, always coming up with great suggestions and feedback. Of all the editors that I have had the privilege to work with, you are the best. To Amy Changar who kept an eye on the design, supporting me big time in making this book look as good as possible. And last but not least, to Nancy Ruenzel who had the vi-sion to make it all happen in the first place. Also thanks to Irv Kanode, my tech reviewer at Adobe, for his patience, persistence, and expertise.

Thanks to ...

Michael Adolphs; Florian Allgayer; Florian Anwander; Sabine & Christopher Bach; Friedericke Baumgardt; Heike Baumgardt; Hermann and Renate Baumgardt, my parents, to whom I owe everything; Annette Baumgardt-Thormälen; Maribel Becker; Nina Bergengruen; Marion & Reimund Bienefeld-Zimanovsky; Karen Bihari; Tim & Jenn Bruhns; Ulrike Brüser; Claudia Brütting; Hajo Carl, my long time buddy who I want to thank for his help on this book; Angela Carpenter; Mark Dolin; Albert Dommer; Tim Dorcey; Ronan Dunlop; Paul Ehrenreich, what would I do without your photos?; Lisa Faragallah; Cordula Fischer; Andreas Florek; Susanne Flörsch; Sabine Frischmuth; Anja Gestring; George Geyer; Isabelle Girard and Allonzo; Alejandro and Christina Gjutierrez Viguera; Fritz Goßner; Christine Graf; Harry Greißinger; Silvia & Armin Günther; Tammi Haas, my sunshine; Juliet Hanlon; Mirko & Agniescka Hauck; Hubert Henle; Carol & Terry Hoare; Ernst & Kathie Hofacker; Peter Hoffmann; Larry Jackson; Nina Jakisch; Wolfgang Keller; Christopher LaRiche; Theresa Lee; Katja Lerch and Günther; Roger Libesch; Anja Maurus-Lang; Laurie Anne McGowan; Shari Mitchel; Julia Moreva; Meagan Murphy; Tom Nakat; Sabine & Joseph Plenk; Uschi Reible; Mark Rodgers; Manfred Rürup; Stephen Salters; Wieland Samolak; Andreas Schätzl; Andreas & Verena Schiebl; Anja Schneider-Beck; Michael Seipel; Gia Stemmer; Lisa Tran; Katja Verdier; Lars Wagner; Ilona & Vera Waldmann; Corinne Werner; Udo Weyers; Ulli Wiedenhorn; Klaus Wittig; and last, not least, my great friend Steve Zierer.

The first edition of this book was written in June to October 98 in New York, Munich, Verona and Istanbul; this translated and updated version in New York and Port Chester (July to November 99).

TABLE OF CONTENTS

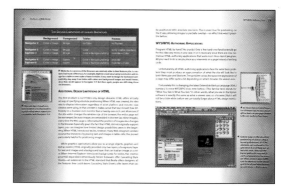

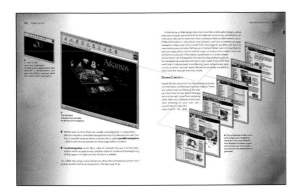

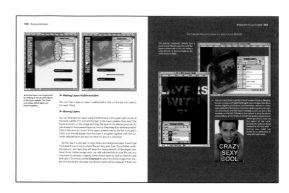

DESIGNING WEB ELEMENTS

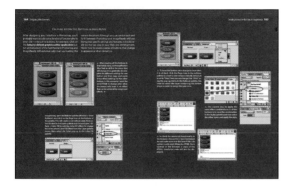

GIF ANIMATION

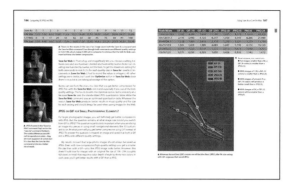

COMPARING GIF, JPEG AND PNG

GIF

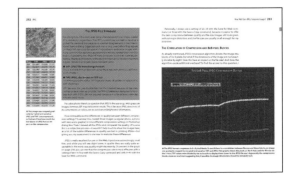

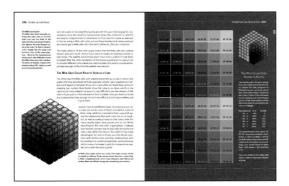

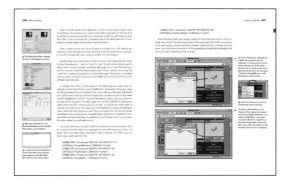

INDEX

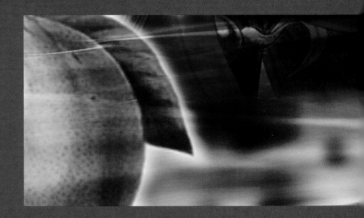

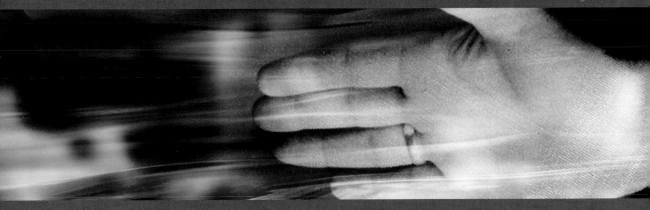

Illustration: Michael Baumgardt

THE BASICS OF WEB DESIGN

From Desktop Publishing to World Wide Web: The Basics of Web Design

Just as California has Silicon Valley, Manhattan has Silicon Alley—a stretch of Broadway that runs from 28th Street in midtown to Spring Street in Soho. The Alley is home to a huge number of Internet and WWW companies. In fact, New York has experienced a boom from the Internet like no other city. Jason McCabe Calacanis, editor of the magazine Silicon Alley Reporter, considers the city to be the new media capital: "In a short time," he notes, "Silicon Alley has grown from being almost nonexistent to employing 100,000 people and 5,000 companies. Though Silicon Alley is still in its infancy, it has already become the center of the Internet media world."

That success is partly based on the broad variety of ideas and trends in advertising, music, content, software and services that are available in this city. New York is the ideal ecosystem for an Internet company because all the world leaders of the entertainment industry are represented here: Viacom, Time Warner, Sony, NBC, CBS, ABC, NBA, Columbia Records, and RCA Records. Most Northern California agencies have to open New York branches because this is where the big money is made. For example, the Web agency Organic had eighty employees in San Francisco when it started its New York subsidiary with a staff of four. In only four months, the New York office had grown to thirty-five employees; currently, Organic New York employs a bigger staff than the home office in San Francisco.

This demonstrates the great potential for design opportunities on the Internet and the World Wide Web. If you have design experience it is only natural to enter the field of Web design as well. But while in 1996, Web design skills could be mastered in a week, the field is constantly growing in complexity—and with that process comes more and more specialization. This book focuses on three important aspects of Web design: design itself, graphic compression, and conversion into HTML using Adobe GoLive.

Although I will give you some basic information on HTML, it's not the book's prime focus. Still, some basic HTML knowledge can be helpful, so this chapter will provide you with important information on the limitations of HTML in Web design.

A BRIEF HISTORY OF THE WEB

Don't worry, this is not the beginning of a long-winded historical essay. Still, I would like to cover a little of the Web's past because many people use the terms "Internet" and "World Wide Web" without fully understanding what they stand for.

"Internet" describes the actual data highway, i.e. the fiber-optic cables and other physical links that connect Internet servers around the world. The Pentagon created this infrastructure more than twenty years ago, with the intention of decentralizing its computer communication system so an enemy would be unable to destroy the entire defense system with a single missile strike.

To achieve this, the Internet was designed with a unique capability: rather than following a pre-determined path, data is split into small packets, each carrying information about sender and receiver that allows it to find its own way through the system. The packets actually pick the best route to their destination via the Internet servers. Because universities also had access to it, scientists and students were the earliest non-military users of the Internet. But in those early days Internet operations were very complicated even for professionals. Finding specific information could give even computer specialists a headache. Things changed when the World Wide Web was developed.

In 1989, Tim Berners-Lee and Robert Cailliau created a special communication system. It allowed all the researchers and scientists at the Swiss Research Center CERN to access data on the CERN computer from anywhere in the world. Part of this development was HTML, HyperText Markup Language. This relatively simple computer language makes it possible to place structural "tags" in the text, which, for example, tell the browser to display text as a header or a listing. To cut a long story short, the boom of the Web went hand in hand with the success of Mozilla, a browser developed by Marc Andreessen, founder of Netscape. The company's Navigator software was a gigantic success. And even though many browsers were in use in the early days, currently only two browsers—Internet Explorer from Microsoft, and Navigator/Communicator from Netscape—rule the market.

HTML BASICS

HTML is the language that allows information on the Web to be displayed correctly in a browser. One big advantage of this language is that since it's

SOME USEFUL SITES FOR WEB DESIGNERS

Do you work freelance, or run your own company? Do you want to know what's happening in Silicon Alley, the heart of the Internet Industry? Or do you just want to find out more about HTML or JavaScript? You may find the following online sources helpful:

wwwac.org
The homepage of the WWW Artists' Consortium (WWWAC) is the best way to contact Web designers, programmers and Internet fans in New York. WWWAC holds a monthly meeting, and you can find special interest groups (SIGs) that focus on a variety of topics like interface design and database integration.

www.nynma.org
The New York New Media Association also hosts meetings and provides job postings on its Web site. If you live in New York and are looking for a job, this is a great place to find it.

www.siliconalleyreporter.com
If you want to stay on top of the latest trends in the New York City Internet scene, and happen to be in the City, you can pick up a copy of the Silicon Alley Reporter; out-of-towners can get a subscription. Also, every Friday, Jason McCabe Calacanis hosts an Internet radio show you can tune into on the Pseudo online network (www.pseudo.com).

www.searchenginewatch.com
This site provides really excellent information that will help you to optimize your site to get good results in a search engine.

www.webposition.com
WebPositionGold is a software to optimize your site for better ratings. It generates HTML pages designed to rank near the top of search results, and it submits your pages to the major search engines automatically. I use it myself because it does excellent reports for the position of a Web site in each search engine.

virtual-stampede.com
One of the first programs available to do batch registrations for Web sites, Spider Software has now been rewritten and released as NetSubmitter Professional. A great (and affordable) tool to register your site with the search engines. I highly recommend it.

ftp://ftp.cdrom.com/pub/perl/ CPAN/CPAN.html
This is an excellent archive of PERL scripts. It has no fancy interface but it is really comprehensive.

www.w3.org
The World Wide Web Consortium is the organization that develops and approves new HTML versions. Check it out whenever there is an abreviation that you don't know; most likely it is something the W3C is currently working on.

developer.netscape.com
Not quite sure which HTML tag was supported in which Netscape browser? This site will have all the information for you. If you want to learn more about HTML, this is a particularly great source.

msdn.microsoft.com/workshop/ default.asp
The Microsoft Developer Network is online source to find out about the HTML implementation in Explorer. It also has a very good introduction to HTML.

www.cauce.org
Coalition Against Unsolicited Commercial Email (CAUCE) wants to ban spam. Check it out to get information on the latest laws.

written in ASCII characters, it works on multiple platforms. (ASCII stands for "American Standard Code for Information Interchange, "and has been a standard in the computer field for many years.) This means that a Web page created on an IBM-compatible computer can be read and interpreted by a browser running on another platform, such as a Macintosh.

Incidentally, it is quite easy to see the HTML source code that defines a Web page in your browser. If you choose Source from the View menu in Explorer or Netscape, a new window will open and display the HTML code. The code will look something like this:

<B>This is bold text.</B>.

An HTML tag generally consists of a beginning and end tag, both of which are placed in angle brackets. The end tag sports a slash ("/"). In the example above, the text between the two tags will be displayed in bold in the browser.

Despite the long list of HTML tags for headers, paragraphs, justification, and so on, the language is relatively easy to learn, and a Web page can be created by writing HTML code in an ordinary text editor. In the beginning, this is exactly how most HTML authors worked, since the WYSIWYG HTML editors available at the time generally produced incorrect HTML code. These days, you can choose from many WYSIWYG HTML authoring applications that work quite reliably.

```
HTML: www.nny.com/nny/index2.htm
        <!--MORE FILLER-->
        <TD WIDTH="54" HEIGHT="62" VALIGN="BOTTOM"><IMG SRC="Art/1x1.gif" WIDTH="54" HEIGHT="62" BORDER
</TR>
</TABLE>

<!--**********************************************************-->
<!--LINES AND TITLES TABLE-->
<TABLE BORDER="0" CELLPADDING="0" CELLSPACING="0" WIDTH="525">
<TR>
        <!--GREY BAR-->
        <TD WIDTH="1" HEIGHT="51" VALIGN="BOTTOM"><IMG SRC="Art/greybar.GIF" WIDTH="1" HEIGHT="14" BORD

        <!--GREEN LINE-->
        <TD HEIGHT="51" VALIGN="TOP"><A HREF="about_us_intro.htm"><IMG SRC="Art/linea.GIF" WIDTH="131"

        <!--BLUE LINE-->
        <TD HEIGHT="51" VALIGN="TOP"><A HREF="talents_intro.htm"><IMG SRC="Art/lineb.GIF" WIDTH="130" HI

        <!--PURPLE LINE-->
        <TD HEIGHT="51" VALIGN="TOP"><A HREF="clients_intro.htm"><IMG SRC="Art/linec.GIF" WIDTH="131" HI

        <!--RED LINE-->
        <TD HEIGHT="51" VALIGN="TOP"><A HREF="contact_us_intro.htm"><IMG SRC="Art/lined.GIF" WIDTH="131

        <!--GREY BAR-->
        <TD WIDTH="1" HEIGHT="51" VALIGN="BOTTOM"><IMG SRC="Art/greybar.GIF" WIDTH="1" HEIGHT="14" BORD
</TR>
</TABLE>

<!--**********************************************************-->
<!--NICHOLSON NY TABLE-->
<TABLE BORDER="0" CELLPADDING="0" CELLSPACING="0" WIDTH="525" HEIGHT="125">
```

▲ **The HTML code of a Web page can easily be viewed in a Web browser: in Internet Explorer use View > Source.**

The HTML Source Code of a Page

HTML documents are ASCII files, and can therefore be opened and edited in any word processor. HTML tags are identified by angled brackets. Every HMTL document needs to contain at least <HTML>, <HEAD> and <BODY> tags. Tags need to be paired; a tag that opens a block of text (<HEAD>, for instance) needs a paired tag to close that block of text (</HEAD>). Closing tags are identical to opening tags except for the "/" character.

<HTML>:This tag identifies the document as a Web page.

<TITLE>: The TITLE tag identifies the text that will be seen as a headline in the browser window.

<BODY BGCOLOR="#ffffff">: The BODY container holds all the text and graphics of the Web page between the start tag and the end tag. A tag often has several attributes. In this example, BGCOLOR defines the background color of the browser window.

<P><CENTER>: This is a paragraph tag. The embedded CENTER tag means that the paragraph is centered.

<MAP NAME="maintop">: MAPs are picture files, parts of which are defined as hot links. You can click a hot link to connect to another Web page.

<IMG SRC="images/maintop.gif" WIDTH="301" HEIGHT="27">: The IMG tag places a picture on the Web page. The attributes WIDTH and HEIGHT tell the browser the size of the picture. This way, text and layout can be displayed properly before the image elements finish downloading.

```html
<HTML>
    <HEAD>
        <META NAME="GENERATOR" CONTENT="Adobe PageMill ">
        <TITLE>Eye2Eye Mainpage</TITLE>
    </HEAD>
<BODY BGCOLOR="#ffffff" LINK="#ff0000" ALINK="#0017ff">
<P><CENTER>
    <MAP NAME="maintop">
        <AREA SHAPE="rect" COORDS="211,2,300,26"
          HREF="press/indpress.html">
        <AREA SHAPE="rect" COORDS="148,0,205,25"
          HREF="bio/bioindex.html">
        <AREA SHAPE="rect" COORDS="69,1,144,25"
          HREF="tour/tourindx.html">
        <AREA SHAPE="rect" COORDS="2,1,61,27" HREF="cd/cds.html">
    </MAP>
    <IMG SRC="images/maintop.gif" WIDTH="301" HEIGHT="27"
    ALIGN="BOTTOM"
    NATURALSIZEFLAG="3" USEMAP="#maintop" ISMAP BORDER="0">
</CENTER></P>


<P><CENTER>
    <IMG SRC="images/e2e_main.gif" WIDTH="301" HEIGHT="211"
    ALIGN=„BOTTOM" NATURALSIZEFLAG="3">
</CENTER></P>

<P><CENTER>
    <MAP NAME="mainbttm">
    <AREA SHAPE="rect" COORDS="94,3,167,26" HREF="exit.html">
    <AREA SHAPE="rect" COORDS="12,2,68,26" HREF="map.html">
    </MAP>
    <IMG SRC="images/mainbttm.gif" WIDTH="176" HEIGHT="27"
```

```
    ALIGN="BOTTOM" NATURALSIZEFLAG="3" USEMAP="#mainbttm"
    ISMAP BORDER="0">
</CENTER></P>


<PRE><CENTER>Click on CDs to listen to check out Eye2Eyes two
available records or ... To get on our mailing list, please send your address
and telephone number to
<A HREF="mailto:email@erols.com">email@erols.com</A>
</PRE>


<H6><CENTER>
    <A HREF="cd/cds.html">CDs</A> | <A
    HREF="tour/tourindx.html">TOUR</A> | <A
    HREF="bio/bioindex.html">BIO</A> | <A
    HREF="press/indpress.html">PRESS</A><BR>
    <A HREF="map.html" TARGET="_top">MAP</A> | <A
    HREF="exit.html">EXIT</A>
</CENTER></H6>


</BODY>
</HTML>
```

<A HREF="mailto: email@erols.com">:** A link is a connection to another Web page. It is identified by an "A." Links are not restricted to the addresses of other pages or files; in this example the link creates an email and sends it to the specified address.

<H6>:** There are six different headline sizes and categories, numbered H1 through H6. H6 is the smallest headline size, and is often smaller than body text. The most common use of H6 headlines is for text links at the bottom of the page.

◄ This is the page generated by this particular HTML code.

DESIGNER HTML TRICKS
To solve the problem of absolute positioning, many designers used tricks and techniques as workarounds. For example, invisible tables were used to bring together the different pieces of a larger image previously sliced in Photoshop. This technique was very useful, especially if you wanted to have some parts of the image be interactive. Another trick was to use invisible images to push certain elements into position. While those tricks still will be around for quite some time to create backward–compatible Web sites, the new XML standard will hopefully be the final solution and give designers everything they've always wanted. XML, which stands for Extensible Markup Language, is something you should become familiar with as it's destined to be essential for Web designers.

There are several reasons that a book concerning Web graphics and images needs to discuss HTML. On the one hand, it is important to know the limitations and possibilities of HTML when designing a Web page. On the other hand, many design solutions are based on special HTML features. So there is (almost) no way around having some basic knowledge of HTML.

WHY STRUCTURAL CODING IS UNSUITABLE FOR DESIGN

HTML is primarily a structural code. While there are some format tags, the main idea of HTML involves defining structures. Let's take a header, for example: in HTML it is embedded between two "H" tags. Accordingly, the browser is told only that the text is a header, but not which font to use or how large the characters should be. Each browser sets those parameters independently, based on user preferences. Therefore the same header may be displayed in sixteen-point Arial in one browser and fourteen-point Times in another. Obviously, this is a nightmare for designers, and many designers sidestep it altogether by avoiding the use of structural tags (like "H") in favor of the FONT tag with the SIZE attribute:

<font size="2" face="Arial,Helvetica">This is text in size 2</font>

I don't recommend avoiding structural tags altogether, since doing so sacrifices one of the main advantages of HTML—its ability to mark content. For-

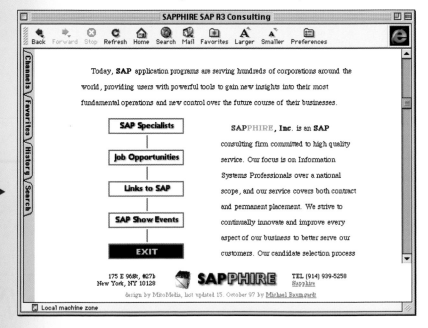

A web site can look good in one browser but be the worst nightmare in another. This could be due to incompatibilities of the HTML implementation in the browser or simply because the visitor's preferences override the settings of the Web site. In that case the color and size of links or text is beyond your control.

◀ This is the same page in Navigator; if the user has changed the browser preferences to override, all the formatting of your fonts might be lost and the design can look very different than what you intended.

tunately, there are other ways to deal with the font issue. HTML has been steadily improved, and currently allows you to set the definition for structural tags via Cascading Style Sheets (CSS). You can even transmit a chosen font to the browser using Dynamic Fonts. This technology was created to solve a basic problem: every font you want to display in your Web site must be installed on your viewers' computer. Since there's no guarantee of this except for basic faces like Helvetica, Times, and Arial, Dynamic Fonts send postscript information about the chosen fonts along with the HTML file. For licensing and legal reasons, fonts can't be transferred in their entirety. Therefore, Dynamic Fonts embeds only the characters that are actually used in your design—which make it less likely that someone can capture and convert them to a useful (and free) PostScript font. But don't get too excited about Dynamic Fonts; they have their own set of problems. For one thing, it's not easy to get them to work properly. For another, older browsers can't handle Dynamic Fonts at all, and will display text in the standard font.

If you want to experiment with Dynamic Fonts, check out HexMac typograph (see page 131). A demo version is available at HexMac's Web site (www.hexmac.com), but before you download it make sure your ISP server supports this MIME-Type (pfr).

THE DESIGN LIMITATIONS OF EARLIER BROWSERS				
	Background	**Foreground**	**Tables**	**Frames**
Navigator 2	Color + Image	Image	no Color	no Frames
Navigator 3	Color + Image	Image	Color	(only visible Borders)
Explorer 3	Color + Image	Image	Color + Background Img	invisible + Color
Navigator 4	Color + Image	Layers	Color + Background Img	invisible
Explorer 4	Color + Image	Layers	Color + Background Img	invisible + Color

▲ This Web site is based on a table in which a background image is loaded, which makes it incompatible with Navigator 3.0.

▲ While the 4.x versions of the Browsers are relatively alike in their features, the 3.x versions had many differences. For example, Explorer could set a background color and image for a table or even make a frame invisible. If you want to design for backward compatibility, stay away from tables with colors and background images and avoid frames, since they would appear in Navigator 3.0. But then again, not many people are still using those old browsers.

ADDITIONAL DESIGN LIMITATIONS OF HTML

The font problem is not HTML's only design obstacle. HTML offers virtually no way of specifying absolute positioning. When HTML was created, the idea was to display information regardless of what platform and monitor size viewers were using. In that context it makes sense that text should flow differently on a fourteen-inch monitor than a twenty-one-inch unit. Moreover, if the site visitor changes the window size of the browser, the entire page will be rearranged. Because images are embedded in the text (as inline images), every time the Web page is reformatted the position of images also changes in the browser. Especially given the fact that HTML did not originally support layers, you can imagine how limited design possibilities were in the beginning. When HTML introduced tables, however, many Web designers worked around the limitations by placing text and images in table cells; this proved particularly helpful for positioning images.

While graphics applications allow you to arrange objects, graphics and text as needed, HTML originally provided only two layers, a foreground layer for text and images and a background layer that could load an image or a color. When Internet Explorer introduced backgrounds for tables, the creative potential expanded tremendously. Newer browsers offer Cascading Style Sheets—an extension to the HTML standard that finally offers designers all the features they could desire. Cascading Style Sheets offer layers that can be positioned with absolute precision. This is even true for positioning on the Z-axis, allowing images to partially overlap—an effect that wasn't possible before.

WYSIWYG AUTHORING APPLICATIONS

Program HTML by hand? No thanks! Only a few hard-core fanatics would go for this idea any more. In any case, it isn't necessary since there are now numerous HTML-authoring applications that work much like a layout program. All you need to do is simply place your elements on a page instead of writing code.

Unfortunately, all HTML-authoring applications face the same basic problem: they must produce an approximation of what the site will look like in both Netscape and Explorer. The problem arises because the appearance of a page may differ quite a bit depending on which browser the viewer uses.

Fortunately this is changing; the latest Extensible Markup Language (XML) standard is more WYSIWYG than ever before. (This familiar term stands for "What You See Is What You Get." In other words, what you see in the layout software is exactly the same as what a viewer sees on a browser.) But it will still be a little while before we can totally forget about HTML design restrictions.

▲ In Adobe GoLive's Link Inspector you can see all the items on your page. Broken Links can easily be fixed here.

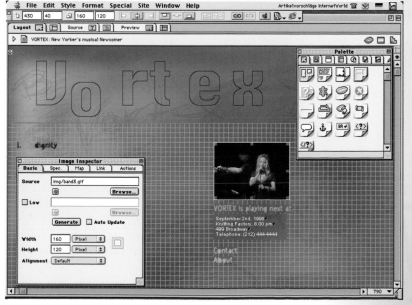

◄ GoLive supports the (absolute) positioning of objects using a layout grid element. All HTML elements can be placed in this grid, which is essentially just an invisible table. Although the layout grid works very well, it can't compensate for the browser offset, which makes it difficult for elements on the layout grid to be aligned with the background image in the browser.

▲ GoLive offers a Preview mode for checking your work. This preview is pretty close to what the page will look like in the browser, but you will still need to double check.

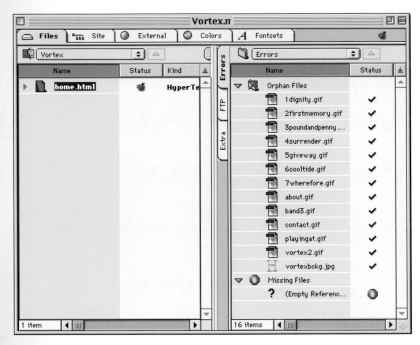

▲ GoLive has a single window for managing the whole site. From files to page hierarchy to colors, everything can be maintained in one place.

Authoring tools always have the challenge of keeping up with the continuously evolving HTML standard. Thus, the two browsers often support many more features than authoring applications can provide. Adobe GoLive (originally developed by the German software company GoLive with the name CyberStudio) addresses this problem by storing the HTML implementation in a database known as the Web Database. This allows programmers and designers to incorporate new tags even before a new version of GoLive is available.

It's no wonder that this program has been highly praised. In fact, GoLive has become the tool of choice for even hard-core HTML programmers, since it has one of the best (if not *the* best) HTML code editors. And while it may not be love at first sight for everyone, the quality of GoLive's HTML code is really remarkable. Even pages with interactivity and JavaScript work flawlessly in both browsers. Manual modifications to the HTML code, which may still be required, are no problem for GoLive's HTML editor. And GoLive offers Dynamic HTML, Cascading Style Sheets, and support for ActiveX and WebObjects. GoLive even offers many JavaScript functions as modules that can be inserted as easily as dragging them onto the page.

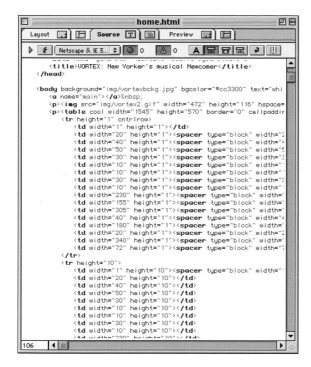

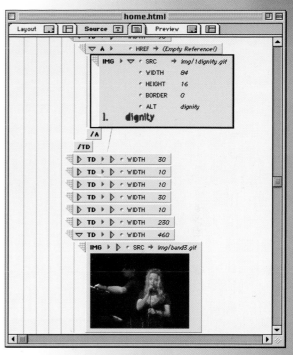

Adobe offers another HTML-authoring tool called PageMill (for Mac or Windows), which is more an entry-level application rather than a full-fledged WYSIWYG editor. I can only recommend it to designers who are looking to save some money. Even so, it's a better solution than assembling your page with a text editor. One advantage of the program is its interface, which is logically structured and easily learned. If all you care about is creating a simple home page, PageMill may be enough for you.

▲ GoLive offers two excellent HTML code editors, which is probably one of the reasons why it's so popular with professional Web designers.

PHOTOS AND GRAPHICS ON THE INTERNET

If you're making the leap from the desktop publishing field, you're probably accustomed to using graphic formats like TIFF or EPS. On the Web, these formats are largely irrelevant. JPEG, GIF, and PNG prevail here. (By the way, these abbreviations are pronounced jay-peg, jiff and ping.) These image formats are popular on the Web because they employ effective compression algorithms that can compress graphics into relatively small files. As you probably know, a big problem with the Web is that most users own slow modems. Even at 4.2K/sec or 7K/sec, large data transmissions are out of the question, given the amount of memory images use. That makes file compression a significant issue.

For you as a designer, this means that if you want to avoid painfully slow downloads for visitors to your Web site, 40-60K of graphics should be the maximum amount of "new" data transferred. The concept of new data is based on the fact that browsers store downloaded text and images in a local cache on the user's hard drive; stored data can be recalled from the cache much faster than having to download it again from the Web.

This means when you develop the design concept for your Web site it's a good idea to use the same image elements as often as possible over all your pages. For example, if you use the company logo on the first page, the following pages can use the logo "for free," since it's already in the cache. As mentioned above, the amount of new data shouldn't exceed 60K. Letting the browser cache images from a previous page allows you add new graphics to each new page with minimal additional download time. For instance, you can use an introduction page with text to load pictures for the next page in the background. This can be done with JavaScript, which is the more advanced method, or simply by placing the image on the text page and scaling it down to 1 pixel so it becomes virtually invisible.

While in the print world colors are combined from the four process colors CMYK (Cyan, Magenta, Yellow and Black), colors on the monitor are based on the RGB color model (Red, Green and Blue). It is important to convert an image into the right color mode before saving for the Web.

But let's go back to the different image formats. JPEG, GIF and PNG all have their advantages and drawbacks, which mainly pertain to their different compression algorithms. Generally, JPEG is used for photographs while GIF is employed for graphics with solid colored areas. The other difference is that GIF is limited to 256 colors, while JPEG can store up to 16 million colors—and compresses substantially better. However, JPEG is not ideal for text or graphics, since the compression algorithm introduces a blurring effect. Text in a picture will get fuzzy and lose contrast, making it hard to read.

Each image format is explained in detail in its own chapter, but to help you get started designing right away, here's a brief explanation of the differences.

➤ JPEG—Joint Photographic Experts Group

The blurring effect I mentioned above results from JPEG's block-by-block compression. Within each block, differences in brightness are retained, but subtle color changes will be lost. You can fool the eye at relatively low compression levels, but as compression increases the effect will become more visible. Nevertheless, it is amazing how good JPEG quality is even at maximum compression. Compression factors range from 10:1 to 100:1, meaning that at the highest compression rate, a 1MB image can be compressed into a 10K file. That is ideal for the Web, but because JPEG compression is not lossless, every time you save the picture as a JPEG you lose some quality. It's a good idea, therefore, to always keep the original.

➤ GIF—Graphical Interchange Format

The GIF compression algorithm operates by pattern recognition: if several adjacent pixels have the same color, GIF can compress them. Here's a comparative example: If a block of text contained the word "yellow" twenty times, it could be shortened significantly by writing "20xYellow." Obviously this approach can be used with repetitive color combinations too; each kind of pat-

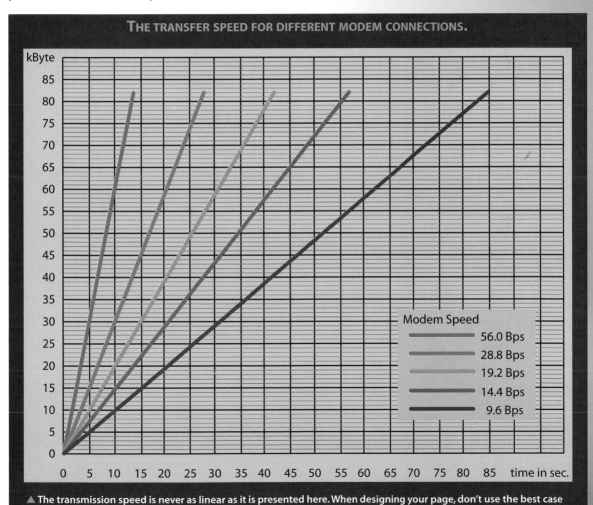

▲ The transmission speed is never as linear as it is presented here. When designing your page, don't use the best case scenario; even if the visitor has a 56 kBaud modem, it is more likely that he ends up with only 50 kBaud or less.

tern makes it easier to compress the image. Compared to JPEG, the GIF compression algorithm works line by line and not block by block.

GIF is not as successful as JPEG when it comes to compressing photographs, but it compresses large areas of flat color perfectly. Although GIF's compression factor with photographs is around 4:1, it has the advantage of lossless compressing—aside from reducing color information to 256 colors through indexing. In this case, lossless means that after decompression the picture looks exactly the same as it did before, and that repeated saves don't degrade the image like a JPEG does. GIF has two more special (and handy) features: it supports transparency and animations.

In order to produce transparency, one color is defined as "Chroma Key Color" during storage. The browser then disables this color and replaces it with the background—the clipping paths of the Web, so to speak. This feature, along with GIF's capability for animation, is one reason for its huge popularity. With animation, foreground images are layered over background images, and switching them creates the impression of movement. You can even set the duration of each image and define whether the animation should run once or in a continuous loop. You can learn more about this technique in the GIF Animation chapter on page 170.

➤ PNG—Portable Network Graphic Format

PNG, a response to the restrictions of JPEG and GIF, is probably the next step in image formats for the Web. PNG combines the best of both worlds: lossless compression with up to 16 million colors, and 256 levels of transparency, which also makes semi-transparent color areas possible. This is particularly important for creating images with transparent backgrounds, because it lets the edges blend smoothly with the browser background. GIFs can sometimes be a pain here—you may end up with a clear edge that appears jagged, or anti-aliased edges that look smooth but can cause a halo effect in front of the wrong background. No matter how you look at it, being limited to only one transparency level can cause difficulties—and PNG solves them in one stroke. At least theoretically.

PNG is not as well-supported by browsers as it should be, which means you probably won't be working with it for quite some time. That's really a shame, since PNG also sports a great Gamma correction function that guarantees images will be equally bright on all platforms. Since Windows monitors are inherently darker than Macintosh monitors, Web sites created on a Mac look too dark when viewed on a Windows browser; and as you would ex-

HOW DO BROWSERS COMPENSATE FOR MISSING COLORS?

Dithering describes a technique that mingles two main colors together to create the optical illusion of an intermediate color. This is basically the same procedure as printing with process colors; all the colors of the spectrum can be created by mixing different amounts (or dot sizes) of the four basic colors (cyan, magenta, yellow, black-or CMYK). The dots are printed at different angles to one another, and are so small they can hardly be discerned with the naked eye.

Browsers use a similar process—if a called-for color is outside the range of the available color depth, the browser tries to create that color by mixing colors that

are available. Two techniques are used—pattern or diffusion dithering. With pattern dithering, the intermediate color is created by using a regular pattern of pixels, which can produce unpleasing, unaesthetic effects. The second technique, diffusion dithering, simulates the intermediate color by placing pixels in a random pattern. Of course this only appears to be random; it is actually based on a mathematical model that can differ from one application to another.

If an application doesn't simulate a color by dithering, it only quantizes the color, which means it is rounded to the next available color and the color shifts become even more apparent. So 99% red, for instance, becomes 100%, while 84% red becomes 80%.

The original image was saved as a GIF with an adaptive 256-color palette and as a JPEG. Both images were then viewed in the browser with the monitor set to 256 colors. You can see the results in the following images.

Explorer (top) dithers the GIF using diffusion dither, Netscape only quantizes the color value (bottom image). *Pictures are scaled to 120%.*

The same image saved as a JPEG (best quality) is displayed in both browsers with diffusion dithering. Explorer (top), in my opinion, yields the better result.

With PNG it is no problem to create objects with a drop shadow and have it integrate seamlessly with the design. As you can see in these images, the drop shadow blends with any background loaded into the browser. ▶

pect, pages designed on a PC look pale on a Mac. PNG's Gamma correction feature cures the problem, so images display with the correct brightness on both platforms.

Does this mean that PNG is about to replace JPEG and GIF? Certainly not— or at least no time soon. For one thing, PNG files are somewhat larger than comparable GIFs or JPEGs, and for another, PNG does not support animation. Still, as transmission speeds rise and animations can be created with other programs, PNG may well become interesting for Web designers.

➤ Vector Illustrations

There's one image format I haven't mentioned yet: vector illustrations. What worked so well in desktop publishing should also make sense online, right? That is exactly what Macromedia's Flash does. Flash is a vector-based illustration and animation program that gives sensational results; animations with text, and geometrical shapes with color gradients can be created in files as small as 20K, with no compromises in quality. Since each item is rendered

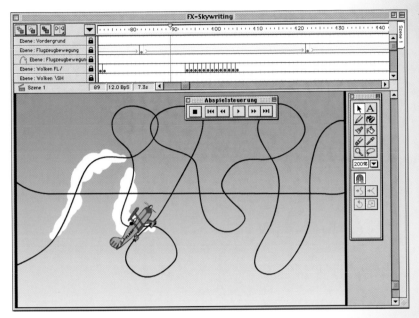

The Flash interface resembles the Director interface—not surprising, since both programs are made by Macromedia. Unfortunately, this is where the similarities end; if you are an experienced Director user, don't expect an easy transition, the learning curve is pretty steep.

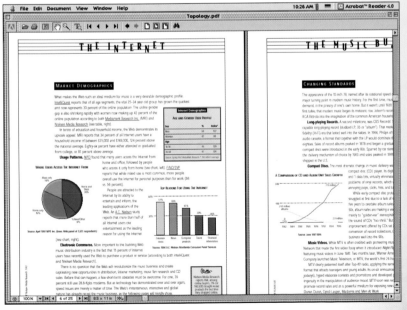

Adobe Acrobat allows you to store layouts with text and graphics in a platform–independent file format (PDF) that can be opened with the free Acrobat Reader. You can even embed those files in a Web page, because Adobe offers a plug-in for PDFs.

with optimum resolution, text can fly towards the viewer without appearing jagged. Flash can also create bitmap images and interactivity! This tool should be a regular companion of every Web designer.

WEB DESIGN WITH ADOBE IMAGESTYLER

It's not so simple explaining what ImageStyler is and what it can do. Imagine a tool that's a cross between a graphics program and an image–creation program, that also creates HTML pages. You design your interface using standard shapes like rectangles, ellipses and polygons, and then assign effects to them—an embossed effect or image, for example. Objects are arranged us-

ImageStyler works with shapes that can either be placed directly using the rectangular, ellipse or polygon tool or by importing shapes from Adobe Illustrator. These shapes can be filled with images or patterns and even have effects like emboss or drop shadows assigned. At the end, ImageStyler creates an HTML page along with all the images and JavaScript functionality like rollover buttons.

ing commands like Bring to Front or Send to Back, just like in Illustrator. The layers palette is only used for layers of an object, a concept that Photoshop would do well to adopt. You can assign rollover functionality to buttons, so their appearance changes as the mouse passes over them. Export the design as an HTML page and ImageStyler will automatically slice the layout and export all the pieces, including the background pattern.

Even though ImageStyler has great features, it is not meant to be a replacement for ImageReady or Photoshop—it lacks their advanced compression export and image manipulation features. But ImageStyler is a great tool for creating a mock–up of a Web site. You can export the images later as Photoshop files, which allows you to compress and optimize each image individually in Photoshop or ImageReady.

◀ This entire composition was done in ImageStyler using only standard shapes and effects. Whenever they're moved around, the water drops will always adapt to the background.

To get a better idea of how the program works, I'll show you step-by-step how to use it to create the water drops:

1. Place a circle in the design and apply the **3D Emboss** effect. To have the light come from both sides, set the **Light** option to **Light only**.

2. At this point the circle is still filled with a color, but you can use the **Layer Palette** to switch it to **Background**.

3. To make your water drop look more realistic, make sure you apply some distortion around the edges of the underlying image. ImageStyler offers this feature in the **Distort Palette**. Select **Displace** and then use the **Distance slider** to set the distortion in pixels.

4. Surprisingly, there is no Drop Shadow effect in ImageStyler. To give the water drop a shadow, you need to duplicate the shape in the **Object Layers**, fill it with black, soften it and offset it on the X- and Y-axes.

▲ Aristotle's promotional Fourth of July Web site shows off Flash's capabilities. Visitors can choose background music (a MIDI file), the location of the fireworks, and finally, they can launch different-colored fireworks using the Launch buttons.

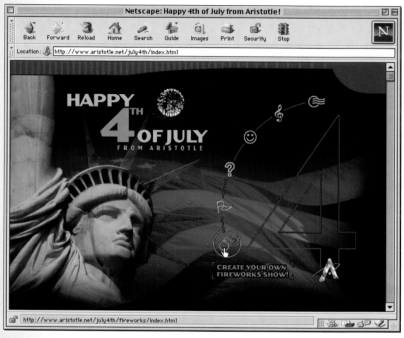

▲ Visit www.aristotle.net/july4th/ to see a well–designed Flash demonstration.

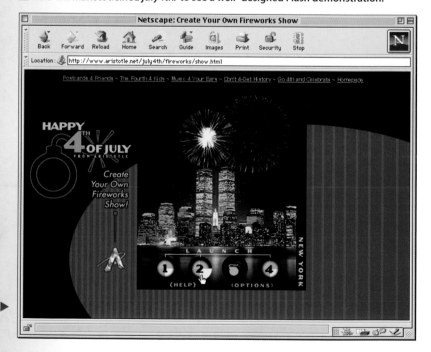

Click on one of the Launch buttons to trigger a rocket that explodes in one of four colors.   ▶

Another format supporting vector illustrations for the Web is Portable Document Format, or PDF. Developed by Adobe before the Web became popular, it was primarily intended to distribute layouts or illustrations in a cross-platform environment. Inspired by the success of the Web, Adobe developed a plug-in that allows browsers to display these PDF documents. This has enormous advantages, because once a brochure or flyer has been created it can be exported to the Web without much additional hassle. In order to create and view PDF files, you need Adobe Acrobat, as well as Acrobat Reader. Acrobat Reader is free, and the latest versions (for Mac and Windows) can be downloaded from Adobe's Web site (www.adobe.com).

PUTTING THIS KNOWLEDGE TO WORK

Now that you've learned the general range and applications of image formats, you can begin to create your own Web site concept.

GIF, JPEG and PNG formats each have their own chapters, with comparison tables that will allow you to pick the best compression setting for your purpose. The chapter "Comparing GIF, JPEG and PNG" will help you determine which image format will yield the best results. These comparison outlines will help you design a fast-loading Web site for your client or yourself. Before you get started, however, you should be familiar with the basic principles of color.

Color, in particular the Web color table, represents a history of omissions and compromises. Using color in desktop publishing is a snap compared to the special problems it causes in Web design. For instance, how much of a color shift do DTP designers have to contend with? Five percent dot gain is realistic, which is worry-free compared to the color variables on the Web: 256-color or one-million-color monitors, wildly varying gamma values on various computer platforms, and competetive browsers that display Web sites differently.

As mentioned before, the imponderables of the Web are a considerable challenge, and if you want to achieve the best results with your Web site on each browser, monitor and computer platform it almost always comes down to a compromise. In an ideal world all Web sites would be accessed with Netscape Navigator on a Macintosh monitor running 16 million colors, or with Internet Explorer under Windows—but in either case it would be with a unified system.

Reality, of course, doesn't work that way. As a result, you had better plan on spending a lot of time optimizing the colors of your Web site and testing the results in the different browsers, again and again.

The three significant problems are:

1. **Limitations of 256-color displays**
2. **Differences between browsers**
3. **Differences in Gamma between the platforms**

The first issue, a video display limited to only 256 colors, creates the biggest challenge, because as soon as you try to display a photo or a graphic with color gradients on your site, you reach the limit of what the viewer's monitor can display; the monitor dithers and quantizes the colors. To make matters even worse, Navigator and Explorer each have their own way of dithering! And finally, the different Gamma values on Mac and PC monitors can cause colors to get "swamped."

HOW TO SOLVE COLOR PROBLEMS?

Color shifts are inevitable with JPEG images, and your only real assurance of quality is to check the final images in all four browsers (Netscape and Ex-

MONITOR OR BROWSER DITHERING

To view a graphic or photograph on a 256-color monitor, you have to change the settings for your monitor in the Control Panel. You'll notice that the same image file is dithered differently in each application. Because every browser and graphics program manages the dithering of images in a different way, (see page 35), when you prepare an image file for the Web in Photoshop or ImageReady, you can only get an approximate idea of what it will look like in a browser. To get a true idea of its final appearance, you must load the image into the browser and then adjust your monitor's color settings.

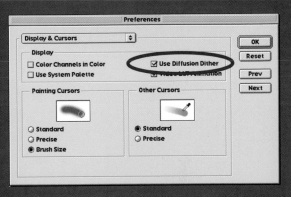

▲ In the Photoshop Preferences you can set the dithering algorithm: Diffusion gives you the best result.

Another little-known fact is that Photoshop has two display modes for dithering. Look in Preferences (**File > Preferences > Display & Cursors**) to find the **Use Diffusion Dither** option. Checking this option significantly improves the display in 256 Color mode. (Browsers also use diffusion dithering, so this mode comes closest to showing what you will see in a browser.)

plorer for both Mac and Windows). GIF images behave a little more predictably, especially when you convert the colors to the Web color table in Photoshop or ImageReady. The Web color palette, also called the Web-safe color palette, contains colors that won't shift on 256-color monitors. (The color table actually only uses 216 colors; the remaining forty colors are reserved for the operating system.)

Converting pictures to the Web color palette guarantees that the browser won't create any unexpected color shifts. The disadvantage is that a color shift is already created during the conversion in Photoshop or ImageReady, and therefore a Web surfer with a high-quality color display will still see the

leaving N2K/CDNOW he started his own consulting and venture capital company called Run Media (run-media.com), together with J.J. Rosen, co-founder and president of N2K & MusicBoulevard. Run Media manages a portfolio of clients and entities in the e-commerce industry and is active in the USA and Europe with a focus on Germany and the UK.

How did you cope with the high volume of CD titles for such a graphic- and image-intensive Web site as Music Boulevard?

We mainly used Photoshop, and for some very specific things we also used DeBabelizer.

Can you give me an example? When did you use Photoshop and when DeBabelizer?

The company N2K, owner of Music Boulevard (which merged with CDNOW), was one of the biggest online CD retailers. With a catalog of 200,000 US records, 150,000 European titles and more than 300,000 sound samples, their Web sites required enormous technical backbone. N2K is short for "Need To Know," which could also apply to Technical Director Tim Nilson, who was in charge of finding the best solutions to cope with this high volume of data. Today he is in high demand all over the world; he shares his expertise in lectures and addresses at international expositions. After

At one point we had eighty different banner ads running on the MusicBoulevard Store, which were all in Photoshop format. We started out saving them as GIFs in Photoshop, but since we wanted to use an adaptive palette we would end up with color shifts in each banner when we wanted identical colors. At that time neither Photoshop or ImageReady had the master palettes feature, which allows you to create one optimized color palette and use it for several images. Considering the time and work involved, we chose to use

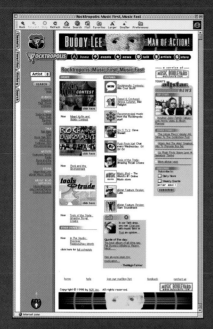

tating all 120,000 CD covers on our server by 20 degrees and supplying each one with a drop shadow. We eventually decided against it, but doing something like that would have been impossible without the Action Palette. DeBabelizer still has some helpful features; for example, it allows you to make certain actions dependent on "If ... Then" conditions. But for most automation and batch processing tasks, Photoshop's Action Palette is a great, easy-to-use tool.

A huge Web site like Music Boulevard probably had its own department for the optimization of picture files, right?

We used to have a specialist who only optimized picture files. He got the graphics from the graphics department and then he processed them in Photoshop or DeBabelizer. Today, all designers do their own optimization, because they have the necessary know-how about compression and dithering. That wasn't the case when we started out. The graphic designers today also have a feeling for when and how to work with the Web color table. The level of expertise in that area has increased significantly over the last few years.

DeBabelizer, because it provides several important features that are very helpful for Web design work. For example, DeBabelizer lets you choose a color that's exempted from dithering, which is nice. We created a macro in DeBabelizer, and used it to optimize all eighty banner ads in a couple of minutes! Today I would probably do the same thing with ImageReady or Photoshop, since handling DeBabelizer is a little complicated.

Was the conversion to GIF or JPEG the only thing you used Photoshop's Action Palette for?

Not at all. In another case we had a row of files that had to be cropped by one pixel each. Then there was the time we were considering ro-

▲ Classical Insites addressed the classics fan.

▲ Rocktropolis and Jazz Central Station were also owned by N2K.

▲ Optimizing an image for both computer platforms requires finding a middle ground. Otherwise, images optimized for the Macintosh will appear too dark on Windows, as you can see in this example. The top image is the Macintosh version, at the bottom, the same image as it appears on Windows. Optimizing images for both platforms is much easier when you use ImageReady; the program allows you to switch back and forth between both Gamma settings.

same "bad" picture. Thus, using the Web safe color palette for images may not always be a wise choice. In general, I prefer saving GIF images with an adaptive color palette and then testing the result in the browser using 256 Color mode. If I can bear the color shift here, I get the best of both worlds because the result will be substantially better on monitors with thousands or millions of colors. Read the GIF chapter to find out how to convert and optimize such GIF images. More information on the Web color palette can be found in the "Web Color Table" chapter.

▲ On the left, a typical GIF with an adaptive 16–color CLUT. The image on the right shows how this GIF will appear in a browser on monitors with 256 colors. You can clearly see the additional dithering.

ANIMATION AND INTERACTIVITY

In closing I would like to briefly address animation and interactivity, since they are important elements of contemporary Web design.

In addition to the GIF format mentioned earlier, browser versions 4.0 and higher also support Cascading Style Sheets. We have already discussed using CSS for defining font formats in structural tags, but since they support layers they can be used to create animation as well.

Layers can be overlapped to create complex image compositions and animation effects. You should definitely try this out when working with GoLive. The program's animation editor resembles those found in 3D animation software, and if you are at all experienced with 3D applications you should get the idea very quickly. The Flash and Shockwave plug-ins provide other possibilities for bringing animation and interaction to a Web page. I've already mentioned Flash in connection with vector graphics (illustrations) at the beginning of this section, but it is also a solid animation program with outstanding interactivity features. Flash's user interface strongly resembles that of Director, which is no surprise, considering that both applications come from the same company.

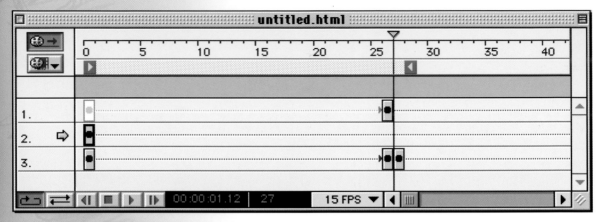

▲ Since the advent of 4.x Browsers it has been possible to place text and images in layers and even animate those layers. This can be easily done in GoLive's Animation window.

▲ GoLive features a couple of ready-made modules that can be implemented via drag-and-drop. For example the very popular rollover feature is as simple as importing the three images. The required JavaScript is handled by GoLive.

Director is the standard application for creating multimedia, and has been used to build quite a few CD-ROMs and kiosk systems. Years ago, Macromedia realized that multimedia was moving onto the Web, and developed Shockwave, a plug-in that allows Director movies to be played in Navigator and Explorer. Over the years this technology has been continually improved. For instance, Streaming Shockwave will now only download the elements you actually need—the single most important breakthrough yet for this technology. Anybody who needs complex and sophisticated interactivity and animation should look into Director and Shockwave.

If you're interested in interactivity, you will surely encounter two important terms: Java and JavaScript. Despite their similar names, they are actually two entirely different things. Java is a high-class (and relatively advanced) programming language, similar to C++, which allows you to create platform-independent applications—at least theoretically. For some time now Sun, the company that developed Java, has been in the crossfire because Java hasn't truly delivered on its promise of cross-platform compatibility (this is partly Microsoft's fault, since it extended Java's functionality and made the two products incompatible again; it's the same thing that happened with HTML and the browsers.) Nevertheless, Java can open many new worlds, because Web site developers aren't limited by the functionality of Shockwave, Flash or any other specific technology. Java has enough power to program complete solutions.

JavaScript, on the other hand, is a scripting language that can be inserted into HTML code and interpreted directly by the browser. Any experienced HTML programmer should be able to handle JavaScript. The reason I mention

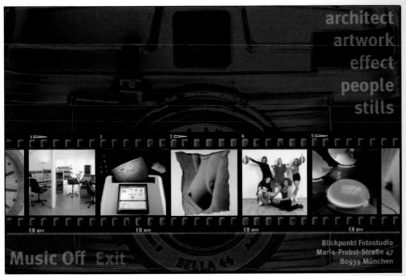

◀ The interactive portfolio of the
German photographer Paul
Ehrenreich (this book features a
lot of his work) was done in
Macromedia Director. Originally
created for use on CD-ROMs, this
projector was later embedded
using Shockwave, another
technology developed by
Macromedia.

JavaScript in connection with interactivity is that many interactive elements
(like rollover buttons, and so on) are created using JavaScript. As in many other areas, Microsoft has managed to make the world a little bit more complicated by introducing its own version of JavaScript, called JScript. And yes,
you guessed it: JScript is not totally compatible with JavaScript! But if you
just work with the ready-made JavaScripts that come as modules in GoLive,
you should be fine.

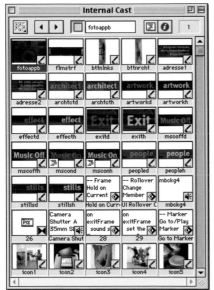

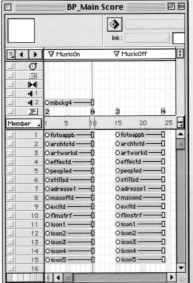

◀ Macromedia Director is a
standard program for all multimedia designers. It started out
as a pure animation program
and only later got extended with
a programming language called
Lingo, which lets you program
even complex tasks. Even now,
Director's interface reveals its
roots—the cast members of a
movie (left) are placed in a
timeframe (right).

DESIGN CONCEPTS

Developing a Design Concept for your Web Site

Even if you are an experienced designer in the world of Desktop Publishing, you still need to learn some basics about the medium of the World Wide Web before you start designing your Web site in Photoshop. This chapter is designed to give you a sense for how the medium will affect your designs.

INFORMATION ARCHITECTURE

These are (or I should say *were*) major buzz words among Web designers in the early days. Clement Mok, founder of Studio Archetype, a well-known San Francisco-based design firm, actually went so far as to rename his company a few years ago, and gave it the subtitle "Identity & Information Architects." The invention of the Web created several new professions so to speak, and today many Web design companies are looking for new hires who have experience in this field—simply because it can make the difference between a good and bad Web site. What does "information architecture" actually mean? The best way to describe it in one sentence is that it refers to struc-

Left: DAT's main page. DAT is a Web site for distribution of digital music.

Right: Since this Web site requires various plug-ins to hear the music, a dedicated page helps users find the necessary plug-ins. ▼

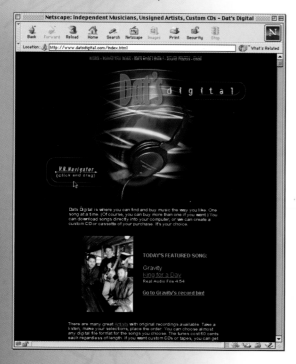

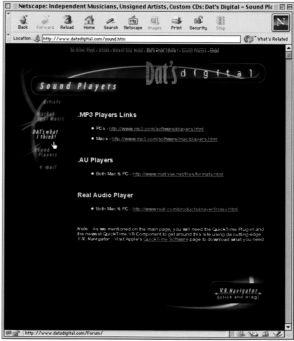

turing information and content based on a logical and consistent navigational concept.

It may seem simple at first sight, but in reality it's the biggest challenge when designing for the Web. Designers who come from the print world may have a particularly hard time here, because designing for print uses an established set of rules and concepts, to which we are all so accustomed that we don't think about them any more. For instance, every book has a table of content, an index and chapters that divide the content into units. Book designers and readers are so familiar with this navigational concept that nobody has to think about how to design or use a book.

On the Web, navigation is handled quite differently, since information may not be organized or accessed in a linear way. There are many more options for how to structure content and navigational elements.

You can draw a parallel to the development of the user interface on computers. In the very beginning, computers and computer applications did not provide standard functions—not even simple, familiar commands like Cut, Copy and Paste. Today it seems the most natural thing to copy something to the clipboard and paste it into another application—but if you've ever observed someone learning to use computers for the first time, you remember how hard it was to get your mind around these concepts at first.

It is important to keep this in mind when you start developing Web sites, because not everything that seems logical to you will seem that way to your visitors. Increasingly, large Web design companies use test groups to study how users respond to the site, giving them specific tasks like looking for a particular document or service, in order to gain some sort of feedback.

Only a few years ago, when the Web first became popular, many sites were laid out like printed brochures, including the navigation and the content, simply because those sites were built by DTP designers who were using concepts they were familiar with from the print media. Fortunately, Web design has matured, and a process you could call "survival of the fittest" has established standards that you now find on many, many successful sites. Looking at these sites is a good way for print designers to make the transition to the Web. But still, Mark Crumpacker, the Creative Director at Studio Archetype, believes that multimedia designers have a much easier time making the transition to Web site design because multimedia is interactive and therefore much closer to the Web.

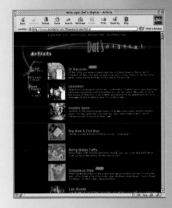

▲ On DAT's Web site, visitors can order music as a sound file.

▲ After selecting a CD title, the visitor can select an individual song.

▲ Christopher Stashuk of Aristotle used JavaScript to create rollover links/buttons. Rollover buttons are not only trendy, they allow the designer to use navigational elements that integrate very well into the design, as in this example; instead of using buttons, the links are all blurred text, but as the mouse rolls over them, they are replaced with an unblurred version of the text.

Many of today's Information Architects have an editorial background, and they spend a great deal of time analyzing current trends, and looking at how comparable sites are structured. But in smaller agencies, the designer has to cover that responsibility too. If you are interested in this subject, you should check out my other book, *Creative Web Design*, published by Springer, which features extensive in-depth interviews with well-known Web designers like Clement Mok and Mark Crumpacker from Studio Archetype, Peter Seidler from Avalanche (now part of Razorfish) and many more.

This chapter will give you a brief overview of what constitutes good (and bad) information architecture. It introduces some of the basic concepts, and outlines the questions you should ask yourself before beginning a Web design project. If you have already done a lot of Web design, feel free to skip this chapter, or save reading it for a later time—but even experts may find some interesting new information here.

➤ Without Structure There is no Architecture

Many Web sites are so confusing that the user gets lost, can't find what he is looking for, or—in a worst-case scenario—can't even comprehend what the site is all about. Even Web sites that have a clear and consistent navigational structure can make the fundamental mistake of not structuring the content clearly enough. A common mistake that you used to see (and sometimes still do) on large corporate Web sites is that they inundate you with hundreds of products or throw content at you from various areas of the site. It is just one of the traps to avoid when creating a Web site; building a site that reflects an existing structure, rather than taking a step back and rethinking the whole process. For instance, Motorola structured its first site to reflect the company's internal divisions. As Mark Crumpacker points out, that might make sense to the people in the company, but not to the end user. To Crumpacker, information architecture has failed if it doesn't focus on the target audience and its needs. This is utterly crucial for the success of a Web site.

The UPS Web site is a great example of Studio Archetype's work, and of how a thoughtful analysis of the audience and its needs can make a huge difference. When UPS approached Studio Archetype with the task of redesigning their site, they were faced with the challenge of dealing with a lot of existing content—and ensuring that the user wouldn't get lost. It was apparent that the problem lay in the site's structure, and in the way it broke the content up into categories.

To get a better idea of how to approach the problem they looked at the user model. The typical customer was interested in either tracking the current location of a package, calculating shipping costs, or in learning where he can drop off a package or how to schedule a pickup. Studio Archetype simply re-organized the information and the content around those four central tasks. After the new version went live, phone calls to UPS dropped by 20% according to Crumpacker—which shows how much impact a well-structured Web site can have on customer support.

➤ Reduction is Construction

Reducing the amount of information on a Web site, and consolidating similar topics into a single topic set are essential for a good site. Rikus Hillman, from Pixelpark in Berlin , who has worked on the online magazine *Wildpark*, is quite familiar with this problem. *Wildpark* started as a very complex site, but the creators soon decided that they should reduce the number of categories from ten to four. With this simple change, suddenly the magazine's structure became much clearer, and it became easier for the editors to point out new content to the viewers. But reducing the number of categories was just a start; the information itself also needed to be reworked. Most articles and

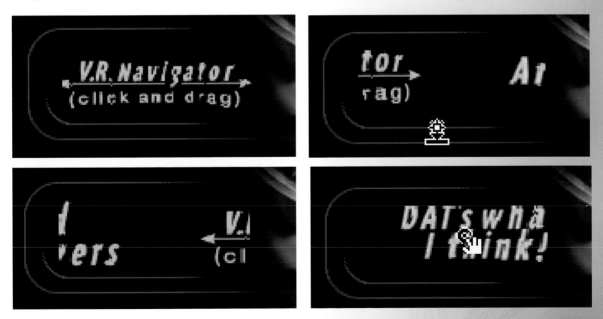

▲ Christopher Stashuk used QuickTime VR to help users navigate DAT's Web site. Because QTVR allows for a 360° view of a scene, Christopher used it to put text links at the imaginary "wall." QTVR can also embed hyperlinks, which makes for a really innovative navigational element. Not everyone will get the concept right away, though, so Christopher also included traditional text links.

COMMON INFORMATION ARCHITECTURE MISTAKES

How do you approach the concept of a Web site and achieve effective information architecture? The easiest way to show you is to point out the most common mistakes:

1. Too Many Categories

Reduction is the key to success. Combine information, and avoid too many categories. The Golden Rule on this subject declares that there should be no more than seven categories; scientific studies have established that this is the most that most users can remember.

2. Getting Trapped in Established Structures

Does the structure of the Web site make sense, or is it simply based on the company's departmental structure or some other preexisting concept? Always ask yourself if the categories are logical from the user's point of view.

3. Lack of Consistent Navigational Organization

Is your navigational concept simple and straightforward? If you can't answer this question with a clear Yes, you should start over. Make sure your concept includes clear global, parallel, and local navigational structures.

4. Burying Information in too Many Levels

Many Web sites are structured in a tree hierarchy, but if your tree includes more than four hierarchy levels, it is probably too complex for most users. Creating a visual representation or chart of your design will help maintain control of hierarchy levels.

stories in online magazines are too long, says Hillman, a problem that arose early on because many editors came from traditional print magazines. The Internet requires a different approach to text.

The Adobe Web site, also designed by Studio Archetype, presents another example of the importance of grouping content. (And I am not mentioning this just because this is an Adobe Press book!) When Studio Archetype was given the job of reworking the Adobe site, their Information Architects set themselves the goal of reducing fourteen sections to six. Together with Adobe, they worked on regrouping the information to make navigation simpler for the user. For example, the original site drew a distinction between graphic and prepress products—but for the user, those two categories overlap, so making them into separate categories only created confusion. "We

didn't quite achieve the goal of reducing everything to six sections," says Mark Crumpacker, "but we came close. We ended up having eight categories on the Web site."

➤ Navigation in the Information

Many Web designers make the mistake of creating a fancy interface with the expectation that users will be able to understand it. Very often this is not the case, and the user may have serious difficulties finding the desired information. This pitfall can be avoided by using clear and consistent global, parallel and local navigation. What does this mean?

● **Global navigation** allows the visitor to move between the main sections of the site. It should be present on every page.

▲ The Studio Archetype Web site is one of the better-known promotional sites. Designed by Mark Crumpacker to embody Studio Archetype's philosophy of information architecture, it's a great example of a clean and consistent navigational concept. This shot also shows the concept of content surfacing, in which images are updated regularly and are linked to new content within the site.

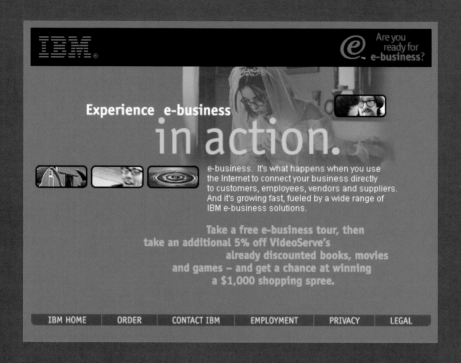

INTERVIEW WITH TOM NICHOLSON, NNY

Tom Nicholson is an unassuming man. When he occasionally hangs out with his coworkers and employees after work, he's just one of the crowd. It's hard to tell that he's the owner of one of the oldest and most successful Web design agencies in New York.

But when he gets into talking about information architecture, both customers and employees are under his spell. No question, he is a man with a lot of experience who can provide highly valuable input.

His company, Nicholson NY, started with interactive media way back in 1987. At that time the Web boom was far in the future, and Nicholson was working on multimedia. Today, the company has over 100 employees and occupies several floors in the Puck Building on Lafayette Street in New York's SoHo.

You worked with interactive media back in 1987, at a time, when computers were still relatively new technology. What was that like?

We have been in the business for twelve years now, from 1987 to 1999, and we started with interactive media, which was quite different back then from what it is today. Using computers to create interactive media was not as common at the time, and I had to spend a lot time on core issues like how do you balance "user drive" versus what we call "editorial drive" in order to get something communicated in this new medium.

Do you remember any particular project from back then? It would interest me to see what you were thinking about interactive media ten years ago as opposed to what you think of it today.

The first project that I did and that really launched my career in that area was a pretty large scale project involving six million visitors to the World's Fair in Knoxville, many of whom had come to the US to learn about energy. I developed six or seven interactive programs using touch screens and computer graphics, and merged them into interactive experiences, such as an energy glossary that listed 500 words—all dynami-

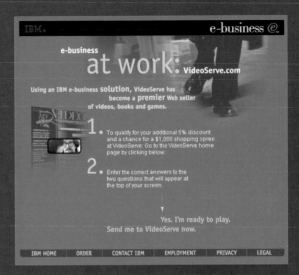

▲ IBM, one of Nicholson's clients, wanted a special Web page for their e-commerce campaign.

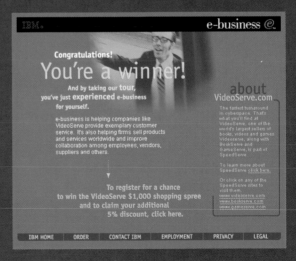

▲ The IBM site also reflects the visual style of Andreas Lindström (see interview at the end of the chapter), who acted as art director of the site.

▲ The splash screen of the Sony Web site.

▲ For a corporate Web site, the Sony site is amazingly hip and cool—another Andreas Lindström creation. Tom Nicholson and his team tried to group as many categories as possible to make it easy to locate products and information.

cally animated on screen. They included videos and a lot of technical terms. We also did projects for IBM and Citibank.

When did you get into Web design?

It was many years after that...around 1991 when Newscorp came in and wanted to create an AOL-killer; it was supposed to knock AOL out of the box. It was our first online experience, and it led to the first Internet Web site developments. That was when the company started to grow from fifteen people to 100.

You really watched Silicon Alley rise, so to speak?

We were the first interactive agency in Silicon Alley. When we started, there was basically nothing here.

When you look around on the map there is CKS Modem who were founded in 1987, the same year we were, but that was it.

What would you say is the strength of the agency? I suppose it is the strong background in interactive media?

Yes, I think so. We were leveraging what's possible with interactive media at a time when nobody else was doing it. But we have certainly grown beyond being just a design firm. What is happening in the Internet industry is that it's becoming more and more important to incorporate all aspects of Web Design and Internet and offer a full solution for the client. Besides working with interactive content and information design or information architecture, we have been building e-businesses for our clients—doing everything from Internet business strategy through creative execution and technology development.

That brings me to my next question. Information architecture is one of the buzzwords of the Internet. What does it mean to you?

Information architecture is nothing more than formatting information in a way that communicates. It's kind of a mental model, where you try to share your mental model with another person by using words, pictures, and so on. The user interface plays a big part in this. For instance,

in the print world the information architecture is very much established and fixed; with a book you have three ways of accessing information: from the front with the table of contents, from the back with the index, or by just browsing through the content. But in a flexible environment like Web design there are an almost infinite number of ways of representing the information.

Can you give an example?

Let me tell you about a project that's coming to completion right now. It's a kiosk system for a museum, but it could just as easily become a Web site once bandwidth is not a problem any more. An archeologist discovered something new on this Indian reservation: he found these stains

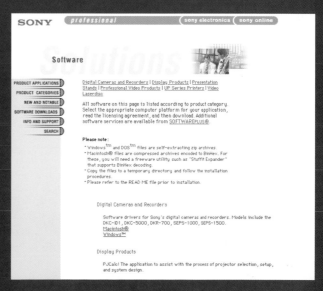

▲ Although the Web site uses a conventional sidebar, the use of different colors gives each section its own identity.

in the ground that he concluded were from a seventeenth-century fort. He started digging, and sure enough he learned that it was a fort, and he found all these components of life in a village.

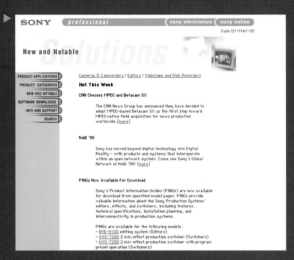

So if somebody came to you saying, "I want to convey this to the public," well, one way to start might be to get an editorial person to figure out what the content is. It might look like "Tell us everything about the fort: Who lived there? Where? Why were they there?" and then you could present it interactively on the Internet. Somebody else might break it down to the fortification itself: arms and defense mechanisms, daily life, food, social interactions, and so on. This version of the Web site would proba-

bly have buttons labeled "Life in the Village," "Food," "Arms," and so on. That's a lot like what you see on the Web today.

Yet another way of approaching this would be to ask yourself, "What is the closest mental model to the subject?" It happens that in this case it is the fort itself, because that's the artifact that offers all the information. So why not just give the fort to people and let them move through it, and interact with it; eventually you would learn all about life on the eastern seaboard. The key to designing an interactive environment is that you can have many different interfaces, which offers great possibilities for adapting to people's different learning styles. The more you can adapt to those differences, the better.

That example really illustrates the possibilities of interactive media. Instead of simply communicating linear information you can model it around the real world. Do you have any more examples? Or can you make a general assessment about what you think constitutes good and bad information architecture?

There are many basic principles that apply. You have to start by thinking about basics like the graphic user interface, what makes for good graphic design, and how well the information has been put in an hierarchical structure.

Then there is the rule of seven: people can only remember seven independent things. They can hold in their short term memory seven independent entities that have no relationship to each other. Some people can do eight, or maybe nine, but most people are limited to seven. That's why telephone numbers have seven digits; that's not an accident. So when it comes to designing a Web site you should stick to seven groups, and then work out a hierarchy with a consistent interface for those seven.

But what happens far too often is that a company has several different sections and departments, and each of them has its own Web site. Sometimes they put an umbrella site on top, but then you don't have any consistency, and the deeper the people get into the site the more confusing it gets.

There are many sites that have that kind of "bad" information architecture. It's a common occurence, because the Web is changing so fast. Our Sony project is a good example. Under the professional products group they had a number of different marketing groups, all of which were independent and all of which used their own printed material. That didn't matter, because those customers didn't cross paths with each other. Now, all of a sudden, Sony needs to come together on one Web site—as a Web design agency we were faced with the challenge of re-

organizing all this content without getting trapped by the structure of the company.

Sony had several departments, which was an efficient way for them to run their business, but the customers had no perception of that. All the user cared about was that he wanted to buy a monitor, for example, and he didn't care which prod-

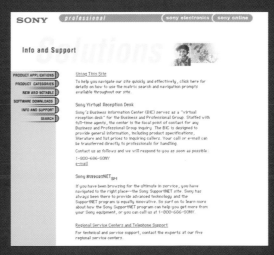

◀ An e-commerce site must have a dedicated page for customer contact.

ucts group the monitor department belonged to. So the first thing we had to do was to go in and work across the groups to create consistency, which was essential for the success of the Web site.

▲
**In most of his
Web sites, Christopher
Stashuk uses a splash screen
that features a GIF animation
and gives the visitor a summary
of the site's content.**

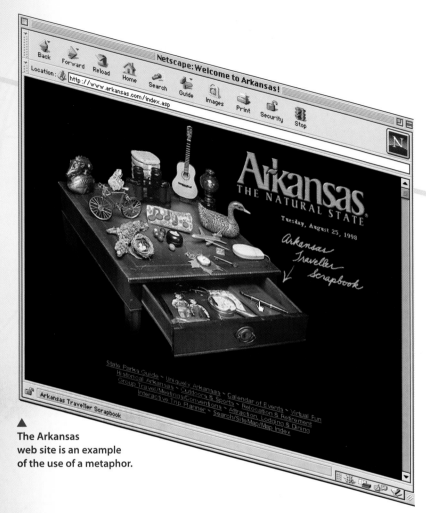

▲
**The Arkansas
web site is an example
of the use of a metaphor.**

● Within each section there are usually subcategories or subsections
that also require a consistent navigational structure. Because you are moving in a parallel manner within a section, this is called **parallel navigation**
—and should also be present on every page within a section.

● **Local navigation** works like a table of contents. You use it to find information within a page. It may look like a table of contents at the beginning
of the page, or it might be a list of links in a sidebar.

For a Web site using a classical tree structure, this navigational system (with
global, parallel and local navigation) is the best way to go.

In the future, as Web design becomes more like multimedia design, and as new technologies are embraced by the Internet community, information architecture will have to solve ever more complex problems. With extensions to HTML, information is becoming more dynamic, and the conventional page metaphor, where you click yourself from one page to another, will be only one solution among many. Perhaps, as in Clement Mok's vision, future Web interfaces might allow users to walk through a virtual world in which they hear ambient sounds, and information is presented in a three-dimensional world. I am intrigued by the idea of using ambient sounds for navigational purposes, but that is light years from now. But wait! Aren't Internet years more like dog years, where every year counts as seven "normal" years? We will be probably amazed at how soon this concept becomes a reality.

DESIGN CONCEPTS

Hopefully this excursion into the underlying issues of information architecture has been helpful. There are some books out there on the subject, but most of your know-how and experience will come from analyzing other Web sites. However, before you start working on your own site I would like to take this opportunity to offer

▲ The architecture of the site is very simple and straightforward. But whether the user finds his way through it depends on how clear the sections are and how well the information is grouped.

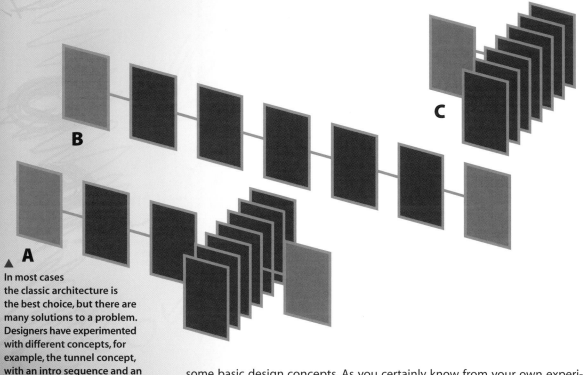

▲ **A**

**In most cases
the classic architecture is
the best choice, but there are
many solutions to a problem.
Designers have experimented
with different concepts, for
example, the tunnel concept,
with an intro sequence and an
exit page (see example A & B).**

some basic design concepts. As you certainly know from your own experience, the design of your Web site needs to stand out in order to attract visitors and inspire them to return. Here some tips and techniques that you may
or may not be aware of:

➤ Content Surfacing

Content Surfacing is a crucial part of Information Architecture, since it allows
a visitor to immediately locate new content on your site rather than having to
look for it. In the same way a newspaper "grabs" readers with a headline and
breaking news, you can pull the reader into your site with something new
on your first page.

This might be just a photo and a headline, or it could provide a little summary or the story's lead-in sentences. Either way, it is a great way to grab the
visitor's attention and tie him to the site. A very good example can be found
on Studio Archetype's site (www.studioarchetype.com). The main page is
built using a modular structure, meaning that the images in the middle of
the interface can be easily exchanged. A click on the image brings the view-

On the Baldor Web site, the navigational elements are placed inside a Frame, which will always be visible.

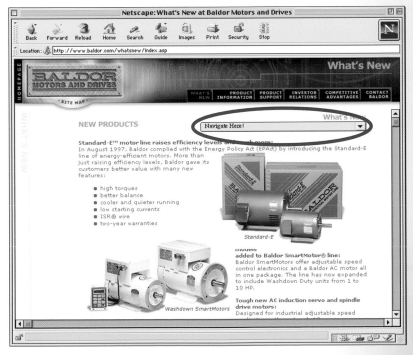

▲ Web sites that work with frames should use a splash screen (without frames) so that search engines don't get trapped in a frameset.

◀ A pop-up menu, like the one Christopher Stashuk used on the Baldor Web site, is another great navigational element.

er right to the story within the site. This technique should always be used on Web sites with frequent updates, since it is one of the most important ways of motivating your visitors to return on a daily basis.

➤ Metaphors

The goal in using a metaphor is to give a site a central visual theme, and to use it consistently throughout the site. Finding and creating a metaphor is not easy, because not every Web site is really suitable. Very often you see metaphors used for navigational elements, like a mailbox for email, but this doesn't really qualify as a metaphoric Web site. To see an example of a Web site where a metaphor is used tastefully for the entire site, check the Arkansas Web site (www.arkansas.com/index) designed by Christopher Stashuk from Aristotle (see p. 64). This site uses a table with several objects to represent the different areas of the site. Another example is the Web site of the DJH (German Youth Hostel), designed by Pixelpark (www.pixelpark.de). It used a backpack and all its contents to do the same job.

Web sites that use metaphors are certainly more interesting than sites that just use text links, but at the same time if you overdo it, or use an inappropriate metaphor, you run the risk of crossing the line between good and bad

As with all his Web sites, Christopher Stashuk designed the "Arkansas Museum of Discovery" completely in Photoshop because it gives him the most control and flexibility. It's only important to know how the design will translate later into HTML. For the presentation to the client he uses always a layer showing the browser interface.

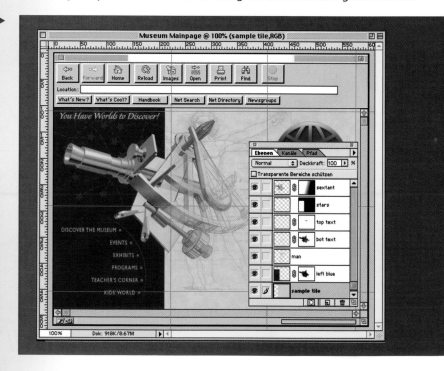

design. So unless you can find something really catchy and appropriate, stay away from visual metaphors.

➤ The Tunnel Concept

Printed brochures can use a great looking cover to grab the reader's attention. In a way, the tunnel concept tries to do the same thing by using a splash screen—an attention-capturing image that appears briefly before giving way to another image. The visitor has to click through one or more splash screens before he gets to the main screen with the content and the navigational interface. A Web site using a tunnel concept might also use a flashy exit page, which can leave a big impression, but you don't see this very often any more.

In the beginning of the Web era, many companies were primarily concerned with having a nice looking site, mostly as a way to show off and provide the company with a cool image. These days most companies are more sophisticated, and want to utilize their sites as a customer service tool. Forcing a visitor to click through a bunch of pages before he gets to the main page is just not smart any more, especially in a time marked by a decreasing attention span.

▲ The "Museum of Discovery" is a wonderful example of a Web site that looks great without relying on the latest plug-ins. The navigation bar at the bottom is a nice detail; although it's a frame, the background pattern makes it appear curved.

You Have Worlds to Discover!

SIDEBAR LAYOUT

If elements are placed over the edge of the sidebar like here in the "Arkansas Museum of Discovery"-Web-Site, it is important to take browser offset into account. As you can see in the smaller picture, the sextant and the navigational links were saved as transparent GIFs (grey area). Since there is enough room between the navigational links and the edge of the sidebar, they can compensate a browser offset of several pixels in either direction.

NAVIGATIONAL TECHNIQUES AND CONCEPTS

When building a Web site you have to decide which HTML features you want to use to create your navigational tools. If this is the first time you are designing for the Web, and have only a rough idea of what HTML is, or what it allows you to do, this section will help you make the right choices for your design. (If you are already familiar with HTML, you can skip this part.)

One very common technique is to slice up a larger image and put it back together in an invisible table. It was used in this example to place animations and interactive buttons on the page.

As it happens, there are not that many ways of creating navigational tools; it basically comes down to three choices: links, frames and image maps.

➤ Navigational Concepts Based on Links

The most common way of providing navigation is by using text or image links to connect pages and information. If you've ever seen a Web site with several buttons, then you saw a set of images that were defined as hyperlinks. Pop-up menus are becoming increasingly popular for navigation; if you want to see a good example, check out the Viagra Web site (www.viagra.com) designed by Andreas Lindström, the Art Director for Nicholson NY. Creating pop-up menus is a breeze with Adobe GoLive: Simply open the palette (**Window > Palette**) and select the tab called CyberObjects (the third tab from the right). When you drag the module to your page, the URL Pop-Up Inspector comes to the front and you can enter the text you want to appear and the URL to which it links.

➤ Navigational Concepts Based on Frames

Using text and images as links has the advantage of being backward-compatible to Netscape Navigator 2.0. The only problem is that navigational elements may scroll out of reach if there is more content on your page than the browser can display on a single screen. To compensate for this, frames were introduced after HTML 2.0. Frames allow you to split a browser window into two or more independent areas. This allows designers to create a sidebar or topbar in which they can place all buttons and navigational elements. No matter what happens to the main frame, the navigational sidebar remains on the screen at all times.

Frames require an additional document (called a Frameset) that contains all the information about the frames (like dimensions and settings), and also holds the information about which HTML page is loaded in which frame. Each individual frame can be addressed using a target attribute; this is essential in creating navigational bars.

Do you want to give it a try yourself? Start up GoLive and open the Palette (**Windows > Palette**). As you have probably realized by now, the Palette is one of your most important tools in GoLive, since it contains all the HTML elements (modules, effects, and so on) that you need—including frames (sixth

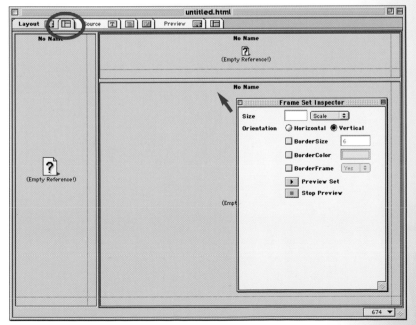

▲ Various framesets are stored in the Frame Palette and just need to be dragged over into the frameset view of the document.

◄ The second tab in the document window hosts the frameset view. Once a frameset is dragged from the Frame Palette, click on the frame itself and the Inspector will show its properties for example, Border Size.

tab from the right). Before you can drag a frameset into your document, you need to switch to the Frame Editor; click on the second tab from the left in your work area. Now you can place a frameset by simply dragging and dropping one of the presets. To create more complex framesets, just keep adding additional frames by dragging them to your page. Adjust the size of the frames by clicking in the frame and resizing it; just hold the mouse button while you position the frame.

By default, these frames appear with a six-pixel border, and in gray – two settings that I seriously doubt you want to use for your page. Usually, frame borders should be invisible. To ensure that they appear that way in both Netscape Navigator and Internet Explorer, you have to set the size of the border to zero pixels, and the BorderFrame attribute to "No." To do this, click on the border (rather than inside the frame), and the Inspector Palette will change from Frame Inspector to Frame Set Inspector. Here you will find the options for Size and BorderFrame; simply change their values. If you have several frames placed, you must repeat this step for each frame.

Frames are a great improvement over no frames at all, but in the first version you couldn't make the borders invisible. The attributes that I have just mentioned didn't exist when frames were first introduced. Only later did Explorer and Navigator offer these essential attributes, but by then frames had become slightly unstylish.

WebPosition is a very powerful tool to check the ratings and position of a Web site with the major search engines. You can find more information at www.webposition.com. If the search engine rating is very important to you, try to avoid using frames—they have a negative effect on the search result.   ▶

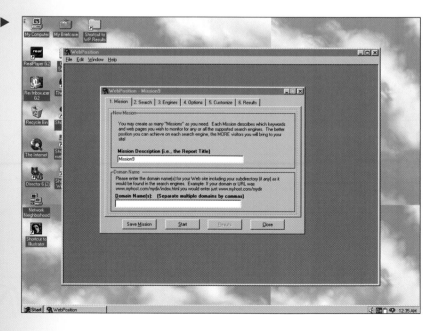

These days, designers have come to realize that frames have some serious drawbacks. The most important is that Web sites with frames fail to get good results when search engines like Infoseek or Excite check them out. This has to do with the way search engines work: they index the text in an HTML document, and count how often a certain keyword appears on a page. Unfortunately, if you use frames the search engine never gets to see or index the real content of your Web site, since it "sees" only the Frameset Document, which contains only a few lines of HTML code; to make matters worse, the pages with content replace each other in the frame.

I don't want to go into too much more detail on this; all you need to know is that using frames can be counterproductive if you want to create a content Web site. There are ways to use frames and still appear high in the ranking of a search engine search, but the subject of how to optimize your Web site for search engines is so complex that it would fill a small book all by itself. Most Web designers, knowing the importance of a good search engine ranking, have gone back to frameless designs.

If you are interested in finding out more about how to optimize your Web site for search engines, log onto one and search for the key words "Search Engine." You will come across a number of sites that offer information, or even the service of optimizing your Web site for you. Use careful judgement if you decide to use this service, because truly effective site optimization for search engine promotion requires someone to monitor the changes that happen constantly among the search engines. These engines change the way they index more frequently then you might think, because they are constantly trying to improve the accuracy of their searches. A good place to get more information about what's happening is www.searchenginewatch.com.

Search engine indexing is not the only problem that frames bring with them. There are also design issues: for instance, if there is more content in a frame than it can display, it shows a scroll bar. (This can be prevented by setting the Scrolling attribute to "No" in the Frame Inspector). While a scroll bar in a frame with content is not really an issue, it is if it appears in a control bar. Keep this in mind if you decide to use frames when you design your page.

➤ The Sidebar Design

One of the most popular Web design concepts is using a sidebar in which all the navigational elements can be placed. This can certainly be done with frames, but as discussed before, frames have some disadvantages. So most sidebar designs use a different trick: they place a background image in the browser that has a rectangle on one side, usually the left, colored differently. (See the chapter "Designing with Photoshop") The only drawback is that all the navigational elements in the sidebar will eventually scroll out of reach if there is a lot of content on the page; that's why every designer places a copy of the links as text links at the end of the page. This way a visitor doesn't have to scroll back up to move to another page.

➤ Image Maps and Image Tables

Another navigation feature of HTML is image maps. These are images in which certain areas have been designated as hot spots, or hyperlinks. This has some advantages over slicing up an image and putting it together in a table (another popular technique among Web designers, called image tables). One advantage is that your hot spots can have any shape you like, from rectangular to elliptical, even polygonal. You can even knock out areas from a shape—all things that you can't do with an image table.

ImageReady supports both image maps and image tables. To create an image map, simply select a layer in the layers palette, double-click on it, and select the Image Map option in the dialog box that appears. You also use this

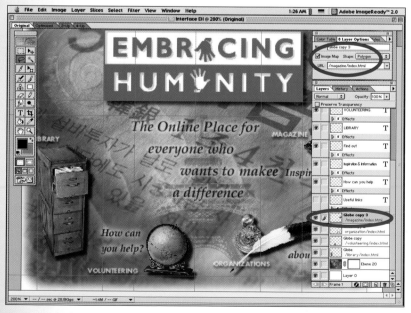

▲ A layer can be turned into an image map by activating the Image Map Option.

dialog box to choose which shape you want the image map to have (rectangle, circle or polygon), and the URL to which it should link.

Another thing you should know about image maps is that they come in two variations: client-side and server-side. The main difference is that with the server-side image map the information needs to be sent first to the server, who then determines if the mouse is over a clickable area. With the client-side image map, the local computer does this task. Stick with the client-side map, as the server-side is somewhat obsolete now. A server-side image map may still fulfill a purpose here and there, but client-side image maps are easier to set up and they work faster.

I mentioned image tables and I still owe you a better explanation of what they are. The basic idea is to slice up an image into pieces, and to drop each piece into the appropriate cell of an invisible table so the image appears to be in one piece again. The advantage of slicing an image up is that you can optimize each fragment, and achieve a much better compression rate than if you were to compress the entire image at one time. Also, you have to use an image table if you want parts of your images to be rollovers. You have probably seen this effect on a Web site—as you move the cursor over a button or image, its appearance changes. If you wish to differentiate separate areas within a larger image where this happens, you have to slice up the image in order to do so (this is not possible with image maps). Fortunately, ImageReady makes this process easy by giving you a slicing tool you can use to define rectangular areas on an image that will be sliced up and put into a HTML table automatically.

▲ The Slicing Tool in Image-Ready allows you to divide one large image into several smaller ones that are then are put back together in an invisible table.

➤ Using the Slicing Tool

You have several ways to create an image table, one of which is to use ImageReady's slicing tool, which allows you to draw rectangular areas in your image. Then ImageReady will automatically slice up the image accordingly; it even works with overlapping areas. Another great feature of the slicing tool is that you can optimize each area differently. Just open the Optimize Palette (**Window > Show Optimize**) and select an area with the Slice Select Tool. Change the settings in the Optimize palette and when the area is exported, ImageReady will save it with its own individual settings. But beware: if the colors in one slice shift, the edges where it adjoins the next area may not be seamless any more.

A ndreas Lindström, a native of Sweden who has been living and working in New York for several years now, has achieved something that only a few designers can claim: he has developed a totally unique Web design style. His work for Carnegie Hall and the Viagra site, among others, carry his signature. He is one of the best-known and most in-demand Web designers in New York today.

How did you get into Web design?

I attended a special high school for design in Sweden, and was lucky to get a job offer from an advertising agency in Malma, Sweden, right after my graduation. So instead of going to college I went directly to work, which I think is an advantage. I learned so much at that time that after five years I felt that Malma was a little bit too small for me. I wanted a

this new medium and how to push the limits. It was a great experience.

You designed the Lost Highway site, which is a good example of your style, because it used large, dimmed images in the background combined with smaller images in the foreground. What can you tell me about the site?

I think the use of large images in combination with smaller images

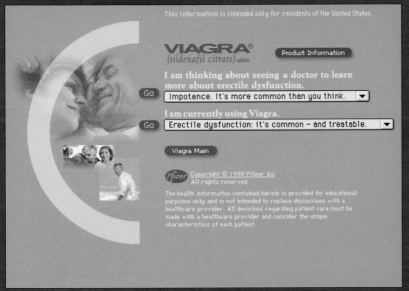

Pfizer, the company that manufactures Viagra, hired Nicholson NY to do a web site for their customers. Andreas Lindström was art director of this site: "the color combination in this web site is based on the printed brochure, other then that the design is very different. The main navigational element is a pop-up in which the visitor can select the information that he is interested in. This has the advantage that the site can easily be extended and at the same time the design remains very clean and clear. To align the elements on the first page with the background pattern we used JavaScript to compensate for the browser offset."

bigger challenge, so I applied to the Parson School of Design in New York, and was accepted. After I finished there I started to work in the print field. When the Web started to happen, I got in contact with Avalanche, a company that was just starting up in New York. They did cutting edge stuff on the Internet, and I worked there for two years, learning about

creates a real dimension and depth to the page. For example, on the Lost Highway site I used a large face that blended into the black background, and in the foreground I placed smaller images of the actors in the series. This created tension and depth at the same time.

What was really neat about this site was the navigation elements that we came up with. The site didn't have traditional navigation. Instead of buttons or any other kind of visual indication of where to click, we based the navigation on how the story of the movie was going. We also linked the pages so that you would get more images if you clicked on an image, and you would

get more text if you clicked on a text link. Since every visitor has individual preferences, I thought this was a great way of giving them a choice.

There are quite a lot of Web sites for movie companies in your port-folio, for example the Polygram Filmed Entertainment Web site.

Yes, that was actually the first Web site I created. I used film props to create the tone of the site, and tried to associate various objects with different sections. This is one of the few sites where we actually had a real photo shoot, and didn't have to use stock photos. I think you end up with a much better result that way, because it gives you control over the outcome and you can get closer to your vision as a designer. The same applies to the Carnegie Hall site, where we had a photographer come in and shoot pictures. It made a big difference in the quality of the design.

You also worked for Nicholson in New York. What are some of the projects you did there?

The first site I did as art director for Nicholson was a site for Sony, a business solutions site. We had to create a site that could handle something like 50,000 products. The important thing was to consider Sony's brand, which has a very clear look, as well as creating a navigational system that could pull all this information together—so whatever search results you would get, it would fit into the template we created. Another project was a Web site that was part of IBM's e-business campaign. We did that in conjunction with a company called Video Surf that sells videotapes online. It was just a demonstration of how e-business works, an opportunity to see e-business in action. The site reflected the advertising campaign that was going on at that moment, as well as taking you through a couple of IBM pages and a contest.

Another big project was the official Viagra Web site. I think it has a very unusual and appealing charm. We used a very simple user interface with a very unconventional navigational system. Instead of using traditional buttons and links, the main navigational element is a pop-up menu. I was almost surprised that a customer like Pfizer agreed to do it, since big corporations lean more and more toward standard sidebar navigation.

That indeed is the overwhelming trend. When you develop a Web site, how do you approach the navigation?

Personally, I wish clients would experiment with a few more navigational possibilities. I try to break out of that standardized sidebar concept as often as I can by creating navigation elements in different places, or by trying to come up with different page layouts. Usually clients prefer the standardized model, because they have seen it so often, so most of the time it's a battle. My overall goal is to develop very clear navigation. I prefer to avoid designing with buttons, although they have become such a standard that sometimes I

have to use them. Buttons are not necessarily the worst choice, but I prefer to use them more delicately, maybe as a subtle sub-element.

When you start a project and get the outline, how do you come up with a concept and a site design?

Generally I sit with the client and show them different kind of designs and see what they like; it's important to find that out. Then, after we have established the creative direction, I experiment with different kinds of imagery. I usually do sketches by hand and try to develop two or three different solutions—solutions that might work together, because sometimes you show the client three solutions but they may like certain

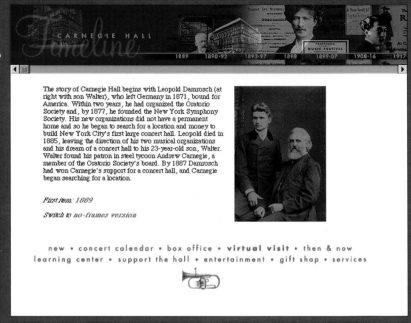

▲ The history of Carnegie Hall is presented on its own page.

things here and there, and want to pick pieces from different solutions. At least that's been my experience.

Another thing that's important, particularly when you create a Web site for a location, is to go to that location, which is what Avalanche did for the Carnegie Hall Web site. I walked through the aisles and halls, listening to the noises and trying to visualize sound as a color. Colors and images are my strength, and I try to use these elements for my designs.

How do you think Web design is going to change with the development of dynamic HTML and layers?

Since most of my clients are corporations, I really have to keep the low-end user in mind. I still do my designs so they will be compatible with older browsers, because a lot of people are not using the latest versions. Of course I would love to experiment with the high end, but now that I'm mostly working on corporate Web sites, I have to stay away from really fancy design features.

What do you think the future of the Web will be?

I think the Web will merge with television. WebTV is definitely where the Web is going, and I'm really looking forward to that, since in the future, bandwidth will allow for different kinds of design and functionality.

new & notable
concert calendar
box office
virtual visit
carnegie then & now
support the hall
learning center
entertainment lounge
gift shop
services guide
about this site

MAIN MENU

©CHC 1996, 1997

Andreas Lindström on the Carnegie Hall Web Site: "The main challenge was to capture the the ambience of the hall and bring it online. We managed this by using dimmed images and the combination of blue and orange. For the font I used Monterey because it has a very music like flow for me."

VIRTUAL VISIT

timeline   photo bubble   walk through

Try this month's Carnegie Hall Quiz in the Entertainment Lounge. Enter to win free tickets!

new • concert calendar • box office • **virtual visit** • then & now
learning center • support the hall • entertainment • gift shop • services

What's your vision of a Web site without any limitations?

It would be like interactive video, where everything is in motion all the time, almost like a computer game. I can see that being used in very interesting ways in corporate Web sites, when they finally get there.

The Web is so serious right now, it's not as experimental as it was in the beginning. Now it's all corporate—I'm really waiting for the next step, because at the moment everything looks the same.

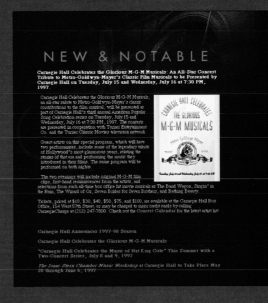

NEW & NOTABLE

Carnegie Hall Celebrates the Glorious M-G-M Musicals: An All-Star Concert Tribute to Metro-Goldwyn-Mayer's Classic Film Musicals to be Presented by Carnegie Hall on Tuesday, July 15 and Wednesday, July 16 at 7:30 PM, 1997.

Carnegie Hall Celebrates the Glorious M-G-M Musicals, an all-star salute to Metro-Goldwyn-Mayer's classic contributions to the film musical, will be presented as part of Carnegie Hall's third annual American Popular Song Celebration series on Tuesday, July 15 and Wednesday, July 16 at 7:30 PM, 1997. The concerts are presented in cooperation with Turner Entertainment Co. and the Turner Classic Movies television network.

Guest artists on this special program, which will have two performances, include some of the legendary talents of Hollywood's most glamorous years, relating the stories of that era and performing the music they introduced in their films. The same program will be performed on both nights.

The two evenings will include original M-G-M film clips, first-hand reminiscences from the artists, and selections from such all-time box office hit movie musicals as The Band Wagon, Singin' in the Rain, The Wizard of Oz, Seven Brides for Seven Brothers, and Bathing Beauty.

Tickets, priced at $18, $30, $40, $50, $75, and $100, are available at the Carnegie Hall Box Office, 154 West 57th Street, or may be charged to major credit cards by calling CarnegieCharge at (212) 247-7800. Check out the Concert Calendar for the latest artist list.

Carnegie Hall Announces 1997-98 Season

Carnegie Hall Celebrates the Glorious M-G-M Musicals

"Carnegie Hall Celebrates the Music of Nat King Cole" This Summer with a Two-Concert Series, July 8 and 9, 1997

The Isaac Stern Chamber Music Workshop at Carnegie Hall to Take Place May 28 through June 6, 1997

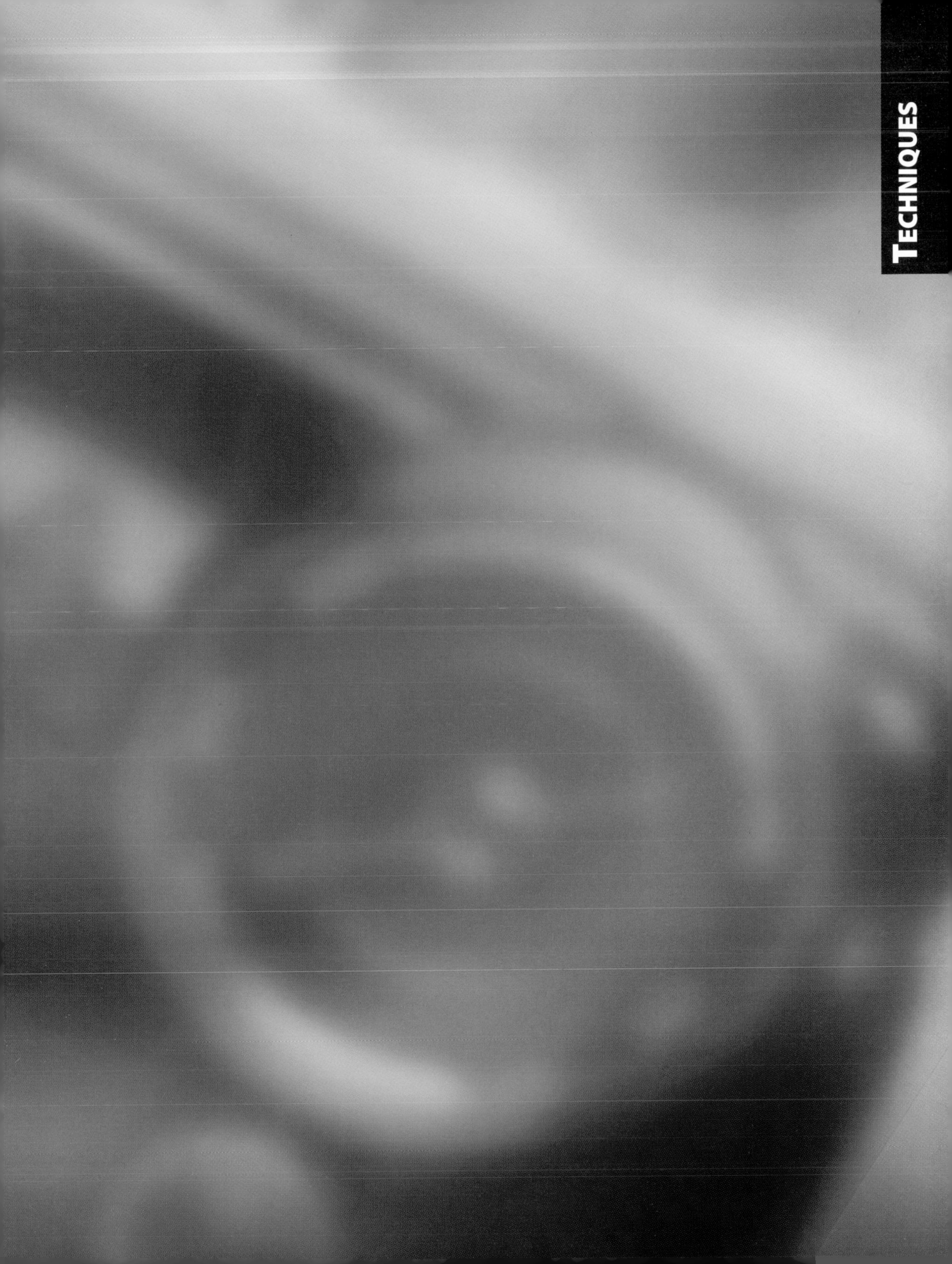

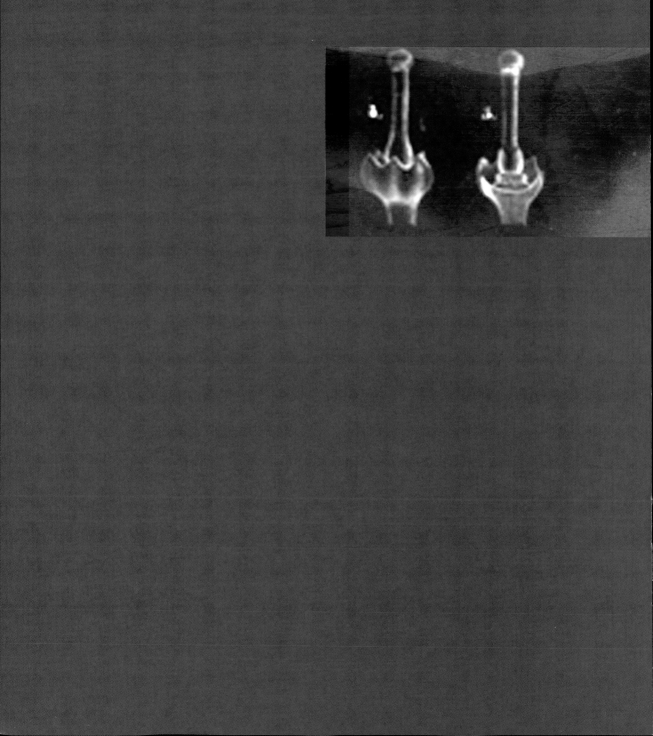

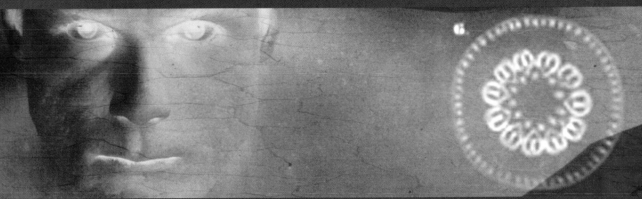

OPTIMIZING PHOTOSHOP

Optimizing Adobe Photoshop

Photoshop was originally developed for the print medium, but over the years it has become the primary tool for multimedia and Web designers as well. Because of its "print" history, not all the default settings in Photoshop are optimal for Web designers, but it takes only a couple of minutes to change this.

OPTIMIZING THE COLOR PICKER

You are probably familiar with Photoshop's color picker, which you can access by double–clicking on the colors in the tool palette. This color picker shows you color values of several color models at once, but choosing colors from the Web–Safe Color palette used to be tedious because you had to enter the numerical RGB values. In 5.5 Adobe introduced a little enhancement that makes it easier to select only Web–safe colors: the option **Only Web Colors** will lim-

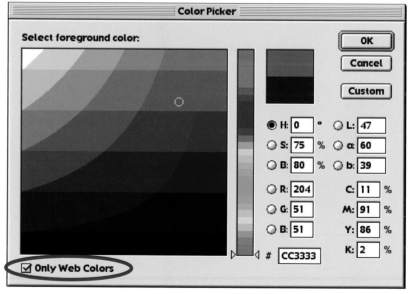

▲ The Adobe Color Picker features now an option that makes the selection of web safe color much easier.

it the color spectrum to the 216 colors of the Web palette. Still, if you want to work with an alternative color picker, you can select **Apple** or **Windows** (depending on which platform you work in) in the Preferences (**File > Preferences > General**). Apple has implemented a special HTML color picker with the OS 8.0 release that makes picking a Web-safe color a breeze, particularly if you need to enter the colors as hexadecimal values.

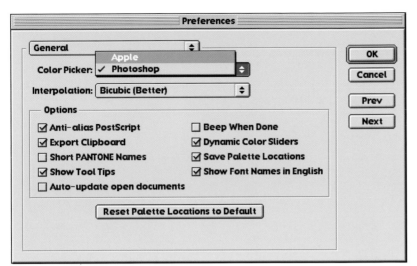

◄ If you want or need to work with a different color picker, you can switch to Apple (or Windows) in the Preferences dialog box.

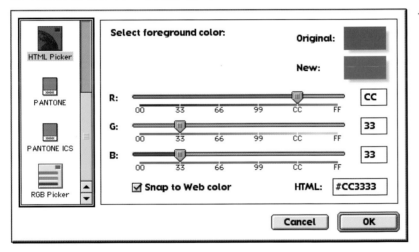

◄ The Mac OS offers a special HTML color picker that makes it easier to work with the Web-safe color palette—especially if you have to enter the hexadecimal color values.

USING THE RIGHT INTERPOLATION METHOD

When you scale images in Photoshop, the pixels and their colors are adjusted using one of three methods: Bicubic, Bilinear and Nearest Neighbor.

Usually, Photoshop uses the Bicubic method because it gives you the best result when resizing an image. In this method, Photoshop analyzes the values of adjacent pixels and calculates the middle value between them (when sampling down) or creates additional intermediate colors (when sampling up).

The original 2 x 2 pixel image (left) was enlarged by 1000% using Photoshop's three Interpolation Methods. The effect can be seen in these three images: with Bicubic and Bilinear scaling, Photoshop introduces additional colors to smooth out the appearance of your image. Only with "Nearest Neighbor" the enlarged result looks like the original. ▼

Bicubic

Bilinear

Nearest Neighbor

In general, Bicubic gives you the best results—but not necessarily in every case. The top two images here compare Bilinear (on the left) and Bicubic (on the right). You can clearly see that the blurring effect is much stronger in the image scaled with Bicubic, but Bicubic also produces halo effects in images with hard contrasts. And while Bilinear (bottom left) creates a blend between only two colors, the Bicubic method (bottom right) generates even more colors. My advice: If you are scaling up an image by a fairly large percentage, you are better off using Bilinear for all images where two solid colors are adjacent, as in this example. If you are scaling up by a smaller percentage, you probably won't even notice the difference between the two methods.

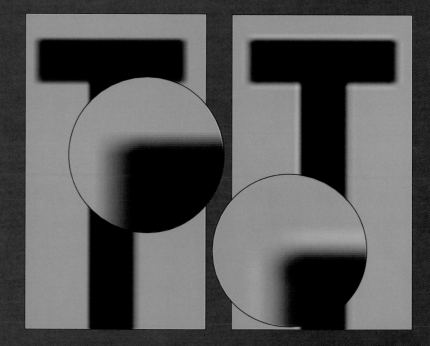

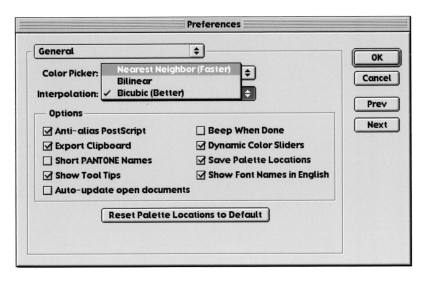

◀ There are several interpolation methods in Photoshop. Although Bicubic is the default setting, it might sometimes be a better choice to use Nearest Neighbor.

However, Bicubic's creation of colors may create a problem if you want to work with GIFs or colors from the Web-safe color palette. Imagine, for example, that you have created an illustration using only colors from the Web palette, but when you resize you get a lot of non-Web-safe colors at the edges that will ultimately dither on monitors with 256 colors. Moreover, these additional colors may have a dire impact on how well the image compresses. Therefore, use Bicubic only for photos that are to be saved as JPEG images. Any illustration that you plan to publish as a GIF is better resized using the Nearest Neighbor color adjustment. If you resize using the Resize command, you can select the method in the dialog box, but if you use the Layer Scale command Photoshop automatically uses the default method set in the **Preferences**.

The Bilinear method works similarly to the Bicubic method, but according to the Photoshop manual it uses a simpler algorithm, and is therefore less accurate. Even though this is true, my experience has been that the Bilinear method is better for images with strong contrasts. The side effect of the Bicubic method is a blurrier picture, as you can see in the example with the character "T," where it creates something of an aura, while the Bilinear method creates a blend. The bottom line is that if you resize a graphic that you later want to save as GIF, use Bilinear color adjustment. You'll end up with fewer additional colors in your image; while this may seems like a minor point, it is much better to do it right in the beginning than to try to fix it later when you index the image.

When transmitting files to the server, the preview for GIFs gets stripped away automatically. That is not the case for JPEGs, so it is best to always deactivate the Image Preview preference.

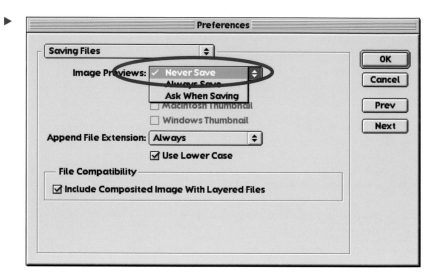

PREVIEW

When creating a Web site you want to keep an eye on how many images you use and how much data has to be downloaded to display those images on a user's computer screen. I usually keep a folder with all my images in one place, which makes it very convenient to select the folder with the Mac Finder, select the Get Info command (command-I), and let the system tell me how big the folder and its contents have become.

By default, Photoshop creates a preview when you save images, which adds 25 percent to the size of your file. Even though this preview is stripped away when you FTP your images up to the Web server, it confuses things if you want to know exactly how much data all your images comprise. To prevent Photoshop from creating the preview, call up the Preferences (**File > Preferences > Save File**) and set the Image Previews option to **Never Save**. The option **Ask When Saving** allows you to choose whether you want a preview when you save an image, but this is more annoying than useful.

APPEND FILE EXTENSION

Whatever format you choose—GIF, JPEG or PNG—your files need to have the appropriate extension in order for browsers to display them correctly. The extension always consists of a dot and three letters. A GIF is saved as filename.gif and a JPEG as filename.jpeg (or filename.jpg); PNG has the extension '.png'.

Photoshop will automatically save files with the right extension, but to activate this feature you must select **File > Preferences> Saving Files**, and choose the Append File Extension option: **Never, Always,** or **Ask When Saving**. If you select **Always,** go ahead and select **Use Lower Case** as well. Sometimes UNIX Servers won't recognize an extension if it is in capital letters.

RULERS IN PIXELS

The most important unit in Web and multimedia design is the pixel, so it makes sense to set the preference unit for **Units & Rulers** to pixels. If the ruler is not visible in your document, select **View > Show Ruler** to have it appear.

GUIDES AND GRIDS

Using guides and grids makes it much easier to slice up an image. It is a very common technique to export pieces of an image and put them back together in a table using the HTML authoring tool. Depending on the color of your image, you might want to adjust the color of the guides and grids— which you can do in **File > Preferences> Guides & Grid**.

LOADING THE WEB-SAFE COLOR PALETTE

It is very important to use as many Web-safe colors as possible in your illustration, because you don't want colors to dither on low-end computers with only 256 colors. Instead of typing in the color values by hand, it is easier to work with color swatches.

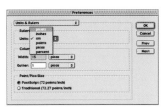

▲ Photoshop will automatically add the correct file extension if this option is selected in the preferences.

▲ Set the ruler unit to pixel in the preferences.

You can open the Web-safe color swatches via **Window > Color Swatches**, and then use the palette menu to replace the standard swatches (**Replace Swatches**). In the file dialog box that appears, navigate to the Goodies folder in the Photoshop folder.

To select a color from the swatches palette, simply click on it. Saving a color is as simple as clicking on an empty field; the tool switches momentarily to the paint bucket and fills the swatch with the current foreground color that is selected in the tools palette.

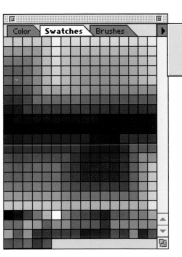

▲ Using Web–safe colors is much easier if you load them into the Swatches Palette using the Load Swatches command.

Beginning with Photoshop 5.0 ▶
Adobe included its own Gamma
Control Panel: this panel has the
advantage that it comes with an
"assistant," which is basically just
a Wizard that guides you step by
step through the calibration
process. If you want to optimize
your images for the web, you need
to preview them with a Macintosh
and a Windows Gamma, but instead of switching the Gamma in
the control panel, I suggest that
you use ImageReady for this
step. ImageReady has a Win-
dows/Macintosh preview as
option in the View menu.

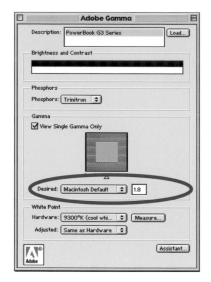

GAMMA

As you probably know, the brightness
of a monitor is measured on a Gamma
scale. However, Macs and PCs use different Gammas, which means the image you optimized for one platform
may look too bright or too dark on the
other. The differences in Gamma between the two platforms is roughly 20
percent; you can use **Image > Adjust >
Brightness/Contrast** to correct an image. As a rule of thumb, if you work on a
Macintosh make your images a little
brighter than you normally would; on a
PC make them a little darker.

If you want to have more precise control, you can simulate how your images will look under a different Gamma setting by simply changing the Gamma curve. In Windows, you can do this in the Monitor Control Panel; on a Mac,
go to the Adobe Gamma Control Panel. In the Desired popup menu in the
Adobe Gamma Control, you'll find **Macintosh Default** and **Windows Default**. Adobe has simplified the calibration process substantially; you have
the choice of using the assistant to walk you through the calibration process
step-by-step, or you can use the control panel.

If you work on a Macintosh, make
your images a little bit brighter
(around 10-20%) to have them
also look good on Windows.   ▼

But in Photoshop 5.5, you can also use ImageReady to create your GIFs
and JPEGs. ImageReady makes it very easy to control your Gamma, because

Photo: Paul Ehrenreich

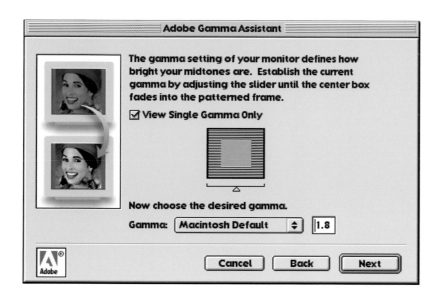

How to calibrate correctly
1. Turn the monitor on half an hour before you calibrate so that it can warm up.
2. The Brightness and Contrast controls on the monitor should be in a neutral position (not too high, not too low).
3. Turn off any image or pattern background for the monitor. Use instead a neutral gray.
4. Use the assistant if you have no experience with the monitor calibration. It will guide you through the process step by step.

you use a command to switch Gamma within the program. **View** > **Preview** gives you a choice between Windows, Macintosh and Uncompensated Colors. This way you don't have to switch Gamma in your control panel. If you haven't already upgraded to Photoshop 5.5, this is a good reason to do so, since ImageReady comes with a set of features that are invaluable for Web designers.

THE INFO PALETTE

The info palette shows both the color value and the position of the mouse, and updates both sets of information constantly. Open the info palette from the Window menu, then click and hold on the cross icon in the bottom-left corner, and select Pixel from the popup menu. The two eyedropper icons in the upper part of the palette

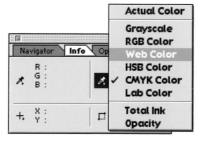

◀ In the Info Palette you can switch to the Web Color model by clicking on the eye dropper icon.

allow you to display two different color modes (RGB and CMYK, for example). You can select the settings for these the same way as you did the units—click on the icon to display the pop-up menu with your choices. Make sure that you select the Web color mode for at least for one of the displays; this shows the hexadecimal values (HTML) of a color and also—if the image is indexed—its position within the Color Look Up Table (CLUT).

Photo: Paul Ehrenreich

THE ACTION PALETTE

The action palette is a kind of macro processor, and one of the most useful tools for Web design. It allows you to record, and automatically repeat, several actions in Photoshop. You can even assign an action to a key, allowing you to trigger it with a single keystroke. I use this feature extensively; it makes working with Photoshop much more efficient.

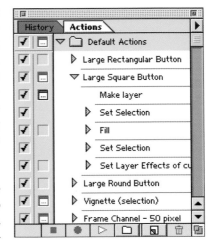

▲ Tasks that need to be performed over and over can be recorded in the action palette, then you can even batch process an entire folder with images.

Open the action palette from the Window menu, and if you want to trigger an action with a keystroke, click on the palette menu (the triangle in the upper–right corner) and select Button Mode. To record an action, you work with the palette as if it were a tape deck, using the buttons at the bottom of the palette. The red circle is for recording, the square stops the current recording, and the triangle plays back the macro. Before you start recording, click on the icon that looks like a sheet of paper to create a new action; otherwise you will record over an existing action.

Even though using the action palette is virtually self-explanatory, here are some tips on how you can optimize it for Web design.

➤ Toggle Dialog On/Off

When you record an action, you also record the settings in dialog boxes. To use a action flexibly, for different purposes, it is important to be able to change the settings in a dialog box. For instance, if you wanted to set up an action to automatically create several versions of one image, all indexed with a different color depth, you would need the ability to override the previously recorded settings. Here's how you would set up such an action:

1. Open an image and create a new action by clicking on the new action icon. The recording button should automatically switch on.

2. Select the entire image (Command-A), and copy it to the clipboard.

◀ Sometimes, when dialog boxes are recorded in an action, it might be necessary to use the "Toggle dialog on/off" switch to be able to change some settings. For example, whenever this action plays, it will stop at the New command and display the dialog box to allow the user to set the image size manually.

3. Select Command-N to create a new file, and a dialog box appears in which the new document has the same measurements as the image in the clipboard! Click OK, and paste the content of the clipboard into the new file using Command-V.

4. From the Layer palette menu select **Flatten Image.**

5. With Image > Mode > Indexed Color you can choose the color depth. For example, select **Adaptive** from the Palette popup menu, and 3 bit from the Color Depth popup menu. Steps 3 to 5 can be repeated as often as you want to make copies of your image. For example, you could create two more copies, one with 4 bit and one with 5 bit, before you stop the recording of the action. By replaying this action, you can create several views of your image with different color depths, compare them, and pick the one that gives you the best quality and the best compression.

The only problem now is that Photoshop will always use the same dimensions that are recorded in the script or the same color depth. This makes this action useful only if you are always dealing with the same size image (and the same color requirements)—which is very unlikely. If you want Photoshop to always use the current dimensions in the **New File** dialog box, then you have to open the action in the palette. Just click on the triangle next to the action name, and Photoshop lists all the individual tasks within that action. Then activate the modal control for all the **New File** commands. The **Toggle dialog on/off** control is in the second column from the left, and looks a bit like a dialog box. If you run the action again, Photoshop will open the **New File** dialog box, fill in the current dimensions and wait for you to confirm them. By the way, you can also activate the modal control for all dialog boxes at once within an action. Just click next to the **Toggle dialog on/off** icon next to the action entry in the palette

➤ Inserting Stops

If you want to create an action that allows you to make some manual changes with one of the tools, like creating a selection with the lasso for instance, you must insert a stop in the action. You can select this command from the **Action palette menu**. Select the step after which you want to insert a stop, and choose **Insert Stop**.

In the dialog box that appears, you can enter a comment to remind you what you are supposed to do. My favorite is: "Wake up ... make coffee," but you will probably want to write something more serious, like "Select the part of the image that you want to copy." Later on, the action will display the dialog box with a stop button for you to confirm the stop. Once you are done, a click on the play button in the palette will pick up where the action stopped.

Because it might not always be necessary to make changes, you can select the **Allow Continue** option in the Stop dialog box. Then, in addition to the

▲ Sometimes you have to include a Stop in an action, to make a selection with the Lasso Tool, for example. You can type in some instructions as a reminder when you are inserting the Stop command.

Stop button you will get a Continue button, saving you the hassle of clicking the play button in the action palette.

➤ Recording Paths in your Action

Paths are an alternative to Alpha Channels as a way of creating selections. If you create an action that requires a certain path, you must insert this path into the action rather than just selecting it; otherwise the action palette gives you an error message in a new document if the path doesn't exist.

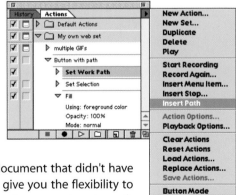

Suppose you want to create an action that builds a rounded button in each document. If you created the path in the original document and then recorded your action, Photoshop would only record the name of the path that you selected. This means you would not be able to use this action in another document that didn't have this path. To avoid this, and to give you the flexibility to use a path across many documents, you can insert a path in the action by first selecting the path, and then choosing the **Insert path** command from the **Action palette** menu.

➤ Batch Processing

One of the best features in the action palette is the ability to apply an action to several images automatically. This is called batch processing, and is partic-

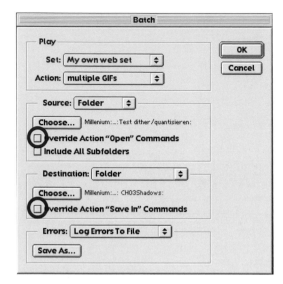

▲You might think you're being safe by choosing the Override options regardless of whether the action contains any Open or Save commands, but this will confuse the Batch command, and you'll get an error message.

Web Photo Gallery is a special Batch processing command that makes it easy to display a couple of images on the Internet: just choose the image folder and all the required HTML pages will be created along with the images and thumbnails.

ularly useful for Web designers, as they often have to convert several images with the same settings. To activate batch processing, first create the action that you want to apply, then choose **File > Automate > Batch**. The Batch dialog box displays all the sets and actions listed in the Action palette. Pick the right set and action and then—by clicking on **Choose**—select the folder (for Source) containing the images you want to be processed.

The **Override Action "Open"** Commands option is only important if your action actually has an open command. (Note: It is usually better to open a image before you start recording an action.) If you have no embedded **Open** command, this option must be deactivated! It might seem that this shouldn't matter, but it does and I have to emphasize this because more than once people have overlooked this and been frustrated because batch processing will display an error alert. By the way, the same is true for the option **Override Action Save In Commands** in the Destination section. If you have no **Save** command embedded in the action, don't activate the **Override** option!

If batch processing doesn't work as expected, use the Log Errors to File command. This simple text file contains all the events and errors that Photoshop encounters while running the script, which will usually give you enough information to fix the problem.

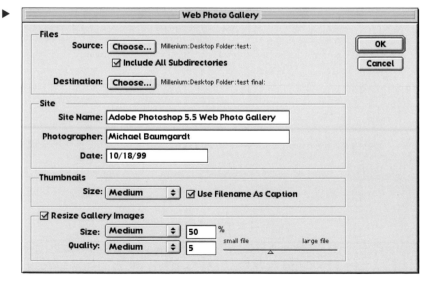

Photoshop also comes with a set of ready-made batch processing scripts that are all listed in **File > Automate.** One that might be particularly helpful to you is **Web Photo Gallery.** Just select an image folder and this script will generate a main page with all the images as thumbnails. A click on one of the images will bring you to an HTML page with an enlarged version of the image. Best of all, these pages include all the navigational elements to move parallel between the pages.

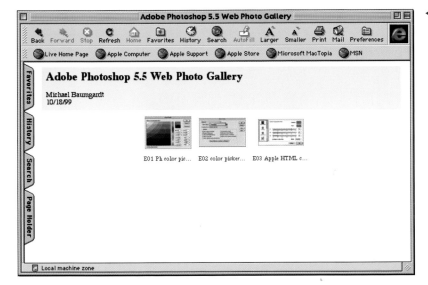

◄ In the top image you see the main page with the thumbnail images. On the bottom is the HTML page with an enlarged version of one of the images (a set of screenshots) along with all the navigational elements.

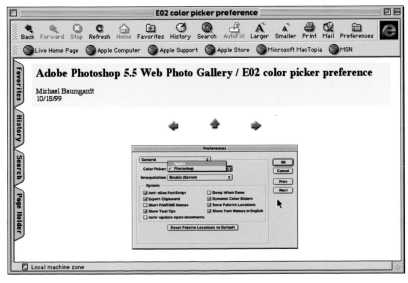

Illustration: Michael Baumgardt

PHOTOSHOP TECHNIQUES

Photoshop Techniques

Many designers these days start out by designing their Web sites in Photoshop to present their ideas. Only after the client has approved the plan does the designer actually build the site with an HTML authoring tool like GoLive. This process makes a lot of sense, since it is much easier to create and change a Photoshop design than one in HTML. Also, thanks to their low 72-dpi resolution, those Photoshop files stay relatively small and manageable even if you use plenty of layers.

In this chapter you will learn all the basic Photoshop techniques you'll need to create a Web site quickly and efficiently. For example, I'll cover how to work with the Layers palette, and how to use guides to split up an image into smaller pieces. The next chapter will focus on creating some of the fancier design elements.

HOW LARGE SHOULD YOUR CANVAS BE?

When you design a site, you should have a clear idea of who your target audience is going to be and what kind of equipment they will be using. For instance, since not everyone has a twenty-one-inch monitor it doesn't make much sense to create a design that requires that kind of viewing space. Many

For my documents, I usually choose a width of 550–600 pixels and a height of 1000 pixels. Even though the smallest screen is 640 pixels the browser's scroll bar and other elements take up some of that space. The document's height is more flexible, but it's a good idea to make it about 2.5 times the monitor height so viewers with small screens won't have to scroll too much.

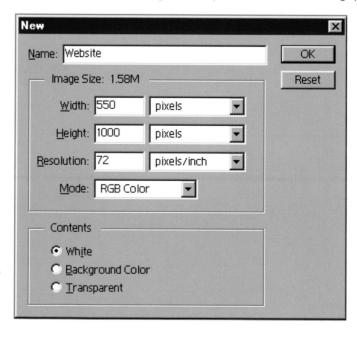

When creating a new document ▶ via File > New it is important to consider the monitor size of low–end computers.

Web design books recommend designing for fourteen-inch monitors running at 640 x 480 resolution, but this can be very limiting. Recent surveys show that most computer users these days have sixteen-inch monitors running at 800 x 600 resolution; however, there is a growing user base for WebTV (which uses fairly low resolution). You'll have to decide if you want to play it safe and go for 640 x 480, or take a chance on using a higher resolution. (You can always split the difference and base your design on 640 x 600. This way the width of your design won't cause problems on smaller screens, like forcing users to scroll left and right to view the entire page.)

▲ As a reminder of how much of the web site can be seen on smaller monitors, a horizontal guide is placed at approximately 350 pixels. When designing the site, you should place the main and key elements in the top part.

Select **File > New** (Command-N/Ctrl-N) to create a new, empty Photoshop document. Designate 72 dpi as the resolution, and anything between 640 and 800 pixels for width. Since it's easy for people to scroll down in a browser, you are, of course, free to use any length that you like, but it's a good idea to keep the main visual elements within an area of 340 vertical pixels. That's the area that everyone will be able to see, even on the tiniest screen with all the browser's navigational toolbars displayed.

WORKING WITH THE LAYERS PALETTE

The Layers palette is one of the most important tools in Photoshop; if you're not already familiar with it you should start by reading the Photoshop manual. Working with layers is essential for Web design. To get you started, here are some basics:

► The Layers Palette Quick Guide: Opening the Palette

You can open the Layers palette via **Window > Show Layers**. When you start a new document you will usually see only one layer (the background layer), but as soon as you paste some-

▲ Open the Layers palette from the Window menu. Just click on the Create New Layer icon to create a new layer.

thing from the clipboard into your new document, it becomes an additional layer. You can easily see this, as each layer usually has its own icon which helps you to find certain elements. You can also use the **Palette menu**, which is hidden behind the triangle in the upper-right corner, to create additional layers. The third way to create a layer is by using the **Create New Layer** icon at the bottom of the palette. Regardless of how you create layers, they all work the same.

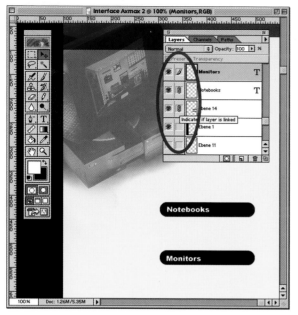

▲ Several layers can be grouped by clicking in the second column in the Layers palette. The chain icon shows which layers are linked together.

▶ Making Layers Visible/Invisible

You can hide a layer, or make it visible with a click on the Eye icon next to the layer listing.

▶ Moving Layers

You can arrange your layers using the **Move tool** in the upper-right corner of the Tools palette. First activate the layer in the Layers palette, then select the Move tool, click on the image, and drag the layer to the desired position. It's just as easy to move several layers at once so they keep their relative position. Click in the second column of the Layers palette (next to the Eye icon), and a chain icon should appear. Now the layer is grouped together with the currently selected layer, and you can treat the group as one layer.

By the way, if a new layer is larger than your background layer it won't get truncated if you move it outside the working area. Even if you flatten multiple layers to one layer, they will keep the measurements of the largest one. Since those hidden image areas can add substantially to your file size, you may want to consider cropping some of your layers to save on memory and disk space. To do that, use the **Crop tool** to select the entire image, then double click inside the rectangle and all your layers will be cropped. If that's not

THE LAYERS PALETTE: OPACITY AND LAYER MODES

The opacity parameter defines how much a layer blends with the layers underneath it. You can enter a value directly, or click and hold on the arrow to use a slider. ▶

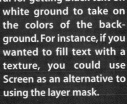

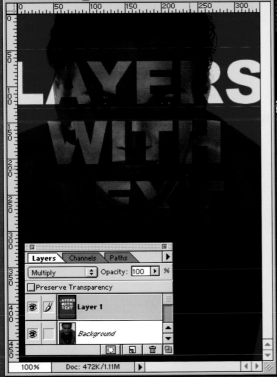

◀ You can select from a variety of layer modes: Dissolve, Multiply, Screen, Overlay, Soft Light, Hard Light, Color Dodge, Color Burn, Darken, Lighten, Difference, Exclusion, Hue, Saturation, Color and Luminosity. Multiply is useful for combining the color values of one layer with the layers beneath, as you can see in the example on the left. Difference (see below) is great for photo compositions, while Screen is helpful for getting black text on white ground to take on the colors of the background. For instance, if you wanted to fill text with a texture, you could use Screen as an alternative to using the layer mask.

what you want, you can use the **Rectangular Marquee tool** instead—activate the layer you want to crop, then select the portion of it you want to keep. Invert the selection via **Select > Inverse**, and press **Delete** to delete the unwanted area. If you want to keep a larger area of the layer, you'll have to move it with the **Move tool** first, and then use the **Select tool** before you move it back. There is no other way to accomplish this, since you can't go outside the working area with the **Select tool**.

➤ Layer Modes and Opacity

Layers can have a opacity level of anywhere from one to one hundred percent. You can use the **Opacity slider** in the **Layers palette** to select how much the current layer will be blended with the layers underneath. In addition, you can combine layers using one of several mathematical algorithms like **Multiply**, **Overlay** or **Soft Light**.

➤ Layer Masks

Sometimes you want to make a layer only partially transparent—this is where you can use layer masks. To add a layer mask to a layer, select the layer and either choose **Layer > Add Layer Mask > Reveal All**, or click on the **Add Layer Mask icon** in the **Layers palette** (the leftmost icon at the bottom). A new (white) area should appear next to the layer thumbnail in the palette. You will see a chain symbol between the icons, which works just the same as it does with layers: click on the symbol to group or ungroup the **Layer Mask** and the Layer.

After adding a Layer Mask, a white or black area (depending on whether you choose Reveal all or Hide all) is visible next to the layer preview. You can then use the Airbrush Tool to change the transparency of the Layer Mask.

▲ The black areas in the layer mask reveal the background. To make sure that you paint with the Airbrush inside the Layer Mask, click on the Layer Mask Preview.

◀ The Layer Mask can be deactivated temporarily: a Shift–click on the Layer Mask will do the trick.

◀ If you want to see just the Layer Mask, hold the Alt/Option key and click on the Layer Mask.

To make part of your layer transparent, select the Airbrush tool (or any other tool that may seem appropriate), click on the **Layer Mask icon** in the palette (it should acquire a heavier border, and the color fields in the **Tool palette** should switch to black and white), and start painting onto the layer mask. To see any effect, you have to use the right color: Black represents one hundred percent transparency—if you want to make parts of your image transparent be sure you select black when using the airbrush. The same holds true for the reverse: if some parts of the layer are too transparent, you can use white to make them more visible. By the way, you can view the layer mask by clicking on the icon in the palette while holding the **Command key** (or Alt on a PC). This can come in handy if you place text in the layer mask.

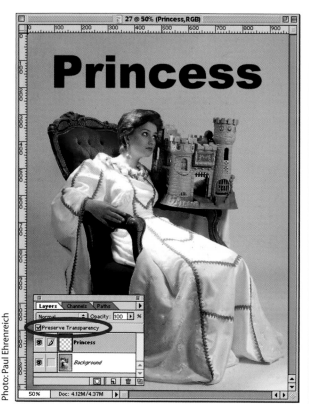

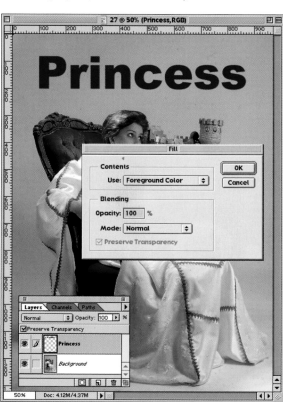

Photo: Paul Ehrenreich

▲ A layer (in this example a converted text layer) can be filled using Layer > Fill. It's important to have the Preserve Transparency option activated in the Layers Palette.

➤ Transparency

For many design tasks that involve layers, you may want to leave the transparent parts out. To make sure the transparent area is not affected by any filter or command, select the **Preserve Transparency** option in the Palettes menu. This won't help you with partially transparent areas like you may have at the edges, but everything that is completely transparent can be protected this way. For instance, take a common task like changing the color of an area with the **Fill command**. If the **Preserve Transparency** option is not selected, the **Fill command** will fill the whole layer.

➤ Adjustment Layers

Since version 4.0, Photoshop has included a great tool to help adjust and ma-nipulate images and layers without permanently affecting the image. This function, **Adjustment Layers**, allows you to apply (for example) **Bright-ness/Contrast** on one or more layers, but since it is handled like a layer you can turn it on and off at any time, or manipulate it pretty much the same way as layer masks or a regular layer. Here's a step-by-step guide to give you an idea of how to work with the Adjustment Layer:

1. In the Layers palette, select the layer to which you would like to add an adjustment layer (the **Adjustment Layer** will be inserted above the current-ly selected layer).

▲ If you forgot to activate the Preserve Transparency option the whole layer will be filled. In that case just use Undo and try again.

◄ Clicking on the Eye icon in the layer palette will deactivate the Adjustment layer.

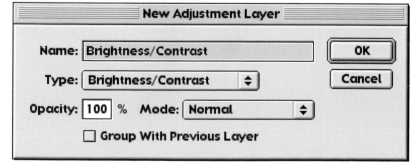

▲ After inserting an Adjustment Layer you can select the type of effect from the pop–up menu.

▲ Clicking inside the document window while holding the Control key (Mac) or the right mouse button (Win) will show a pop-up menu where you can select one of the layers directly.

◀ Like the Layer Mask, the Adjustment Layer can be manipulated using a tool like the Airbrush tool, which gives you precise control over where and how much adjustment you get. In this example the background of the photo is blacked out so the Brightness/Contrast Adjustment Layer is only affecting the person in the photo.

2. Choose Layer > New > Adjustment Layer to bring up a dialog box in which you can select the command or function that you want to apply. For example, select **Brightness/Contrast** from the pop-up menu and click **OK**. The **Brightness/Contrast dialog box** will appear and you can enter your settings.

3. The adjustment layer has now been added to the **Layers palette**; you can set the transparency level and the layer mode as you do with any other layer. Even more important, you can now paint into the **Adjustment Layer** with the **Airbrush tool** and define precisely how much adjustment you actually want for different areas.

➤ **Selecting Layers**

If you work with the **Layers palette** a lot, sooner or later you will find it tedious to have to select a layer in the palette before you can move and drag it. This process is not very intuitive, especially if you have used a graphics program like Adobe Illustrator where you can simply click on an object to make it active.

Well, you won't find the same convenience in Photoshop, but you will find something that comes very close: if you hold down the **Command button** (or the **Ctrl button** on PCs) and click with the **Move tool** on the object you want to move, Photoshop will automatically select the layer on which the object lies. The currently activated layer will be displayed at the top of the document window.

Sometimes there are just too many layers on top of one another, which makes it hard for you (and for Photoshop) to be clear about which layer you want. In this case select the **Move tool**, right-click (Windows) or

Control-click (Mac OS) in the image, and choose the layer you want from the context menu that appears. The context menu lists all the layers that contain pixels under the current pointer location. By the way, the context menus are available for almost all the tools. For example, if you're using the **Pencil tool** you can select a different brush form and size.

> **Layer Preview**

There are different preview sizes for the layers in the Layers palette; to switch between them, select **Layers Palette Options** from the palette pop-up menu in the upper-right corner. You can select one of three preview sizes, or you can turn off the preview altogether.

▲ Layer Palette Options lets you choose the size of the layer preview.

CHANGING COLORS

One of the most common tasks you'll encounter while designing Web pages is changing the color of an object. Like in the example on page 108, the easiest way to do this for a solid colored area is using the **Preserve Transparency** option of the **Layers Palette**. A typical example would be if you discover that a button is not using a Web-safe color, and it dithers too much on monitors with less than 256 colors. So now you want to change its color to the closest color in the Web-Safe Color palette—here's what you do:

1. Activate the layer that contains the object you want to color. Make sure the **Preserve Transparency** option is selected.

2. Pick up the color of the object that you want to change by clicking on it with the **Eyedropper tool** (it now becomes the foreground color in the **Tool palette**). Double-click on the color field in the **Tool palette** to open the color picker and change the color to the closest Web color by activating the **Only Web Colors** option.

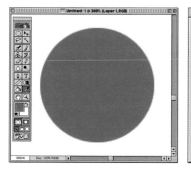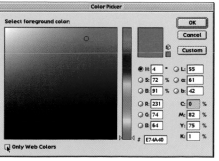

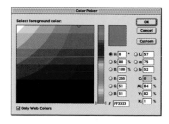

▲ After activating the Only Web Colors option, the current color will be shifted.

The Paint Bucket tool was used to fill the area. It's important to activate the Anti-alias option in the Option palette. ▶

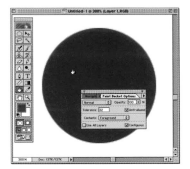

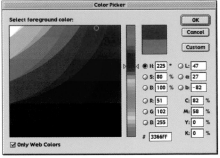

In the mock–up of the Axmax Web site, several paper clips were used as navigational elements. The basis for all these paper clips was a single photo of a blue paper clip that was modified using the Replace Color command. Using Hue and Saturation, the former blue color is changed to red (or any other color from the spectrum). ▼

3. Double click on the the **Paint Bucket** icon to open its options. (Alternately, you could open the tool options via **Windows > Show Options**). In the options palette you will see a parameter for **Tolerance** and the **Contiguous** and **Anti-alias** options. If the Tolerance is set to zero, only the pixels with the exact same color will be filled. The new Contiguous option restricts the selection or fill to areas connected to the area clicked, but the most important option for this example (of changing the color of a button) is Anti-alias. It will

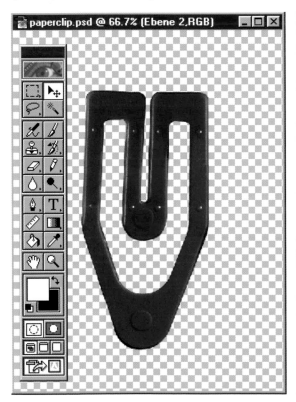

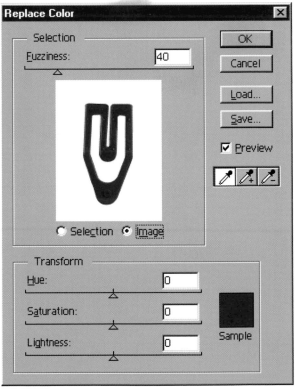

ensure that the intermediate colors at the edges will also be filled. So make sure that it is selected (which it is by default) and then click inside the object that you want to change.

➤ Changing the Color of an Object

If you come from the world of desktop publishing, this technique may be completely new to you, since you seldom need to change colors in a photo intended for print. But if you do Web design, this trick can save you cost of an entire photo shoot, since it allows you to reuse one element of a photo over and over again. On the Axmax Demo Web site, for example, you can see six paper clips in different colors being used as navigational elements. Even though they look quite different, they are all made from one photo of a blue paper clip.

1. To change the color of the paper clip, choose **Image > Adjust > Replace Color**.

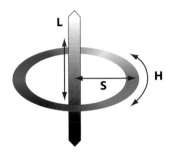

▲ This graphs shows how the Replace Color command works: the Hue slider rotates the colors within the spectrum , the Saturation slider represents the movement toward the center and the Lightness slider changes the colors along the vertical axis.

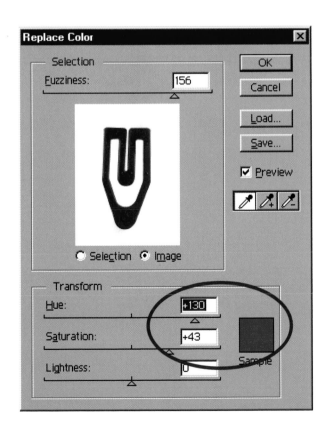

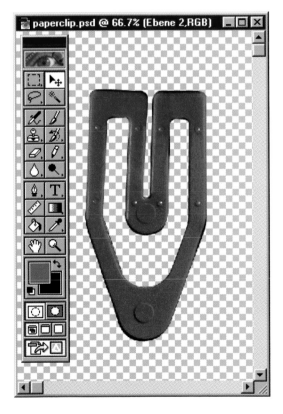

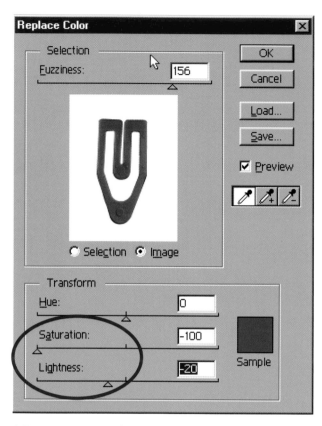

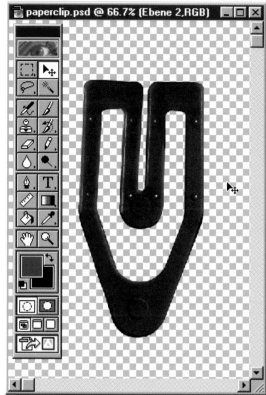

▲ To create variations of gray, reduce the Saturation to zero and
then use the Lightness slider for
various shades of gray.

2. Using the Eyedropper tool, I selected a blue tone that was in between the
darkest and brightest blue tones of the paper clip. Then I used the **Fuzziness
slider** to change the tolerance to 160. You can select additional colors by using the **Eyedropper tool** with the plus sign until the entire object is selected.

3. Once all the color tones of the paper clip are selected, you can use the
Hue slider to shift through the color spectrum. If the preview is activated you
can see how the changes affect your original image. To get white and black,
including various levels of gray, use the **Saturation slider** and set it to -100.
The brightness of the black (gray) can then be set with the **Lightness slider**.

CORRECTING COLORS

One of the standard tasks in Photoshop is color correcting photos. This is particularly important if the photo wasn't shot in a professional photo studio.
Very often those images suffer from a shift in colors due to variations in light-

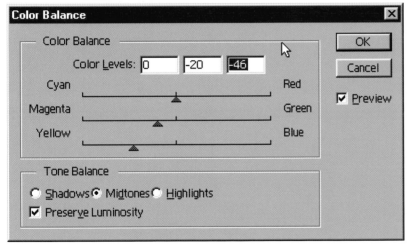

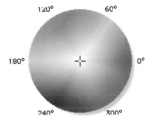

▲ This color wheel shows how Color Balance works. Cyan and Red are on opposite sides of the spectrum, as are Magenta and Green, and Yellow and Blue. Use the sliders to move between the poles. For example, to correct an image containing too much blue, you move the bottom slider to the left.

ing conditions. Daylight, for instance, brings out different color frequencies than neon light, and you have to correct those color differences in Photoshop.

Photoshop offers two commands aimed at color correction: **Color Balance** and **Variations**. Both do exactly the same thing; only their approaches and interfaces are different. The **Color Balance** command (**Image > Adjust > Color Balance**) allows you to change the color via three sliders, while in the Variations command (**Image > Adjust > Variations**) you work with a preview in which you see several variations of the same image and select the one you like the best. Both functions work by shifting the image color toward the value on the opposite side of the color wheel (red shifts toward cyan, yellow shifts toward blue, and so on). For example, to correct a red tone

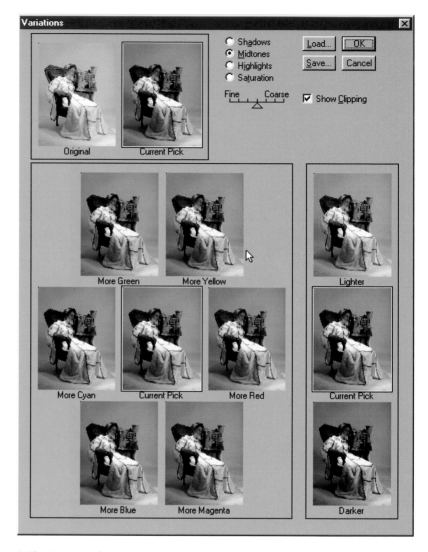

▲ **The intensity of the variation is set with the Fine/Coarse slider.**

in your image you would have to add more cyan, to compensate for too much green you would shift toward magenta, and to correct for blue you would add yellow.

Even though the **Variations** command seems more intuitive, you can actually get a more precise result by using **Color Balance,** because it allows you to set the value for each color between zero and one hundred, while the

Variations dialog box forces you to choose one of only six possible alternatives. The only tricky part of using **Color Balance** is deciding which color needs to be shifted to correct the image. Once you have determined that, making the actual correction is very simple: just move the appropriate color slider in the correct direction. (For instance, if the image has too much yellow, the Yellow/Blue color slider needs to be moved towards blue.)

If you are using the **Variations** command to correct colors, adjust the **Fine/Coarse slider** until one of the previews is just the right color; click on it and it becomes the new **Current Pick**, with new variations around it.

Photoshop 5.0 brought significant changes in the Hue/Saturation dialog box, one of which was direct visual control of the Hue slider. The bottom image shows how much the spectrum has shifted. ▼

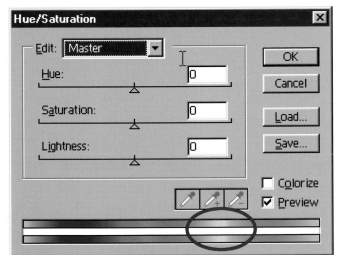

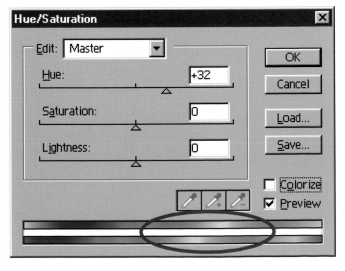

With Hue/Saturation you can also shift and correct only certain parts of the spectrum, like in this example all the red tones.

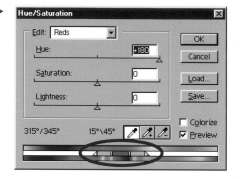

Another great tool for color correction is the **Hue/Saturation** command (**Image > Adjust > Hue/Saturation**). Adobe has improved the interface for this command with Photoshop 5.0, and has added two color bars at the bottom of the dialog box which make it much easier to see what you are doing. Using the **Hue slider**, you can rotate the color wheel. The **Saturation slider** controls the movement towards the center of the color wheel, and the Lightness slider controls the L-Axis (see p. 113).

Consider using **Selective Color** as an additional tool for making color corrections. Although it's generally used for correcting colors for printing, you can use it for RGB images too. The main advantage is that it allows you to

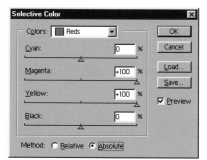

◀ Desktop Publishers might find it easier to do color corrections using the CMYK model. You can do this with the Selective Color command.

The red color of the chair was changed and made brighter using the Selective Colors command (see previous page). ▼

▲ The original image (at the top) was modified twice with the Hue/Saturation command.

Photo: Paul Ehrenreich

USING A DIGITAL CAMERA

A digital camera is a must-have for Web designers. Print design aside, the resolution of these cameras is perfectly sufficient for most applications. If you're building a Web site on a small budget, you will probably have to rely on stock photos—this is where a digital camera may give you a little more flexibility. It also frees you from legal problems, since stock photos are not always license-free or may have other restrictions for online publishing. If you're working on a PowerMac, you most likely have Audio/Video Input already. The three RCA jacks connect your video camera to the computer, and you can use the Apple Video Player software that comes with the operating system to transfer still images into the computer. (If you hook up your VCR, you can even watch videos while working, which might help you get through a long long work day.) To check if you have an video input, just look for a yellow input (audio inputs are marked red and black).

correct the image by using the process colors Cyan, Magenta, Yellow and Black. Most designers who come from the desktop publishing field are far more familiar with defining colors this way, so using this command can make life a little bit easier for them.

HOW TO MAKE WHITE DISAPPEAR IN A LAYER

Very often you will be faced with a situation in which an element on a layer has a white background. Sometimes you can erase the background manually, but it's usually impossible. For example, if you have black text on a white

◀ White areas in a layer can be eliminated by using the Multiply mode. This works best for a layer with a strong contrast, as with this screenshot of text that was laid out in GoLive and then imported into Photoshop.

▲ If Anti-Alias is selected in the Text Window, the edges will be smoothed. When the image is later exported as a GIF with Transparency, this can become a problem, since the extra colors at the edge become visible.

▲ The red of the background was selected as a transparency color, which will make the anti-aliased edge visible.

background, you can't get rid of the white behind all those letters and characters with the **Eraser tool**. One way to solve this problem is to click **Select > Color Range**, choose white with the **Eyedropper tool**, and then delete white with the backspace button—but this solution is not the most elegant one. A better technique is to use one of the layer modes, which are basically mathematical algorithms that control the ways layers are composed. The **Multiply** mode does exactly what you want. Since white is represented by 100 (meaning that the underlying layer and its color values are multiplied one hundred percent), all the white areas disappear. The drawback of using **Multiply** is that it changes the color values of the selected layer; depending on the layer this may be an undesirable effect. However, if your layer has a strong black and white contrast like the screenshot of text on the previous page, this method is the easiest way to make the white disappear.

AVOIDING HALOS

In order to create lines and edges that are not perfectly vertical or horizontal, Photoshop employs an approximation based on the available resolution. To get the best result, many programs—including Photoshop—use a technique called anti-aliasing, in which pixels at the edges of an object are smoothed to blend with the background.

The intermediate colors that anti-aliasing creates are only a problem when you are planning to use transparency with a GIF. If the image is viewed on a browser in front of the same color as the transparency color, you won't have a problem. But if you change the background in the Browser at some point, your image may show a halo at the edges. Fortunately, Photoshop offers you a great way of dealing with this problem. The best way to demonstrate it is with an example that you are very likely to run into: rendering a headline as an image.

Because it is always a bit tricky to get a headline or a subtitle to display in a specific font on the user's monitor, Web designers usually rely on rendering text as an image. To make sure the text-image displays correctly in the browser and blends perfectly into the background, it is important that, before you render the text, you use a background color that's as close as possible to the one on your Web page. To accomplish this, follow this step-by-step procedure:

1. Create a new document, select a color for the font, and click on the working area with the **Text tool**. Photoshop will automatically create a new layer and allow you to select a font and size. Be sure to select the **Anti-Alias** option.

◀ After the text is placed with the Anti-alias option activated, hide the background layer by clicking on the eye icon in the Layers palette.

2. Since you want the background to be transparent, hide the background layer by clicking on the **Eye icon** in the **Layers palette**. A gray and white checkerboard signals that the background is now transparent. Choose **Save for Web** from the **File menu** to display the **Save for Web dialog box**. Click the **Optimized tab**. Set the format to GIF, and (as you will see) the **Transparency option** will be automatically preselected. Now, to make sure the edges are anti-aliased to the background color in the browser, select the **Mat-**

If you are using an older version of Photoshop, or if you want to use the File > Export > GIF89a Export command, you will have to select the background layer in the Layers palette. Since this is a new document, most likely the background layer is white. Use the Tool palette to choose a new color for the background. Then, using the Paint Bucket tool, fill in the background layer. At this point it's a good idea to save the file; in the next step you will have to flatten the layers, and you want to keep them intact in case you have to come back later and change the color again. Finally, convert to Indexed Color via Image > Mode and use the Export command to pick the background color as your transparency color.

◀ Select Transparency and choose the background color from the Matte pop-up menu: the text will then be anti-aliased towards that color.

te pop-up menu. Here you can choose between **Eyedropper Color** (the color in the upper-left corner of the dialog box), **Black**, **White**, and **Other**. If you select **Other**, the **Photoshop color picker** will appear, you can select your color, and Photoshop will immediately adjust the edges accordingly. When trying out this example, use colors that contrast strongly with your text color; otherwise you won't see much change.

3. Click OK. The **File Selector dialog box** appears, giving you the option of saving your work as an HTML file. You can use this to check the result in a browser. Save in HTML, then open the file in Netscape Navigator or Microsoft Explorer to see how your text looks in front of the background color you selected.

VECTOR GRAPHICS: USING ILLUSTRATOR WITH PHOTOSHOP

Even though Photoshop's Pen tool works just like the pen in Illustrator, Photoshop is not the ideal choice for creating vector graphics. It is much more convenient and flexible to use Illustrator—particularly since it's so easy to import those objects into Photoshop. In order to do this, however, you do need to know a couple of things, such as how to define a Web-safe color in Illustrator, and how to match the color that you used in your Photoshop document.

▲ An invisible frame the same size as the target image will allow you to preserve the absolute position of elements when you paste them into Photoshop.

▶ Importing Vector Graphics

You can save Adobe Illustrator graphics as TIFFs or Photoshop files, which you can then open in Photoshop, but it is usually better to do the rasterizing in Photoshop. One advantage is that Photoshop will preserve transparency; if you rasterize a circle in Illustrator you will always end up with a white background. In any case, importing and rasterizing a vector graphic in Photoshop is pretty simple, particularly if you work with Illustrator (or any graphics soft-

◀ Photoshop can't create text along a path, but you can easily do it in Illustrator, then copy and paste it into Photoshop.

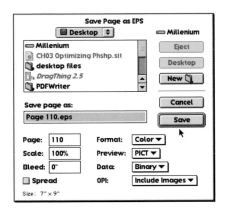
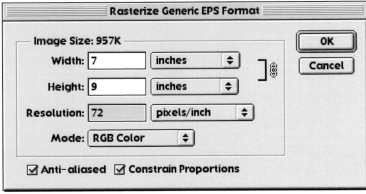

▲ You can even use elements and designs created in a layout program like QuarkXPress or Adobe InDesign and import them into Photoshop. Just save the page as an EPS and open the file in Photoshop.

ware that can save a Illustrator file). Most programs will allow you to copy an element to the clipboard with Command-C/Cntrl-C, and paste it into a new Photoshop layer using Command-V/Cntrl-V, but you can also open an Illustrator or EPS file directly in Photoshop.

As the inventor and developer of the PostScript standard, Adobe created a special file format for Illustrator that allows you to save an editable Post-Script file. This file can be imported into other programs like any other EPS graphic, but you can still open it in Illustrator and make changes.

Most graphics programs allow you to save image files in an editable EPS format, thus making it possible to have illustrations generated in one graphics program easily transferable to another. Macromedia FreeHand was one of the first programs to offer this capability, but other programs like Corel-DRAW now offer it too. In most cases you will find this option listed in the Save dialog box, or as an Export command.

If you are not using Illustrator, but want to import vector-based graphics from any program into Photoshop, save the graphic as a regular EPS file. Because EPS is such a widely used standard, most programs that work with vector-based elements offer this option. Photoshop can even interpret an EPS file that was created in QuarkXPress, although it doesn't always work and you may end up with unexpected results, especially when the layout includes both images and text. This is a combination that causes problems in Photoshop regardless of where the EPS comes from.

Use Points as Units in Illustrator
—every point will translate as
one pixel when importing an
element into Photoshop. ▶

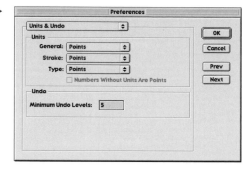

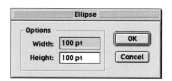

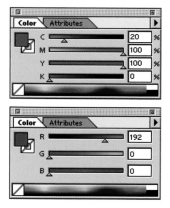

▲ In Illustrator, hold down the
Alt/Option key and click in the
work area to bring up a dialog
box in which you can enter the
dimensions of your image.

▲ If you are working in CMYK
mode on an image for print, use
the CMY color sliders in 20%
increments to create colors from
the Web-safe color palette. When
the graphics are destined for the
Web, use RGB color values in
increments of 51.

▶ The Right Size

Enlarging an image in Photoshop reduces its quality, so
you should plan on designing
your graphics to work in 1:1
scale. Because one point is
equal to one pixel in Photoshop, it's a good idea to
choose points for rulers and
units in Illustrator. You'll find
these settings in Illustrator in **File > Preferences >Units & Undo**. If you prefer, you can always enter "pt" when you create a object using a dialog box.
(Hold the Alt/Option key and click with the tool inside the work area. Illustrator will then display a dialog box for numerical entry.)This way when you
import an object created in Illustrator into Photoshop, either by dragging it
from Illustrator to the Photoshop document, or by opening it via the menu,
the element will have the same size in pixels.

▶ Preserving the Layers

One tiny problem encountered when importing a vector graphic from Illustrator or another graphics program into Photoshop is that all the layers get
flattened. While this may not seem so terrible, it can cause a problem if you
want to change the color of individual elements later on. Because the layers
are flattened you'll have to go back into Illustrator, make the changes there,
and import the object into Photoshop again.

There are two solutions to this problem. The first one involves creating
several layers in the graphics program and dragging each element (or group
of elements) onto its own layer in Photoshop. For example, if you create several buttons in Illustrator you may want to place all the buttons on one layer,
and all the text for the buttons on another layer. Now, if you wish, you can
hide the other layers, save the document, switch to Photoshop and import
this file; of course the hidden layers stay hidden. Or you can drag the layers individually into the open Photoshop document.

The only problem with the latter technique is that you have to position
each layer again. To avoid this, place an invisible rectangle—one with no col-
or attributes—with the same measurements as your Photoshop document in
the back. Every time you want to import an element from Illustrator to Photoshop just make sure your selection includes the transparent rectangle, and

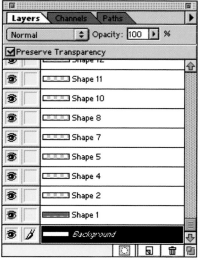

You can use Painter to import an Illustrator file into Photoshop with all its layers intact. First import the Illustrator file to Painter, then save it as a Photoshop 3.0 file, which can then be opened in Photoshop 5.5.

copy it to the clipboard. When you paste the contents of the clipboard into your Photoshop document, your elements will be in exactly the same position as they were in Illustrator.

A second way to bring your graphic elements over to Photoshop while maintaining their layers is with Painter from MetaCreations. Because Painter can use pixel- and vector-graphics at the same time, it's a great tool for designing Web pages—but for now we'll just use it to move the Web design that we created in Illustrator into Photoshop. To do this, save the illustration as an Illustrator–EPS file, open it up in MetaCreations Painter, and select Save As from the File menu. This step is very important, because only here do you have the option of saving the file in Photoshop 3.0 format. Later, when you open this document in Photoshop, you will have all your layers intact, which can save you quite a lot of time if you are working with a complex illustration.

▲ When an illustration (top) gets imported into Photoshop all the CMYK colors will be converted into the RGB color space, and you will end up with shifted colors (bottom). So whenever you plan on importing elements from Illustrator to Photoshop, use the RGB color mode for defining colors.

▲ Using File > Import a file saved as an EPS can be opened in Painter. Painter even keeps the layers intact: all the paths of an Illustrator layer will be grouped together, as in this example.

OPTIMIZING IMAGES

Except for navigational elements like buttons, most images on the Web are photos. Preparing photos for the Web requires different skills than preparing them for printing. Compression, which is not an issue in desktop publishing, becomes a main focus in designing for the Web—along with differences in Gamma and brightness on various computer monitors. Simply saving a photo in JPEG format is not enough to make it Web-ready.

➤ Getting Rid of Noise and Scratches

One of the first steps in preparing a photo for the Web, regardless of whether it will be saved as a GIF or a JPEG, is to get rid of noise and scratches. The print medium is much more forgiving of small imperfections than a monitor is—plus these flaws can actually have an impact on compression. For big scratches, you will probably have to make corrections manually with the Rubber Stamp tool, but smaller problems can be corrected with some of Photoshop's filters.

➤ Eliminating Noise

Noise in a photo can come from imperfections in the film itself, or from a bad scanner. This kind of noise can have an impact when you save a GIF (depending on your settings) or a JPEG. The rule of thumb is the less noise you have, the better compression you will achieve.

The Filters menu provides not one but three filters designed to reduce noise. Each one employs a slightly different approach; you shouldn't select one arbitrarily.

The **Despeckle** filter reduces noise by blurring the image subtly while preserving areas with strong contrasts. In other words, the filter blurs only those pixels with minor differences in color so contours won't become fuzzy. Unlike the standard **Blur** filter, which affects everything in the photo (making it look out of focus), when you use **Despeckle** the photo doesn't lose too much quality. It's great for small amounts of noise, but if the contrast of the noise is very high (for example, if there was dust on the photo you scanned) you may not get the result you want. For smoothing gradations or blended color areas in an image with strong contrasts, the **Despeckle** filter is the way to go. You can apply it more than once until you get the desired blurring effect.

The **Median** filter adjusts the brightness of adjacent pixels by interpolating their color values while disregarding all the values beyond a certain

REMOVING DUST AND SCRATCHES

Here are a couple examples ▶
of how a photo with dust
and scratches can be
repaired. In the original
photo (to the left) are very
heavy scratches that were
treated with the Despeckle
filter. Even though they have
almost vanished, you still can
see parts of the scratches
(right). In cases like this try
using the other filters that
are mentioned here.

Photo: Paul Ehrenreich

With the Median Filter you ▶
can achieve quite impres-
sive results. As you can see
in this example all scratches
were eliminated with
almost no traces.

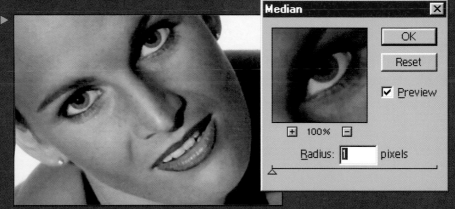

The Dust & Scratches filter ▶
lets you use the Radius
slider to define what will be
treated as dust. The Threshold slider adjusts the
filter's sensitivity to contrast
and Saturation changes.
One side effect of this filter
is that it blurs the image; to
avoid a serious loss of quality, use this filter on selected
parts of the image.

threshold. It works a lot like the **Despeckle** filter, except that **Median** interpolates while **Despeckle** blurs. You use a slider to select the range of pixels that you want Photoshop to interpolate; it's best to stay between one and three pixels. Since a GIF compresses more efficiently if several pixels on a horizontal row have the same color value, this filter can be particularly handy if you are preparing GIFs.

The **Dust & Scratches** filter lets you designate the size of the dust and scratches that you want to eliminate by using the **Radius slider**. If you set the slider to one pixel, only one-pixel scratches will be corrected; all larger scratches will be ignored. Use the **Threshold slider** to define the degree of contrast that Photoshop should use to distinguish a scratch.

➤ Washed-Out Images

Sometimes the situation is the other way around: noise isn't a problem, but the images lack the pep and contrast you want them to have. Most Photoshop beginners make the mistake of using the **Brightness/Contrast** function found under **Image > Adjust** menu, but this is only one of many options you can use to enhance your image—and it's usually not the best one. Here's a list of tools and functions you can use to enhance dull images:

➤ Brightness/Contrast

The **Brightness/Contrast** command allows you to adjust these two parameters. Because everyone is familiar with these effects from their TV, there isn't much to add, except that before you go for Brightness/Contrast, you ought to try the **Levels** command. It often yields better results.

➤ Levels

When you select the **Levels** command (**Image > Adjust > Levels**), Photoshop creates a histogram of the image. That means that Photoshop looks at each pixel and its brightness value, and presents it in a chart. It makes it easy for you to see what kinds of visual information your image is composed of, and obviously it can be a great help in analyzing the image.

More important, in the Levels dialog box you can extend the tonal range of the image. If the majority of your image's tonal values are in the range of twenty to eighty percent, you can expand those values to the full range of zero to one hundred percent. This will instantly give your image much more contrast and detail. To stretch the histogram of an image to the maximum

CORRECTING IMAGES WITH LEVELS

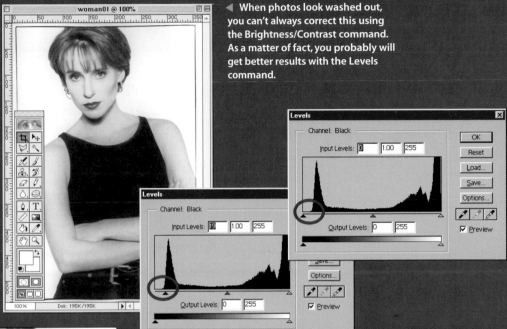

◀ When photos look washed out, you can't always correct this using the Brightness/Contrast command. As a matter of fact, you probably will get better results with the Levels command.

▲ To adjust the tonal range of your image, move the black point and white point sliders to the edges of the histogram (in this example only the black point slider needed to be adjusted). You can also move the grey slider for a non-linear adjustment.

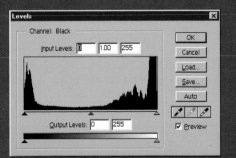

◀ Click OK, then reopen the Levels dialog box to see the results of the adjustment. Now the colors use the full range of 256 levels.

▲ With Unsharp Mask you can get even very blurry photos back into focus.

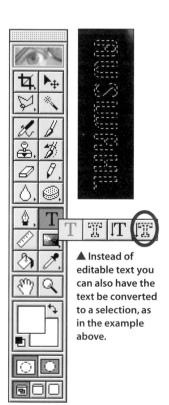

▲ Instead of editable text you can also have the text be converted to a selection, as in the example above.

amount, simply adjust the black and white Input Levels triangles to the left and right of the histogram. Click **OK**, and the shadows and highlights will be adjusted. The slider triangle in the middle sets the value for fifty percent, meaning it will indicate the middle of the tone range. Checking the **Preview** checkbox lets you watch the effect the sliders have while you are changing parameters. Once you click **OK**, call up **Levels** again to see how the tone range has been stretched.

➤ Unsharp Mask

One common cause of a bad image is soft focus. Photoshop provides a set of filters to enhance sharpness; they are all gathered in the **Filters** menu under **Sharpen**. The most useful filter in this collection is **Unsharp Mask,** which allows you to set the precise amount, radius and threshold for sharpness enhancement. As with **Levels**, you can watch the effect of adjusting these parameters if you check the **Preview** checkbox. If you plan to save the image as a JPEG you should use this effect sparingly, because JPEG's compression algorithm actually works best on slightly blurred images.

WORKING WITH TEXT

When creating headlines for use on the Web , rendering them in Photoshop is still the surest way to get the font and appearance you want. HTML has progressed a lot, and now includes the FONT tag as well as dynamic fonts (PFR format) which allow you to save the outlines of a PostScript font and install it on your Web site. Nonetheless, rendering text in Photoshop is still the easiest and safest way to go because you don't have to worry about compatibility issues. That's reason enough for me to dedicate part of this chapter to working with text.

➤ The Text Tool

Since the release of Photoshop 5.0, it has become much easier to work with text. In earlier versions, text was automatically converted into pixels, which made it uneditable. Luckily, you won't have that problem any more, and you can make changes to text and fonts as often as you like.

If you have never used this tool before, give it a try; click in your work area with the **Text tool**, select font and point size in the dialog box, enter the text, and click **OK**. Now bring the **Text tool** on top of the text again, and the tool changes its appearance (the dotted outline disappears) to signal that with the next click you will be able to edit the text instead of placing new text.

And indeed, if you do click, the same dialog box reappears, and you can select your text and change it. (I know, this doesn't sound like that big a deal, but it was a major improvement when version 5.0 was released!) The **Text tool** is even flexible enough to allow you to use mixed fonts; just select a couple of characters in the dialog box and change the font setting.

DYNAMIC FONTS WITH HEXMAC TYPOGRAPH

At one time, the only way to incorporate fancy fonts in Web design was to convert them to a GIF in Photoshop. With Dynamic Fonts you can now save any font as a PFR file and use it on your Web site. The PFR file format was specifically developed for online use, and lets you file one or more fonts for your Web site. Navigator and Explorer (4.0 and higher) can interpret PFR files, so if backwards compatibility is not an issue, Dynamic Fonts are a great feature.

Typograph 2.0 is an inexpensive program that creates PFR files. It is available as either a stand-alone application or as an extension to BBEdit. You can download a demo from their Web site at www.hexmac.com.

Creating Dynamic Fonts with Typograph is easy: start by clicking the Burn button in the main palette, choose the fonts you want from the list in the dialogue box that appears, and burn the PFR file. To increase download speed, you can remove single characters from a font with the subset button. To prevent Dynamic Fonts from being stolen, the URL is embedded into the PFR file.

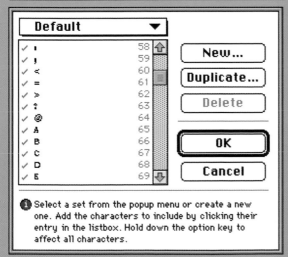

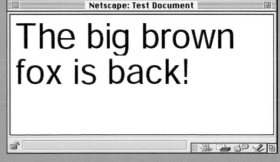

▲ This text uses a font that may not be installed on the viewer's computer. A PFR font embedded in the Web site makes it viewable.

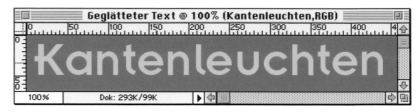

▲ Anti-Alias will smooth the edges to create a better display. Make sure that the background matches the one in the browser (or use Matte) to avoid halos with transparency.

By the way, there are two variants of **Text tools** hidden in the Tool palette. One is a **Vertical Text tool** that allows you to place each character below the previous one. The other tool creates a selection instead of a layer.

➤ Simulating HTML Text

When presenting a site design to a client, you want it to look as authentic as possible, so you probably want to use some body text with the same look and feel as text in a browser. You can simulate this within Photoshop by using Helvetica, Arial, or Times (whatever you plan on using as default font in the browser) and deactivating the anti-aliasing option in the text dialog. But you can get an even more authentic look if you create the text in an HTML authoring program like GoLive and make a screen capture of the result.

▲ Photoshop 5.0 introduced a Text tool that allows the text to be edited even after the dialog box has been closed. An editable Text Layer is represented by a capital T in the Layer palette.

Here's the screen capture of the text laid out in GoLive. Later, you can paste it onto a Layer Mask and easily change the text color. Although you could achieve the same effect using the Paint Bucket tool, your aim would have to be very precise. It's a lot easier when you use a Layer Mask.

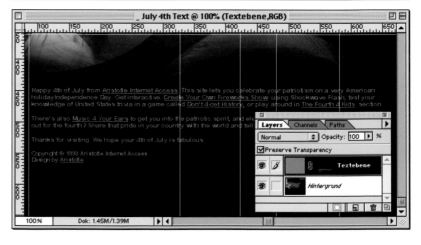

MAKING A SCREEN CAPTURE
Use Command-Shift-3 to create a screen capture on Macintosh. A noise of a shutter will indicate that a copy has been saved as "Picture 1".

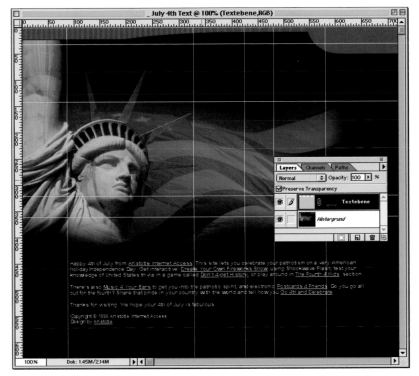

◀ Using a Layer Mask lets you color the screenshot of body text as in this example. The trick is to use the screenshot of the text in the Layer Mask instead as a regular layer.

▲ To add a Layer Mask to the Layers Palette, select the Layer you want to apply the Mask to, choose Layer > Add Layer Mask > Reveal All, and a Mask thumbnail will appear next to the layer thumbnail.

Both Macintosh and Windows have a screen capture command with which you can save the screen image as a PICT file; just make sure you have selected a white background for the text in GoLive.

Open the screen capture in Photoshop and crop the unwanted parts—or just select the text and copy it to the clipboard. When you paste it into your presentation, it will automatically be placed on a new layer. Make any white areas transparent by using **Multiply** mode in the **Layers palette**, and position the layer correctly with the **Move tool**. The only problem now is that if you want to use colored body text in front of a white background you can't use the **Preserve Transparency** option and fill the layer with a new color. But you can get around this by using a **Layer Mask**:

1. Use the Palettes menu (or the **New Layer icon** in the **Layers palette**) to create a new (empty) layer in the target document. Then copy the text of the screen copy into the clipboard.

2. Activate the new layer, choose **Layer > Add Layer Mask > Reveal All**, and an additional preview (for the **Layer Mask**) will appear in the Layers

▲ Sometimes the most effective compression tool is the Crop tool. Select the important parts in the photo with the Crop tool and then double–click inside the frame.

palette linked to your layer. While holding down the Alt/Option key, click on the preview of the Layer Mask. This will make it active and visible.

3. Use Command-V to paste the screen copy of the HTML text from the clip- board into the Layer Mask. Invert the Layer Mask with Command-I (**Image > Adjust > Invert**). Now click on the layer preview to activate the layer.

4. You won't see any effect yet, since the layer is empty, but if you select a foreground color and fill the layer with the **Paint Bucket tool**, the text will ap- pear as if by magic! To change the color of the layer later, just select another color and use the **Paint Bucket tool** to fill the layer again. Positioning the text is no problem either as long as you keep the layer and the Layer Mask linked (the chain icon should be visible in the **Layers palette**). You can use the **Move tool** to move the layer like you would any other layer.

CHANGING THE IMAGE SIZE

One of the most important commands you will need to master is **Image Size** in the **Image menu**, which allows you to resize your entire document, along with all its layers. You can use it to enlarge an image, but this should only be done in cases of real emergency; the quality of an enlarged image decreases significantly since Photoshop has to interpolate image information.

The **Image Size** dialog box displays the width and height of your work area. Make sure the units are pixels. To the right, you'll see a chain icon that in- dicates which parameters are connected, depending on whether you have selected **Constrain Proportions** and/or **Resample Image** at the bottom of the dialog box. **Constrain Proportions** ensures that if the width is changed, the height changes accordingly (and vice versa). Unless you plan on distort- ing the image on purpose, as a special effect, this option should always be turned on. The **Resample Image** option ensures that Photoshop resamples the image if you make any changes in its resolution. You can choose **Nearest Neighbor**, **Bilinear**, and **Bicubic**. (See the Optimizing Photoshop chapter, page 88.) Here are some standard tasks that you might perform with **Image Size**.

➤ Changing Resolution to 72 DPI

This is more or less a cosmetic task, because to a browser or HTML authoring program it makes no difference whether the resolution of an image is set to 72, 85, or 255 dpi. To the browser, a pixel is a pixel—it will always display the real size of the image. Still, changing image resolution can be valuable if you

If the Resample Image option is deactivated, all three parameters (Width, Height and Resolution) are directly related. ▶

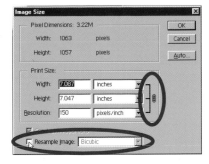

decide at some point to import images into a layout program to print them out for a presentation. If all the images are set to the same dpi they will all appear 1:1 in the layout and you won't have to scale them to get them to the same size. Before you change the resolution of an image, however, be sure to deactivate the **Resample Image** option. Then you won't accidentally resize the image.

➤ Changing Image Size to 50 Percent

Most often you will want to resize an image by a certain percentage. Instead of doing this by calculating pixels or inches, use the **Units** pop-up menu to change units to percent. Now all you need to do is to enter the percent reduction you want.

➤ Changing the Canvas Size and Using the Crop Tool

Changing the canvas size is another important function of Photoshop; it allows you to add or remove space around an image. To enlarge the canvas size, simply enter the new width or height into the **Canvas Size** dialog box (**Image > Canvas Size**) and choose where you want that space to be added by clicking on the squares. The selected square indicates where the original image will be placed on the canvas. For example, if you change the width of the canvas and select the leftmost square, the original image will go on the left, and the additional pixels will be added to the right of the image.

You can use the same technique to crop your canvas size: Simply reduce the number of pixels listed under width or height and click **OK**. Alternatively you can use the **Crop tool** in the **Tool palette**, but the **Canvas Size** command has the advantage of letting you crop the image to a specific dimension by entering a numerical value. You can also enter a specific dimension with the **Crop tool**, but personally I find that takes a little too long—you have to open the palette, enter the dimensions, select the 3, and finally select the area in your document. Using the **Crop tool** is helpful if the cropped area is asymmetrical, but most of the time all you need is to crop a little space on one side or the other. In my opinion, the **Canvas Size** command is the easiest way to do that.

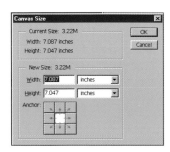

▲ Adding or subtracting pixels to the canvas can easily be done with the Canvas Size command.

Name: Website

Bildgröße: 1,58M

Breite: 550   Pixel

Höhe: 1000   Pixel

Auflösung: 72   Pixel/Inch

Modus: RGB-Farbe

Illustration: Michael Baumgardt

DESIGNING WEB ELEMENTS

Web Elements in Photoshop/ImageReady

Sometimes when I look back to the beginning of the Web, I wish I had taken notes on exactly when certain design elements made their debut. For example, the sidebar concept that is so heavily used today is generally done simply by placing a background image on the page. Because it is just a creative way of using the background image function, and not an HTML feature, some

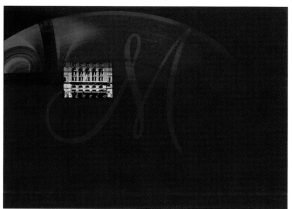

▲ For the Carnegie Hall Web site, art director Andreas Lindström used a background image (see right), and placed the other elements like text and images on top of it.

designer must have had the idea first. I wonder who. We will probably never find out; it's quite likely that any number of designers discovered the trick around the same time. The same holds true for many familiar Web design tricks and standards. This chapter discusses some of those standards; hopefully it will give you a few ideas when you start designing your own pages.

CREATING BACKGROUNDS

One extremely popular HTML function involves filling the background of a Web page with a pattern or image. Nearly all great-looking Web sites use this trick, and it is part of the standard repertoire for any Web designer. There are three variants: background images, sidebars, and patterns.

➤ Background Images

Andreas Lindström, who created the Web site for Carnegie Hall while he was Art Director at Avalanche (now Razorfish), has his own special way of using backgrounds in his Web designs. He likes to use dimmed images that blend with the background, combining them with smaller images in the foreground. This creates an interesting dynamic and lends depth to the Web site.

Monitor sizes and their resolutions (width x height)				
14"	**15"**	**16"/17"**	**19"**	**21"**
640x480	800x600 (SuperVGA) 832x624 (Mac)	832x624	1024x768	1152x870 (Mac) 1152x1124 1280x1024

There is a catch to using the background function, however. Since the background image is repeated in the browser by default, the same image will display again when the viewer scrolls down or to the right. The latest browsers allow you to set the background image to repeat only once (or a specific number of times), but since you have to design with backward compatibility in mind you should stick to the old way of solving this problem. And that means you must append sufficient image space in both directions to prevent viewers with a twenty-one-inch monitor from seeing the repeating pattern.

From the chart above, you can see that you may need to make your background image 1,280 pixels wide and at least 1,024 pixels high to ensure that users with larger monitors won't see the repetition. However, because this creates a lot of unnecessary overhead, many designers limit their background images to 800 pixels in width. Since you will usually place your content in a table with a fixed width, there is little temptation for users with larger monitors to open the window to full size. You could even include a JavaScript in your document that would set the window size automatically, but designers don't usually bother with this. After all, in the worst case all that happens is that the visitor sees you've been using a background image.

▲ The Jazz Central Station Web site (www.jazzcentralstation.com) used a sidebar background as the main design element. A dimmed logo in the main area creates a certain richness and depth when later combined with the content.

▲ The Rocktropolis Web site (www.rocktropolis.com) is another good example of a sidebar background. One problem to cope with is the browser offset. It causes all elements, like the navigation bar, to shift by a couple of pixels.

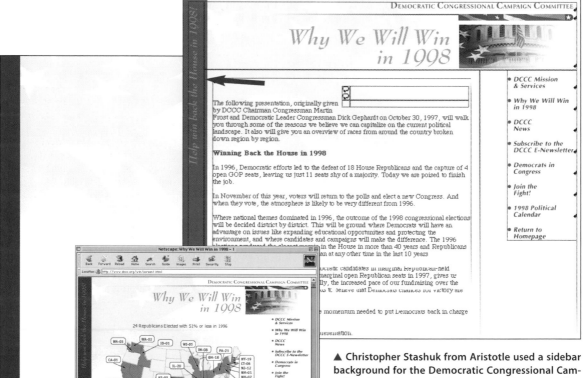

▲ Christopher Stashuk from Aristotle used a sidebar background for the Democratic Congressional Campaign Committee Web site. Because they wanted to display a dimmed image of the American flag, the background had to be wide enough to avoid repeating the image. The blue sidebar uses a table to display the current topic (see top).

➤ Sidebars as Background

You have almost certainly come across Web sites that use a sidebar with text or navigational elements. This is a very popular design concept, since it does-n't require frames at all—it can be done by simply using a pattern as back-ground. All you have to do is color one side of the background, and since the background image is repeated it can be as small as one pixel in height—re-sulting in a very small file size.

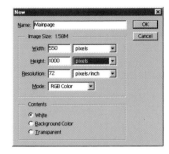

▲ **To avoid having the sidebar reappear on the right side, the background needs to be very wide.**

   Using just one pixel is a bit extreme, of course, and has a drawback that you might not realize: it uses a lot of processor power, since the browser has to render the background every time a user changes the window size or scrolls quickly down a page. With a background image just one pixel high, the browser has to repeat the background more often—and while this may not be noticeable on today's high-speed computers, if a browser is running on an older, low-end machine, that extra demand on the processor can slow down the browser. I suggest using a pattern with a height of forty to eighty pixels. If you are using textures in the sidebar, or even in the main area, you may de-cide to save the image as a JPEG. And remember, you can gain even more of a saving in file size by using values that are divisible by eight, since JPEG's compression algorithm works in 8 x 8 blocks. (Read more on this in the chap-ter on JPEG).

DISPLAY TIME FOR BACKGROUNDS
Theoretically, the height of a background could be as little as one pixel, but it is advisable to use a height of at least 50 pixels, because computation of the background image requires CPU power. If the background image measures only one pixel in height and the page is 700 pixels high, the browser needs to place the file 700 times. While this is hardly noticeable on fast machines, on slow systems it can become an issue. A background with the height of 50 pixels will display almost as fast on slow computers as on speedy ones.

● Designing a Simple Sidebar
Let's start with a simple sidebar. Create a new file via **File > New**. Enter fifty pixels for height and 1,280 pixels for width (or 800 pixels to reduce file size). Use the Rectangular Marquee tool to select a rectangle in the left-hand part of the image; the Information palette will display the width of the selection. Next, choose a foreground color by clicking on the foreground color box in the toolbox. Use the Paint Bucket tool to fill the selected area with color. Then choose **File > Save for Web**. Since images like this are ideally saved as GIFs, choose a color depth of three bits in the **Save for Web** dialog box.

● Designing a Sidebar with Texture
Although the sidebars in the example above are easy to create, they look rather stiff and technical. A sidebar with texture can contribute significantly to the design. To avoid unwanted visible breaks at the edges, the upper and lower edges of the image should fit seamlessly. Follow the steps below:

1. Create a new file and place a background or texture on the left side of the image. Choose the Offset filter (**Filter > Other > Offset**).

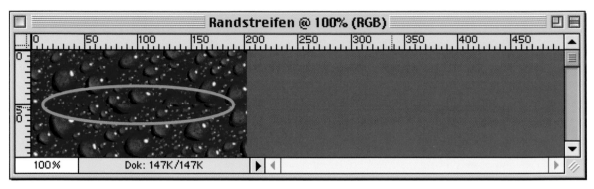

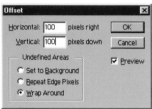

▲ A break in the image is visible after using the Offset filter. This break can be removed with the Rubber Stamp tool.

2. Enter half the height of the sidebar for **Vertical: Pixels Down**, and activate the **Wrap Around** option. This assures that image elements that disappear at the bottom will reappear at the top. Check **Preview** to test the effect prior to clicking OK.

3. Now you need to remove the break in the image. Depending on the image itself, either the **Smudge** tool or the **Rubber Stamp** tool will be most appropriate. Generally, the **Rubber Stamp** tool is more suitable for retouching. With the Option or Alt key pressed, click on the image region you want to use as a source. Release the key and click in the image where you want to fill in the information you've just picked up. As you move the tool around you will see a cross following your movement—it marks the spot that you clicked on the first time while holding the Alt/Option key. To get the best results you will have to change this point frequently; otherwise you will still see an edge.

The first versions of HTML contained only simple background features. The background image was merely repeated horizontally and vertically. Recent browsers are more flexible and allow you to repeat a pattern only horizontally or vertically. You can even define the number of repetitions. This is perfect when you want to display the background only once. Unfortunately, older browsers don't understand these tags (which are part of the Cascading Style Sheets). There are also incompatibilities between Netscape and Explorer. So it's a good idea to use the old tricks and work–arounds for a little longer.

4. After the image has been smoothed out to create a seamless transition, use the **Offset** filter to convert the image file back to normal. (Enter a negative value and use the **Wrap Around** option.) The exported image will appear in Navigator or Explorer as one big image.

● **Pattern Backgrounds (wallpaper)**
When the background feature was first implemented in HTML, many Web sites used textures or patterns to fill the entire page. Amateur Web designers in particular found this very appealing. Today (thank heaven!) you don't see this very often. There's a good reason to stay away from pattern backgrounds—they make text much harder to read. If you want to use one, make sure to use subtle coloring to avoid interference with text, and use a pattern that's large enough to make the continuous repetition less obvious.

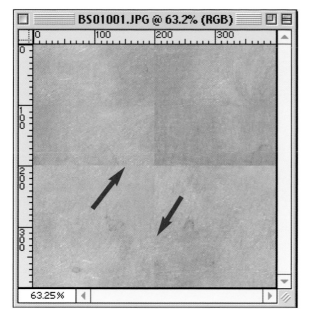 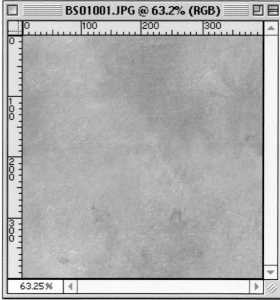

Great-looking background patterns can enhance a Web site. Here's how to design one:

1. Load a file with a texture, and use the **Crop** tool to select the region that you'd like to use (crop by double-clicking inside the selection). Open the **Offset** filter and enter approximately half the pixel size of the image in the vertical and horizontal boxes. Activate the **Wrap Around** option to make sure moved image elements reappear on the opposite end.

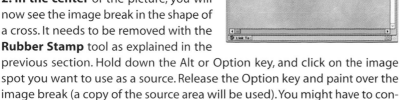

◀ After the breaks have been removed with the rubber stamp tool, the pattern appears to be one continuous image.

2. In the center of the picture, you will now see the image break in the shape of a cross. It needs to be removed with the **Rubber Stamp** tool as explained in the previous section. Hold down the Alt or Option key, and click on the image spot you want to use as a source. Release the Option key and paint over the image break (a copy of the source area will be used). You might have to constantly change the source for the **Rubber Stamp** tool in order to get the re-

This Web site by Christopher Stashuk is a good example of a subtle background pattern, that complements the design. ▶

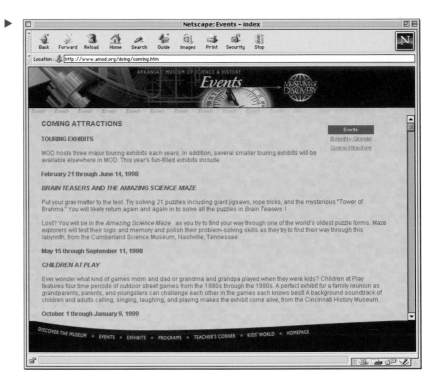

sult you want, but in the end you should have an area that shows no more edges. You can use the **Offset** filter one more time to double check that there are really no more visible edges, or you can just move the pattern into its original position by entering a negative offset with the same values that you used before.

Another important use for an image background is to create colors that are outside the Web-safe color spectrum. This is done by combining two Web-safe colors in a very tight pattern—essentially, you're controlling the dithering rather than allowing the browser or monitor to do it. The advantage is clear: your background will look the same in all environments.

In previous versions of Photoshop this trick was done by using a document with a dimension of 2x2 pixels, coloring each pixel with the pencil tool, designating it as a pattern, and using it to fill a larger document that was then used as background image in a Web page. Photoshop 5.5 makes this whole process much easier with the new DitherBox Filter, which does exactly the same thing.

1. Create a new image in Photoshop with **File > New**. Make sure that the dimensions are a multiple of the fill pattern. These fill patterns in the Dither-Box can be 2x2 pixels, 3x3 pixels, 4x4 pixels, and so on up to 8x8. In most cases the standard fill pattern of 2x2 is enough, so for this example, I'll use a dimension of 50x500 pixels for the background image. If the dimensions don't match up correctly, you will end up with visible edges every time the image is repeated in the browser (see picture on next page).

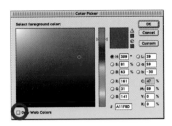

▲ If the dimensions of the background image aren't set up correctly, the repetition of the pattern can be clearly seen, as in this example (see magnified part). To prevent this, the dimension of the image must be divisible by the size of the fill pattern.

▲ Deactivate the Only Web Colors option before you pick a color.

2. Open Filter > Other > DitherBox to bring up the DitherBox dialog box. Click on the RGB color field to open the Photoshop Color Picker. Since you don't want the color to be from the Web-safe color palette, deactivate the **Only Web Colors** option, then choose a color for the pattern and click **OK**.

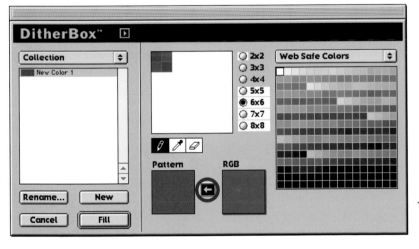

▲ Double click on the listings to name the fill pattern.

◀ Clicking on the arrow and the filter will automatically suggest a fill pattern.

3. Click on the arrow button in the DitherBox dialog box and the filter will automatically generate an appropriate fill pattern. In the **Pattern** field (to the left of the arrow button) you have a preview of how the filled area will look and you can see how closely the color matches the one in the RGB field.

4. To edit the pattern, select the **Pencil** or the **Eyedropper tool**, choose a color from the palette at the right side of the dialog box, and apply it to the fill pattern. Filling the current document with the pattern is easy—just click the **Fill** button.

▲ From top to bottom:
The browser offset in Internet Explorer 3.0 for Windows, Internet Explorer 4.0 for Macintosh and Netscape Navigator 4.0 (Mac).

5. Double click on the listing or click the **Rename** button to rename the fill pattern. To delete the new colors (called Collections) choose **Delete** from the pop-up menu above the listings. But remember, this will delete all the patterns in the listings.

When you magnify the filled document, you can clearly see the checkerboard pattern. You don't have to stick with that look; you get a slightly varied result by placing the same-colored pixels in a row. Although the difference is very subtle, this pattern might look better with your Web site. You can also experiment with larger fill patterns, just click on the radio buttons in the dialog box and edit the extra pixels with the **Pencil tool**.

ALIGNING FOREGROUND WITH BACKGROUND

When you use backgrounds in a design, you may discover that it's difficult to align objects in the HTML page with the background. Imagine working up a complicated print design with your layout software, only to have the Image Setting Service tell you that they can't guarantee the design won't shift slightly!

BROWSER OFFSET				
	BROWSER		**OFFSET (LEFT)**	**OFFSET (TOP)**
MACINTOSH	NETSCAPE NAVIGATOR	1.1	8 Pixels	8 Pixels
	NETSCAPE NAVIGATOR	1.2	8 Pixels	8 Pixels
	NETSCAPE NAVIGATOR	2.0	8 Pixels	8 Pixels
	NETSCAPE NAVIGATOR	3.0	8 Pixels	8 Pixels
	NETSCAPE NAVIGATOR	4.0	8 Pixels	8 Pixels
	MICROSOFT INTERNET EXPLORER	2.0	8 Pixels	8 Pixels
	MICROSOFT INTERNET EXPLORER*	3.0	8 Pixels	8 Pixels
	MICROSOFT INTERNET EXPLORER*	4.0	8 Pixels	8 Pixels
WINDOWS	NETSCAPE NAVIGATOR	1.2	10 Pixels	17 Pixels
	NETSCAPE NAVIGATOR	2.0	10 Pixels	15 Pixels
	NETSCAPE NAVIGATOR	3.0	10 Pixels	15 Pixels
	NETSCAPE NAVIGATOR	4.0	10 Pixels	15 Pixels
	MICROSOFT INTERNET EXPLORER	2.0	10 Pixels	20 Pixels
	MICROSOFT INTERNET EXPLORER*	3.0	10 Pixels	16 Pixels
	MICROSOFT INTERNET EXPLORER*	4.0	10 Pixels	16 Pixels

* Ever since Explorer 3.0 the browser offset can be set by entering LEFTMARGIN=0 TOPMARGIN=0 into the BODY tag. Unfortunately, Netscape Navigator does not interpret these values.

▲ Top: The Viagra Web site uses a three-color background.

Middle: If the web site is optimized for Internet Explorer 3.0 for Windows, the image will appear slightly shifted on the Macintosh (2 pixels to the left). Only a JavaScript can resolve this. The script checks which browser is used and will load an identical HTML document with a modified background image to compensate (right picture).

The problem is caused by the browser offset, which unfortunately is not only different for Netscape and Explorer, it even varies between computer platforms. Browser offset is the minimum distance that content is placed from the upper left-hand corner of the browser window. Since the background is positioned without offset, you can't be exactly sure how a foreground graphic element will align with the graphic in the background.

Although 4.x versions of browsers allow you to use layers for absolute positioning of visual elements, if you want to stay backward-compatible you have to design for 3.x browsers that don't support layers. So we come back to the familiar workaround that designers have used before: JavaScript. JavaScript is a scripting language that both browsers can interpret, and it's well suited to changing elements of an HTML page dynamically. Rollover but-

BROWSER SWITCH

To compensate for the browser offset, a different background needs to be loaded depending on the browser version used. The following JavaScript in HTML code does exactly that: the variable 'skipPage' is defined and all browser versions that are supposed to display the page will write the value "false" into the variable. If the used browser is not listed, the script will go to the end and link to a different document. In this case the document name is "23Browsers.html", but luckily with GoLive you don't have to write any code at all, just drag the Browser Switch icon to the head section of the document.

```
<html>
    <head>
            <title>Welcome to GoLive</title>
    <csscriptdict>
            <script><!--
function CSScriptInit() {
var skipPage = true; bAgent = window.navigator.userAgent; bAppName = window.navigator.appName;
if ((bAppName.indexOf("Netscape") >= 0) && (bAgent.indexOf("Mozilla/4") >= 0)) skipPage = false;
if ((bAppName.indexOf("Explorer") >= 0) && (bAgent.indexOf("Mozilla/4") >= 0)) skipPage = false;
if ((bAppName.indexOf("Netscape") >= 0) && (bAgent.indexOf("Mozilla/5") >= 0)) skipPage = false;
if ((bAppName.indexOf("Explorer") >= 0) && (bAgent.indexOf("Mozilla/5") >= 0)) skipPage = false;
if (skipPage) { location = *URL*/'23Browsers.html'; return; }
}
            // --></script>
    </csscriptdict>
    <csbrowser href="23Browsers.html" ns="0,0,1,1" ie="0,0,1,1"></csbrowser>
    </head>
    <body onload="CSScriptInit();">
    </body>
</html>
```

▲ Dealing with browser offset is much easier with Adobe GoLive. Simply drag a browser switch item into the HTML header and you're done. No need for tedious JavaScript programming.

tons, for example, are done with JavaScript, and it can also be used to compensate for browser offset. You can use a short script to identify the browser and load the appropriate background into the page. In other words, using different backgrounds for different browsers ensures that the foreground elements are correctly aligned with the background.

Because JavaScript is so easy to program, this sounds more complicated than it is. You can even find the scripts you need on the Internet. If you work with GoLive version 3 or higher, you don't even need to look for such a script, since it's included as a little module or head script. It works a bit differently—instead of changing the background in the page it actually switches to a different HTML document. You can do the same thing with the Browser Switch feature. All you have to do is drag it onto the page, select which browser the page is supposed to support, and redirect all other browser types to a different URL.

IMAGE INFLATION

A significant problem in designing a Web site—especially one that uses backgrounds—is that browsers can crash when they run out of memory. You may think this is unlikely, since all those image files are so small, but you'd be wrong. Although a background saved in as a JPEG or GIF may be only 10K, it will be decompressed to full size in the browser. This size can amount to 1 MB, 2 MB, or more. Take the effect of image inflation or decompression seriously, and check the exact memory requirement of your image in Photoshop or ImageReady. The easiest way to do this is by looking at the lower left area of the image window. (If your screen displays something different, click on the triangle icon and select Document Size.) In this exam-

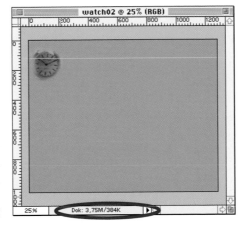

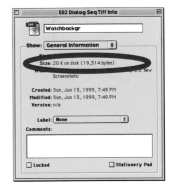

▲ A background image that uses only 20K on the hard drive can eat up several Megabytes of memory when decompressed.

ple, the decompressed background requires 3.75 MB, even though the file only takes up 19.3 K on the hard drive. Users with low-end computers usually don't allocate enough memory to their browsers, and if they view your page the browser may reach its memory limit and crash.

This happens because of additional width that you have to give the background. If all the additional width is a plain color, consider using an invisible frame on the right side of the page instead. Use an empty HTML document in this invisible frame with a background color that matches the one in the main frame.

This trick was used very effectively on the David Bowie Web site designed by Marlene Stoffers and Ben Clemens from N2K. (Unfortunately, that version is history and I can't show you a screen shot of that site.) Because the site used a large background image, they had to limit its width to avoid the risk of browser crash due to image inflation. On the right side, the background image faded to black—the same color as the invisible frame. For this trick to work, it's important that the right-hand frame is set to **Scale** in the **Frame Inspector** of GoLive. Here is a step-by-step guide on how this is done:

1. Create a background with a maximum width of 600 pixels, and select a color from the Web color table (to avoid dithering) with which to fill the rest of the image on the right side. Use the **Airbrush** tool to blend the image with the background color if you need to (in the example on the right I used just a gradient fill to illustrate the principle.) Save the finished background as a GIF or JPEG.

2. In GoLive, define a vertical frameset with two frames. You will find the framesets in the **Frames** tab of the Palette. Switch to the **Frame Editor**; this is the tab in your document window right next to the **Layout Editor** tab. Drag the appropriate frameset to the frame document. Then you can load the HTML document with the background image in the main frame, and load an HTML document with a solid color background in the right frame. Make the left frame 600 pixels, and in the **Frame Inspector** set the right frame to **Scale**. If you switch to the HTML Source Editor, the HTML code for this frame set would look something like this:

```
<FRAMESET COLS="600,*">
<FRAME NAME="mainframe" SRC="main.html">
<FRAME NAME="rightframe" SRC="right.html">
</FRAMESET>
```

Unfortunately, this solution isn't perfect. As soon as you place more text on the main page than can be displayed in the window, a scrollbar will appear on the right side of the main frame. So this simple solution is not suitable for every scenario. If this is a major issue for you, use the browser switch feature to create a version for all 4.X browsers. Those browsers support Cascading

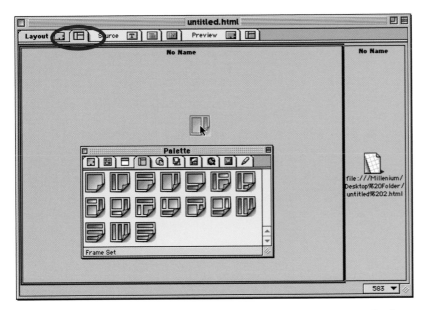

▲ Switch to the Frame Editor, then drag a frameset from the Frame Palette to the document window.

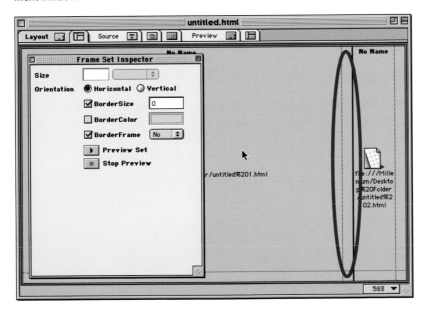

▲ Click on the frame border to show the Frame Set Inspector, in which you need to set the BorderSize to zero and the BorderFrame to No. Next, create two HTML documents, one with the image background (for the main frame) and one with a black background (for the side frame.)

▲ To set the Size attribute, click inside the side frame and set it to Scale. The main frame needs to be set to the size of the background image.

▲ When you switch to the Frame Preview, the two frames will appear to be one background. The dotted line here shows where the two frames meet, but as soon as there is some hidden content, a scroll bar will show up in the main frame.

Style Sheets (which includes the feature of repeating a background pattern only along the vertical or horizontal axis). Redirect visitors with older browsers to an alternative version in which you place the background image traditionally and just accept that those users will see the background image repeat on the right side.

USING BACKGROUNDS IN TABLES

Since Explorer 3.0 and Netscape 4.0, designers have been able to use images as backgrounds for tables. It allows for some nice tricks; for example, this mock-up that simulates computer paper. The great thing about using background images in tables is that (theoretically, at least) you can place your content inside a cell of the table and the background will always adjust to the length of the table. Before you get too excited, I must add that Netscape 4.X does a horrible job of this, and if you want to be compatible with both browsers there are limits to what you can do.

For example, you can't nest tables (place tables within tables) in Netscape, because the nested table uses the background of the table it's embedded in. This doesn't sound too bad at first, but since the embedded table will try to synchronize the background with its own zero origin point, this generally creates an offset. (See picture on page 154.) The same is true for table cells in Netscape: since the background will be repeated at zero origin for every cell, you can't just define one pattern for the entire width of the table. Instead, you have to split the pattern into individual pieces and define each table cell with its own background pattern. Netscape didn't do such a great job of implementing the background image feature for tables.

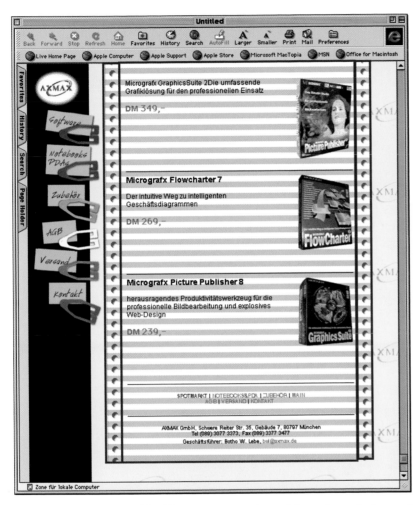

▲ You can create elements like this computer paper by applying an image background to tables. This table contains three columns (marked in blue) and each one contains its own background image.

To illustrate these problems with Netscape, I created a sample Web site that consists of a three-column table, each column using a different background. The left column uses the left-hand guide holes, the middle column uses lines, and the right column shows the outer set of holes. Since you can't use nested tables, you are severely limited in how you position your elements. Ultimately, it all comes down to setting the ALIGN attribute for inline images. The separation of the background in this example at least ensures that text and images don't run over the columns of holes.

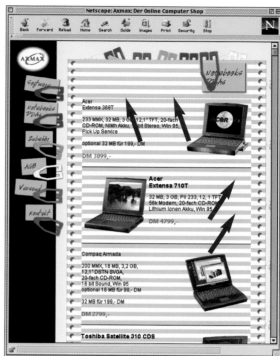

▲ I nested an invisible table containing the computer images inside another table. Although Explorer displays it correctly (on the left), Navigator 4 repeats the background pattern of cells, making it visible (see arrows at right).

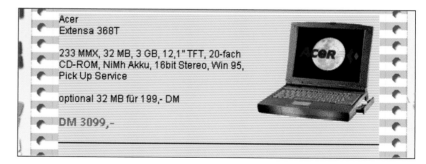

How do Browsers handle background images that use transparency? Navigator 4 doesn't display the transparent color (upper example), while Explorer 4 does so with no problem (bottom). ▶

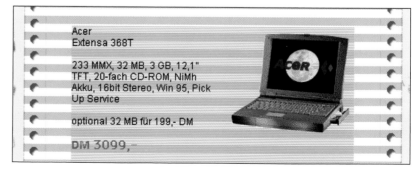

The last table restriction is that you can't use patterns with transparency. Although Explorer renders them correctly, Netscape displays transparent areas as white. If this weren't the case, we could fix the nested table problem by using a transparent image as background for the nested table, but unfortunately that is not an option.

CREATING BACKGROUNDS WITH A GRAPHICS APPLICATION

Graphics applications like Illustrator or FreeHand are great for designing backgrounds. Both programs offer a Pattern feature to define a graphic as a pattern, although that isn't very important in this context. Still, the basic procedures for creating a seamless pattern in Illustrator or FreeHand are outlined below:

1. Draw a one-inch square. The size is really up to you, but be sure to note the value because later on you will need to move your elements by the same amount as the width.

2. Create all the objects and elements inside the square. It's important to use **Wrap Around** so objects that disappear at the right edge of the square will reappear on the left side. Both applications allow you to move elements by entering numeric values in dialog boxes. Illustrator offers a **Move** command that allows you to make a simultaneous copy. FreeHand requires you to

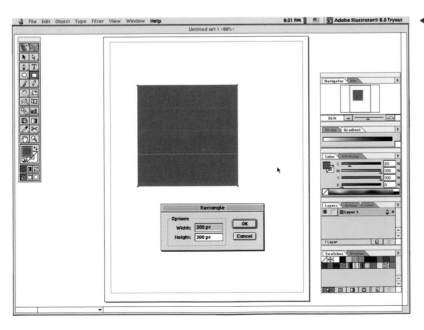

◀ Select the Rectangle tool, hold down the Option key and click in the work space to get a dialog box for numeric entry of image size.

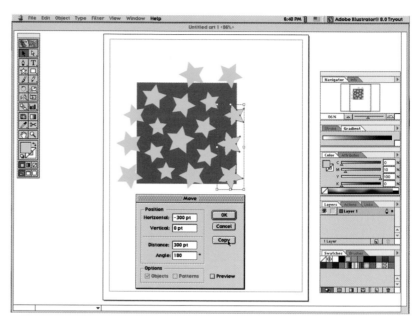

▲ To create a pattern without breaks, the elements need to be duplicated and moved to the opposite side with the Move command.

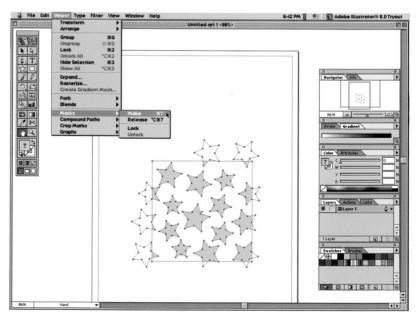

▲ To mask the elements, the rectangle needs to be moved to the front. Then use Mask > Make to crop all overlapping areas.

use the **Clone** feature, which makes an identical copy in the same position, and then move the elements by typing in the width of the rectangle. Follow the same procedure for objects that cross the upper and lower edge of the square.

3. Use the Mask command to eliminate the parts of the elements that are outside the square. In Illustrator, the square needs to be the foremost object. Use **Object > Arrange > Bring to Front**, and then select all objects. **Object > Masks > Make** will mask all extraneous parts.

4. Since Photoshop can interpret Illustrator files directly, simply save the Illustrator file and open it in Photoshop. After saving the image as a GIF, and loading it as background in your document, you will have perfectly seamless wallpaper.

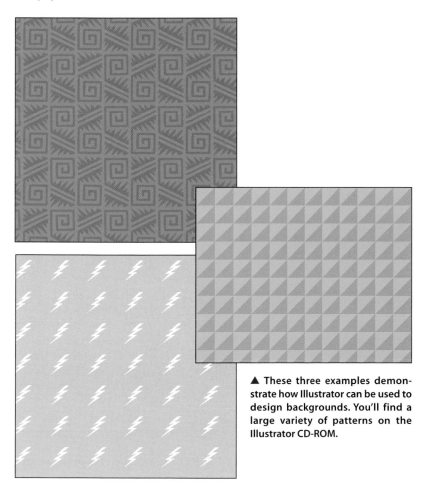

▲ These three examples demonstrate how Illustrator can be used to design backgrounds. You'll find a large variety of patterns on the Illustrator CD-ROM.

IMAGE TABLES

If you were to rank the most commonly used HTML tricks, image tables would be very high on the list. The term itself may seem somewhat confusing, but it simply means invisible HTML tables that are filled with images rather than text. This trick makes it possible to change parts of an image without having to retransmit the whole image. Studio Archetype's former Web site (www.studioarchetype.com), designed by Mark Crumpacker, was a very good (and popular) example of this technique. Basically the design looked like one big image, with a button bar on the top and the bottom. But in fact the entire interface was composed of several smaller images, and, unlike with one large image and an image map, any part of the interface could be changed easily.

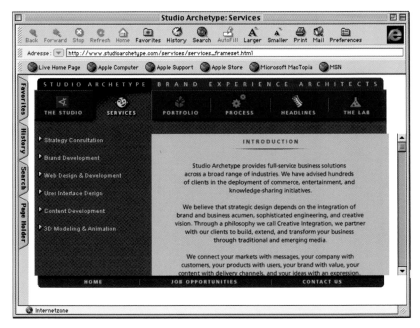

▲ A "pushed-in" version of the button in the top bar indicates which section the visitor is in.

The main area always displayed the latest news (a technique Crumpacker calls "content surfacing") and each part of it could be changed. Also, the buttons in the navigation bar were single images, allowing rollovers. With a click of one of the buttons, a visitor was linked to the appropriate page, and the button replaced with a "pushed-in" version. Since all the other elements were already loaded in the browser cache, only the changed button needed to be transmitted. This reduced transmission time substantially.

Image tables are an important tool for Web designers, and creating them in ImageReady is very easy:

1. Open your design in ImageReady and select the **Slice** tool from the **Tool** palette. Then, while holding the mouse button, mark the area on your image you want to slice. Release the mouse, and special guides will appear that show you how ImageReady will cut the image. Each frame also displays the number of the slice in the upper left corner. Later, the frame numbers will be appended to the filename. Use the **Slice Select** tool to move the areas around or change their dimensions. ImageReady will automatically update the slicing areas, but it is very important to keep the number of slices to a minimum. Very often, beginners make the mistake of overslicing, and this can

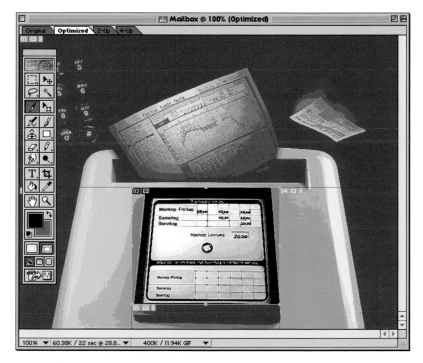

▲ Draw a frame with the Slice tool and ImageReady will cut the image automatically.

ADVANTAGES OF IMAGE TABLES
1. Image tables eliminate the need for image maps, because each of the images in the table can have its own link.

2. Each of the images can be optimized separately, which reduces the overall amount of data.

have a negative effect on the download time, especially if the slices are very small. The myth that slicing improves download time probably comes from the fact that with slicing you can optimize the slices individually. This can save file size for the individual images and indeed improve the overall download time, but as soon as there are too many slices, the browser will make up the time piecing the table together.

When activating the Save HTML File and Save Images option, click the HTML Options and Saving Files Options buttons to make sure the settings match your needs. ▶

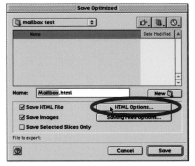

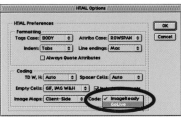

2. Use File > Save Optimized to save your image (including the HTML table). Don't use the regular **Save As** command; it will not give you the option of saving the HTML or the slices.

Be sure to select the **Save HTML File** and **Save Images** options in the **Save Optimized** dialog box. These options allow you to change some very important settings. For example, if you are using rollover buttons and are planning on importing them into GoLive, make sure you select **GoLive** in the **Code** pop-up of the **HTML Options** dialog box. This will ensure that the required JavaScript code is identical to the way GoLive creates rollovers. Or if you have set a background color or image for your design with **File > HTML Background**, make sure that the **Copy background image when saving** option is activated in the **Saving Files Options** dialog box.

The Arkansas Web site uses an image table to combine the animation of the waterfall with still images. ▶

In most cases you can now open the HTML file in a browser and you should see your image just as it was before—only now it is actually sliced and held together by an invisible table.

3. Unfortunately, an image table doesn't always look the way you expected in the browser (especially if you had to create it manually with an authoring tool.) Sometimes gaps can occur, but in most cases you can fix this by changing some of the settings in **HTML Options**. For instance, in the **Coding** section, select the **Always** option for **TD W,H** and **Spacer Cells**. This ensures that the HTML table will have a fixed width and height that matches that of the whole image.

FIXING IMAGE TABLES IN HTML

Joining the individual elements of a sliced image back together in a table doesn't seem particularly problematic, especially if you are using ImageReady (it will actually create the HTML code for you). However, sometimes you choose to or have to do this task manually in GoLive, in which case you can end up with unwanted space between cells. It might also happen that the image table will look fine in one browser and not in another. In any case, you'll have to do some troubleshooting to find the one HTML tag that's causing the problem. As there are several possible causes, here is a little checklist:

1. Check for spaces in the cells. Many authoring programs automatically place a space in a cell, since otherwise the cell will not display the cell border (GoLive is one that doesn't add anything extra). Delete those spaces. If you are not completely sure your image is the only thing in the cell, look at the HTML code. It should read: <td><img= ...></td>.

2. Check justification. You can justify the contents of a cell vertically and horizontally by using the attributes VALIGN and ALIGN in the TD tag. Make sure all the cells use the same justification. It's usually alright to place the attributes in the TABLE tag, but justification attributes in the TD tag will overwrite the global value, so check to see if a VALIGN or ALIGN attribute has accidentally found its way into the code for a specific cell.

3. Adjust height and width of the cells to fit the image. Authoring applications frequently enter vague values here (for example, in percent instead of pixels). You can find the exact measurement for the cell in the IMG tag. After you enter those values, the table should fit the image tightly.

4. The TABLE tag may contain CELLSPACING or BORDER attributes. Remove all unnecessary attributes, or set them to zero.

5. If an image is defined as a LINK, make sure it isn't defined with an additional border by entering the attribute BORDER=0 in the IMG tag. In GoLive, click on the image and in the **Image Inspector,** select the **Spec. Tab**. Select the **Border** option with a value of zero, and that should solve the problem.

Using Images as Links

An interactive medium like the Web couldn't exist without links, and a lot of designers use images as links—let's call them image links. The most common image links, of course, are buttons. Very often designers take the easiest way out and use three-dimensional buttons as image links; it's a simple way of displaying a clickable area. But 3D buttons can give a Web site a rather technical look—Andreas Lindström, Art Director of popular sites like Carnegie Hall and Viagra, tries to avoid them whenever possible. He prefers to search for subtle ways to integrate image links seamlessly in the design.
I'll explore some of the most common concepts for navigational elements.

● Buttons
3D buttons labeled with text are popular because they invite you to click them, and the text ensures that they are totally unambiguous. They are also easy to design. However, I think that there are only a few Web sites where buttons are actually integrated well and look good. One of them was the Studio Archetype Web site (unfortunately, since they merged with Sapient it is no longer available on the Internet). These buttons used pictograms as well as text to communicate where they led. The icons actually seemed to glow when the mouse pointer moved over them.

This interactivity is achieved by using JavaScript, a scripting language that both browsers can interpret. Since older browsers simply ignore JavaScript,

▲ The Legatus Web site features typical buttons, which use an embossed appearance to show that they're clickable. Using JavaScript, each button changes to a clicked version as the cursor comes over it.

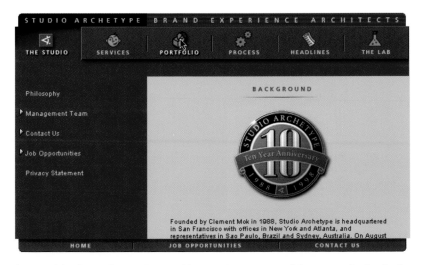

▲ One of the few Web sites that used buttons in a very tasteful way was the Studio Archetype site—which unfortunately is no longer visible on the Internet.

there are very few compatibility issues, which makes JavaScript quite safe to use. The only drawback is that interactive buttons require twice as much data to be transmitted, because the images for both button states need to be downloaded. If you are already using a lot of elements on your page, this could be an issue. Fortunately, it's seldom a major issue, since interactive buttons are loaded after all the main images are in the browser cache.

● Pictograms and Metaphors

Other popular image links are pictograms and metaphors. Pictograms can be very simple, for example, an arrow for the next page, or an X for Exit. Sometimes you may see a telephone icon for the Contact link.

▲ The 4th of July Web site uses pictograms for navigation.

If you want to stay away from buttons and pictograms, try to find a metaphor in the context of the Web site. The Arkansas Web site (www.arkansas.com), designed by Christopher Stashuk, is a good example. On the main page you see a table with many objects, each one representing a different section of the Web site.

Another good example was the old David Bowie Web site, designed by Ben Clemens and Marlene Stoffers. The icons displayed text when the mouse pointer moved over them. This has the advantage of allowing you to use really spaced-out navigational elements but still ensure that visitors will be able to find their way around.

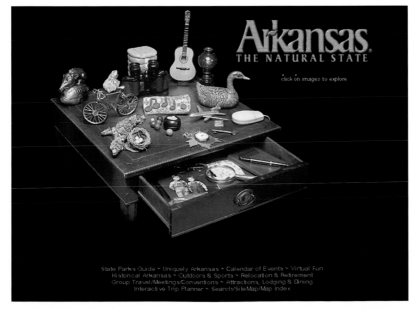

◀ On the Arkansas Web site all objects on the table represent an area of the site. When the mouse is moved over an item, text comes up to indicate where the link leads to.

CREATING INTERACTIVE BUTTONS IN IMAGEREADY

After designing your interface in Photoshop, you'll probably want to add some JavaScript functionality to your site—interactive buttons, for example. Click on the **Jump to default graphics editor application** button at the bottom of the Tool Palette in Photoshop, and ImageReady will automatically start up, loading the current document. Although you can switch back and forth between Photoshop and ImageReady without losing your specific settings and features, it should really be the last step in your Web site development. Here's how to create a series of buttons that change in appearance when clicked on.

◀ After creating all the buttons in their initial state, use ImageReady's Slice Tool to define the areas that will change. It's a good idea to complete the different settings for one button and then copy and paste these effect settings to the other buttons. In this example, I want the word HOME to change color when the mouse rolls over it, an effect that can be achieved by using Layer Effects.

In ImageReady, open the Rollover palette (Window > Show Rollover), and click on the Page Icon at the bottom of the palette. This will create a new rollover state. Then select the text in the Layers palette and choose Layer > Effects > Color Fill to add the Color Fill effect. To change the color, select Color Fill Effect from the Layer palette menu, then select the Color pop-up in the Color Fill palette. ▼

▲ To have the button color change to blue when it is clicked, click the Page Icon in the rollover palette to create a new rollover state. By default, it is set to "Over," but you can change it to "Click" using the pop-up menu in the Rollover palette. You need to select the layer containing the button shape in order to assign the new color.

▲ The easiest way to apply the same effect combinations to all the buttons is to save the combination in the Styles palette and then select the other layers and apply the style.

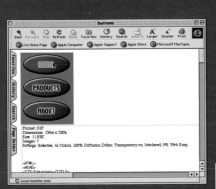

▲ To check the JavaScript functionality in the browser choose File > Save Optimized As and make sure that the Save HTML File option is activated. When the HTML file is opened in the browser, a copy of the HTML/ JavaScript code will also be displayed.

▲ In GoLive, create a text link with Special > New Link, then enter the URL in the Text Inspector.

▲ The colors for text links are assigned in the Page Inspector of GoLive.

● **Text Links**

Creating a text hyperlink is very simple: just select the text in GoLive and select **Special > New Link**. Type the URL into the **Text Inspector**, or use the **Browse** button to navigate to a file you want to link to. Text links allow you to assign up to three colors: one for the unclicked link (Link), one for every link that has been visited (Visited Link) and one for the moment when the user actually clicks on the link (Active Link). To set those colors, you have to click on the page icon in your GoLive document (in the upper left corner), because those colors apply for the whole page and are therefore placed in the BODY tag.

Since people have gotten used to rollover buttons that change when the mouse pointer passes over them, a lot of designers want to use the same effect for text. Unfortunately HTML doesn't offer this option, so they solve the problem by rendering the text as an image and applying a different color, glow or other effect for the rollover image.

▲ What seems to be a regular text link is often just text rendered as an image. This allows for effects that would otherwise not be possible.

Regardless of how you design them, image links and buttons should always be unambiguous and have a tactile quality. But before you start designing your own buttons or image links, here are two more tips:

1. Avoid Transparency

Interactive image links are not complicated, but if you want to use transparency keep one thing in mind: the transparent regions need to be the same for both images, or parts of the other image will remain visible. This is because the browser doesn't refresh the entire display each time, it only updates the parts that change.

2. Have one image link trigger other image changes

A rollover doesn't have to trigger a change in the same image; it could change a different image somewhere else on the page. You can, for example, have a small image as a link, and when the mouse rolls over it, a bigger version of the image appears somewhere else on the page. As a matter of fact, you can have many image changes triggered by just one event, but if you don't use GoLive you'll have to have some good understanding of JavaScript.

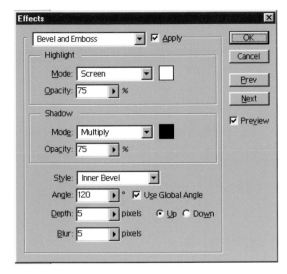

DESIGNING BUTTONS

Photoshop and ImageReady provide layer effects that let you apply drop shadows and bevels to your buttons, and generally make designing buttons a lot easier. One big advantage they have is that they aren't applied permanently—you can modify or remove them at any time. Here's how to create a button in Photoshop using layer effects:

1. Create a new layer in the **Layer** palette, then draw a rectangle with the Rectangular Marquee tool (or the Rectangle tool in ImageReady) and fill it with color. Now select **Layer > Effects > Bevel and Emboss** to open the Effects dialog box. Here you can adjust light opacity as well as many other parameters. The **Layer** palette will show an "**f**" in Photoshop and an "**S**" in ImageReady, indicating that the layer uses effects.

2. In the Highlight section, use **Mode** to define how to combine the light reflections with the layers. You should already be familiar with these modes—they are the same ones that are in the **Layer** palette. To see the light reflections clearly, choose **Normal** or **Screen**. Avoid **Multiply**, because it doesn't produce a visible edge.

You can choose a color for the highlights by clicking on the color field next to the **Mode** pop-up menu. You can also define custom values for **Opacity**. Click the triangle next to the input box to reveal a slider; it's a bit more convenient if you're doing this by trial and error.

▲ To create a button with the Bevel and Emboss layer effect, start with a colored shape on its own layer. Select the desired effect from the top pop-up menu at the top of the Effects dialog box. Check Apply for each effect you want to activate.

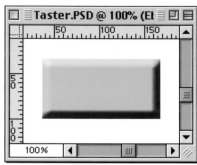
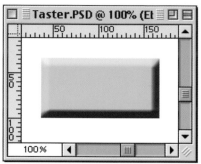

▲ The Blur parameter controls the bevel of the button. Unfortunately, this allows only limited control over bevel width and angle. In Alien Skin's EyeCandy (see right) bevel width can be set in pixel increments.

3. Use Normal or Multiply mode in the **Shadow** section. As with the highlights, you can choose a shadow color.

4. Depth and Blur set the intensity and width of the bevel. If you're using several objects with layer effects, activate **Global Angle**. This way you can change the effect angle for all the layers at once.

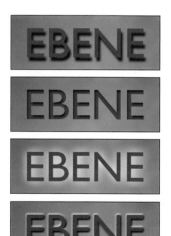

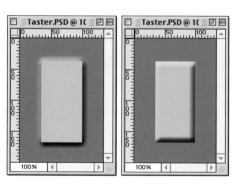

▲ Examples of Outer Bevel (left) and Inner Bevel (right).

Perhaps the most important settings are in the **Style** pop-up of the **Bevel and Emboss** dialog box: Outer Bevel, Inner Bevel, Emboss or Pillow Emboss. **Outer Bevel** and **Inner Bevel** will produce standard buttons, while **Emboss** will process all the edges, making the button appear to be carved out of the background. This can be a very appealing effect when combined with text.

▲ These are some of the new layer effects (from top to bottom): Drop Shadow, Inner Shadow, Outer Glow and Bevel

By the way, a layer can use multiple layer effects. To see which are active, select **Layer > Effects** and note which effects are checkmarked. ImageReady also displays this information in the layers palette.

To deactivate an individual effect, click on it in the menu while pressing the Option (Mac) or Alt (Windows) key.

ALIEN SKIN EYECANDY

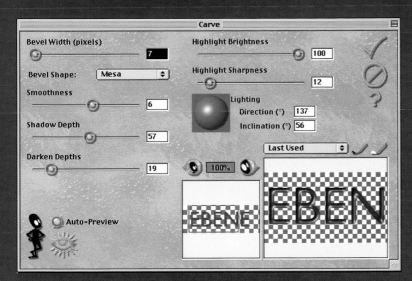

EyeCandy boasts a huge variety of effects that every Web designer needs, plus a simple user interface, making it one of the most popular collections of filters for Photoshop. With the Carve filter, for instance, lighting direction can be adjusted simply using the mouse to move a lighting point on a ball.

The preview windows allow you a lot of control over the effects, because the display can be comfortably enlarged and reduced, and you can name and store your settings under the pen icons.

▲ This is just a selection of the long list of filters shipping with EyeCandy. Left: Carve, Water Drops and Perspective Shadow. Right: Chrome with Drop Shadow and CutOut.

Illustration: Michael Baumgardt

GIF ANIMATION

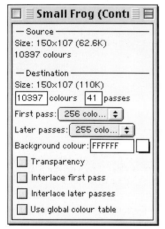

▲ Theoretically it is possible to use a GIF animation to overcome the 256 color limitation of GIFs, since each frame can have its own CLUT. There is only one program I know of that utilizes this. It's called "It's a GIF." There is little practical use for it, but if you want to experiment, download it from www.peda.com/iag/.

Click on the Page icon to create a new frame in the animation. Every change in the layer palette will now be recorded.

GIF Animation

GIF is the most important tool for bringing animation to the Web—and while Flash and Shockwave are steadily increasing in popularity, GIF will hold the top slot for a long time to come. The reason is simple: The files for GIF animations are small, don't require any special plug-ins, and are easy to create. Plus, there are many freeware and shareware GIF animation programs available on the Web, such as GifBuilder 0.5 from Yves Piguet. GifBuilder is one of the most popular and well-known GIF animation applications for the Macintosh; it's simple to use, it works well and is quite stable, and it has a couple of features that are very effective for keeping your files small.

There are many other programs too, such as GIFmation, which is distributed by BoxTop (www.boxtopsoft.com), or the GIF Construction Set for Windows. However, if you have Photoshop 5.5 you already own a fabulous GIF animation program: ImageReady. This application is an excellent Web design tool, and provides great support for GIF animation.

BASIC PRINCIPLES

GIF animation works exactly like cel animation: several frames are displayed in rapid succession, which creates the illusion of movement. For each frame in the GIF animation you can define attributes such as position, a transparency color, a disposal method, and how long it will be displayed. GIF ani-

mations are hugely popular effects because they don't need a plug-in, and even exotic browsers (which may not display GIF animation) can still show the first or last picture of the sequence. So it's a feature you can use without worrying about incompatibility.

To see the Animation window in ImageReady click **Window > Show Animation**. The window that comes up is the same window used for slices and rollovers. If it is already open just select the appropriate tab to see **Animation**.

Let's create a tiny animation to get a feel for the process. To do this, you'll need an additional layer in the **Layer** palette—for example, a layer with text created with the **Text** tool. ImageReady will record the position of each layer (as well as the opacity and effects), all you need to do to create animated text is click on the **Duplicate frame** icon at the bottom of the Animation window. Once the new frame is activated, use the **Move** tool to move the text layer within the **Layer** palette. Now, when you click on the **Play** button in the Animation window you will see your two-frame animation.

◀ The Tween command is the easiest way to create great animations. Tweening will insert a number of frames in between two key frames.

As exciting as this may be, it hardly qualifies for state-of-the-art animation. Of course you could add additional frames and move your text layer around, but your animation probably won't be very smooth; it is quite difficult to position your text with the accuracy required for professional-looking animation. Fortunately, ImageReady offers a really great command called **Tween** that makes it easy to create intermediate frames between two so-called keyframes. To see how this works, select one of the keyframes and

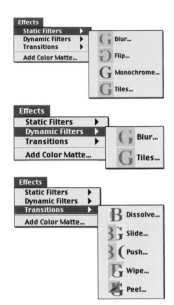

▲ GifBuilder, a very popular and free Gif animation program for the Macintosh, offers a variety of effects that can be applied to frames. Similar to the Tweening command in ImageReady, it will generate all the in-between images automatically. Since GifBuilder is free, you can download it from the Internet if you need these effects.

You can have ImageReady import the animation into a browser to check if everything works. This is particularly important if you work with transparency and disposal methods, since those aren't displayed in ImageReady. In this example you see an animation of a bouncing ball, but the second one (at the bottom) has the disposal method mistakenly set to "Do not dispose."

change the opacity or the effects for that layer. Then choose **Tween** from the **Animation** palette pop-up menu. The **Tween** dialog box lets you decide whether the tweened frames should reflect the changes on just the selected layer or all layers. Next, you can choose to modify **Position**, **Opacity** and **Effects** as mentioned above, and also specify which frame you want to tween with (**Next** or **Previous** or **Selection**). Lastly, set the number of frames that you want ImageReady to add.

After clicking **OK**, you will see your text slowly fade away, or move across the screen, or even gain or lose an effect, depending on what you've done to the text layer. If you want to preview the animation, click the **Optimized** tab, although viewing it in the browser will give you a far more accurate idea of the animation speed. **Use File > Preview in > Internet Explorer** (or **Netscape Navigator**) to have ImageReady place your GIF animation in a temporary HTML file. In ImageReady, even though frames' delay value might be set to the default of **No delay** (0.0 seconds), the animation will still play rather slowly, because Photoshop has to process all the layers. Only after all the layers have been flattened, and the GIF has been optimized, will you get a true sense of the speed of your animation—after which you might want to change the timing on certain frames.

Changing the speed, or delay, of the animation is very simple. The display time (in seconds) is shown beneath each frame; click on it to reveal some preset times. If you don't see a time value that suits your needs, use Other. You can set the delay time within 1/100th of a second.

LOOPING AN ANIMATION

Want your animation to play more than once? No problem. As a matter of fact, you can even have it play forever. The Loop options are set in the lower left corner of the **Animation** window. Choose **Once** to play the animation one time from beginning to end, choose **Forever** to play it endlessly, and **Other** to specify a particular number of repetitions.

Unfortunately, there is no option for backward and forward—if you need that kind of animation you must create it manually. However, that's very simple: After you have created your animation with the moving text layer and the **Tween** command, just shift-click the frames in between the two keyframes to select them. While holding the Option/Alt key (which creates a copy of the frames), drag the frames to the right side of the last keyframe and choose the **Reverse** command from the palette menu.

▲ The standard settings for looping an animation are Once and Forever. To set a specific number of loops, use Other.

SAVING ON BANDWIDTH BY SCALING ANIMATIONS

Since an animation consists of a series of images, its file size is necessarily larger than that of a single image—and as you know, file size is always an issue on the Web. If color reduction and other compression tricks don't shrink the file enough, consider using a little HTML trick that can save you as much as seventy-five percent on file size:

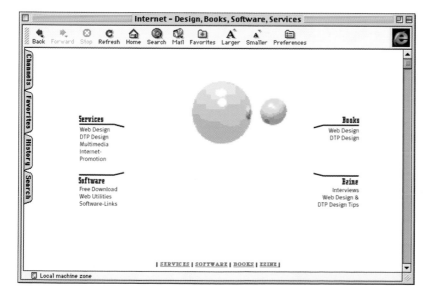

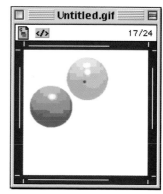

▲ This is the animation of the two rotating balls, later scaled to 200% in GoLive. With this trick, it was possible to keep the file size under 10K.

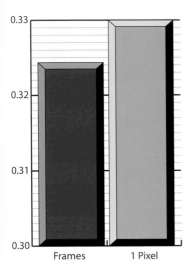

▲ The Zero-Second Trick is certainly a good way to reduce file size. However, even though the frame is reused several times in an animation, the information for Position, Transparency and Delay still require some memory—roughly 25 Bytes. I did a test animation of a line by repositioning a frame containing one pixel. The file was larger than that of an animation done with the Tweening command (see chart above.)

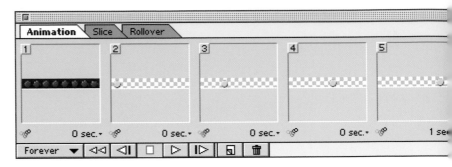

As you know, in HTML you set the dimension of an image with the IMG tag's two attributes, WIDTH and HEIGHT. These attributes are usually used by the browser to determine the size of the image before it has downloaded, but they can also be used to scale an image. So to gain savings in file size, consider shrinking the animation to fifty percent via **Image > Image size**, and then doubling its dimensions in the HTML code. Because it's an animation, the decrease in image quality is in most cases not as obvious as with a regular image. (For those of you wondering how we end up with a seventy-five percent saving when we only reduced the image size by fifty percent, remember that fifty percent reduction applies to both the width and height of the image, and therefore the image is only a quarter the size of the original.)

THE ZERO-SECOND TRICK

Theoretically you can set a delay time of zero seconds (No delay) for each frame in your animation, but this is not really achievable, since a browser

The preview command will display the Gif animation in the selected browser along with the HTML code and basic information about the file such as the file size—in this example less than 10K.

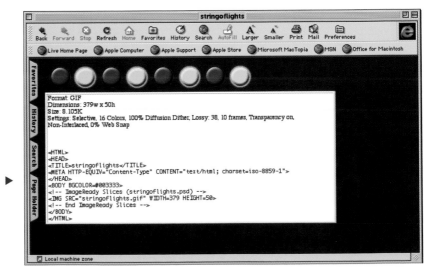

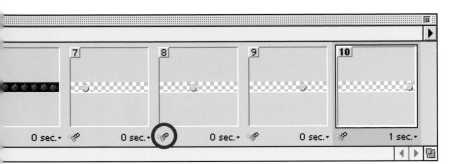

▲ Using the Zero-Second Trick requires a lot of trial and error to get the animation to work right. As you can see, all the frames were set to "Do not dispose", which makes it necessary to copy the background frame. The delay of every frame is set to "No Delay" except the frame with the last light; this one is set to one second.

▲ As you can see in the Layer palette, the entire animation is based on the background layer with all the lights off and one layer with one light on. This layer is just moved and the effects settings are changed. It's important that for all the frames with the light on, the background must be hidden.

needs some time to display a frame. However, this minimal display time is brief enough to make a frame appear almost simultaneously with the previous frame. You can use this to optimize GIF animations by splitting up a frame into two frames and putting them together by setting the first frame to a zero-second delay.

For example, a "string of lights" effect with several blinking lights can be composed out of a background image (all lights off) and one single image with a light on. This single image would be placed on the background image several times, and all the frames would be set to a zero-second delay. If you select **Do not dispose** for your disposal method (this prevents previous frames from disappearing), all the lights seem to blink at the same time. (The delay between each of them will be more visible on slower computers.)

Obviously, it takes more work to create an animation this way than simply using full frames, but you can substantially reduce the amount of data because you get rid of redundant pixels.

This technique is also ideal if you have two animations that you want to run asynchronously. For instance, if you want to animate the hands of a clock, you need a short hand for the hours and a long hand for the minutes. Assuming you use only eight positions for the long hand and twelve positions for the short hand, with this zero-second trick you end up with an animation that requires only twenty-one individual images (twenty for the hands plus one background image). Without the zero-second trick your animation would require ninety-six images (eight times twelve images). I hope I've made the point that certain animations virtually require you to use this technique; otherwise they would be way too big.

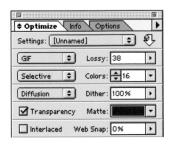

▲ In this particular animation, the glow of the lights needed to fade into the background, so the Matte option was used.

There are limitations to how far you can push this technique, since even a frame containing a pre-loaded image requires some memory—and all the information on position, disposal method and transparency color can add up.

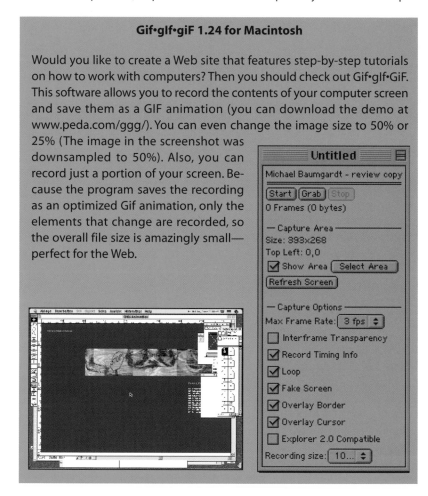

Gif•glf•giF 1.24 for Macintosh

Would you like to create a Web site that features step-by-step tutorials on how to work with computers? Then you should check out Gif•glf•GiF. This software allows you to record the contents of your computer screen and save them as a GIF animation (you can download the demo at www.peda.com/ggg/). You can even change the image size to 50% or 25% (The image in the screenshot was downsampled to 50%). Also, you can record just a portion of your screen. Because the program saves the recording as an optimized Gif animation, only the elements that change are recorded, so the overall file size is amazingly small—perfect for the Web.

TRANSPARENCY AND DISPOSAL METHODS

To use the zero-second trick effectively you have to understand how disposal methods work. Disposal methods control what happens when a frame has transparency. Let's look at cel animation to understand the concept. If you've ever seen the way an animated movie is made you know that the background of a scene, and all the characters, are painted on separate sheets of transparent celluloid. This makes it possible for the animator to reuse the background and animate the characters independently. The same idea lies behind disposal methods. They allow you to hold a previous frame as a background image, while subsequent frames add the animated character.

You can see the disposal method of a frame by right-clicking(PC) or Control-clicking (Mac) on it. A pop-up menu will appear, offering the options **Automatic**, **Do not dispose** and **Restore to background**.

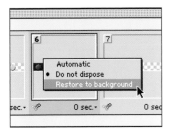

▲ The Disposal Methods are set by clicking on the frame.

Automatic is the default setting, which, according to the Photoshop manual, automatically assigns the right disposal method for you. However, when you use **Automatic** on frames with transparency you are not always to get the desired result—after all, **Automatic** has no artificial intelligence.

Do not dispose keeps frame A on the screen while the following frame (B) is displayed. If frame B has transparent areas, they will be filled with whatever frame A left on the screen. If you start with a full frame (an image that uses the entire frame), define it as **Do not dispose**, and follow it with several partially transparent frames, all the frames with partial transparency will be combined with the frame that was specified as **Do not dispose**.

▲ The Little Rock Web site (www.littlerock.com) uses an animation on the splash screen that might easily be mistaken as a Flash animation, but it is just a cleverly designed Gif animation.

Restore to background allows you to set a background color for your animation, or you could even have the background pattern of your browser be visible. Use this method if you want to have a moving object (with transparency in the frame) blend with the background in the browser.

Important: ImageReady does not simulate the disposal method, so you always have to check your result in the browser by using **File > Preview in > Internet Explorer/Netscape Navigator**.

OPTIMIZING AN ANIMATION

As you may have realized by now, you don't have to use full frames in your animation, which means you can reduce your final file size by cropping frames to only the parts that are important. ImageReady has a special feature that does exactly this for you. It actually goes through your animation frame by frame and figures out if there are overlapping parts in two sequential frames that are identical. If there are, it crops the frame to only the part that changes. Static areas are eliminated and don't use up precious memory. As you can see in in the example of the animation on the Little Rock Web site (next page), each subsequent frame is cropped to just the areas that change. To activate this feature, select **Optimize Animation** in the **Animation** palette

▲ The Little Rock Web site was designed by Christopher Stashuk of Aristotle.

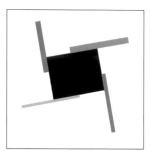 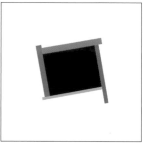  

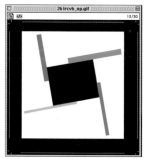   

▲ In the top you can see the some screen shots of the animation on the Little Rock Web site. In the bottom row the individual frames are displayed and you can clearly see how the Frame Optimization cropped each frame to just the parts that change.

menu (upper right corner of the window), and choose **Bounding Box** in the dialog box that comes up. Since this technique is so effective, you should try to create animations where subsequent frames build on the previous one as often as possible.

This feature can be particularly helpful if you are converting QuickTime movies to GIF format. ImageReady can convert entire QuickTime movies for you. Just open the QuickTime file and an Import dialog box will appear in which you can specify the number of frames that you want to import, and so on. Using the **Bounding Box** option when you're done will improve the file's size tremendously. Just make sure that you have **Automatic** selected as your disposal method.

Another great feature is the **Redundant Pixel Removal** option in the **Optimize Animation** dialog box. It improves the animation by replacing every static pixel with transparency. Since this allows for a better compression (remember, GIF uses a pattern-recognition algorithm that makes same-color areas compress really well), the savings can be amazing—particularly in cases where the **Bounding Box** doesn't work so well. Such a case might be if you create an animation that has changing elements in the upper-right and lower-left corners. Since the **Bounding Box** can't crop very much, you still end up with pretty large frames even though all the pixels in between might be static. **Redundant Pixel Removal** fixes the problem!

Case Study: Vino's Pub

Christopher Stashuk, of Aristotle Web Design, is a master of Gif animation. He uses splash screens with little animations to grab the visitor's attention and to preload images into the browser cache so the main page appears right away. He starts with video recordings, which he digitizes and edits on his Mac PowerPC. Here's how he created the Vino's Pub Web site.

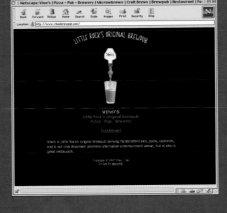

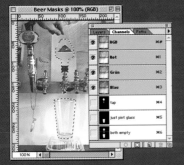

1. After recording the video and saving the individual frames as images, Cristopher selected several elements and saved them in alpha channels. He cut the image into the smallest pieces possible, so the moving parts could be animated and saved separately.

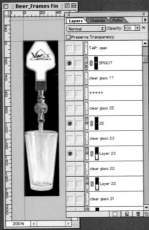

2. He loaded each image into a Photoshop document, then cropped them and eliminated the background. He looked at each layer individually to determine which frames were really essential. Finally, he created an action to index all images with the same color table, then he exported them.

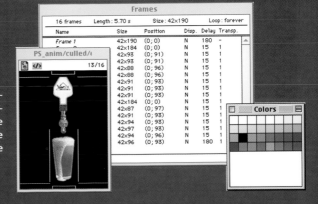

3. The adaptive color palette was exported from Photoshop to GifBuilder. Cristopher positioned each layer/frame, set the delay, and then he was done. Although the animation is five seconds long, the file size is only 25 K, so it loads very quickly.

Illustration: Michael Baumgardt

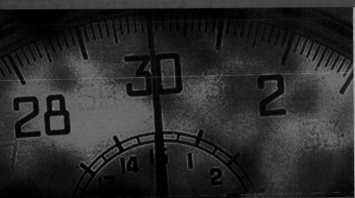

COMPARING GIF, JPEG AND PNG

▲ **These four images are used in the chart on the next page.**

Comparing GIF, JPEG and PNG

Once you have designed a Web site in Photoshop, and gotten your client's approval, your next step will be to recreate the site with an HTML authoring tool like GoLive. The question you face now is this: which graphic format should you choose for each element?

This short chapter deals mostly with when to switch from one format to the other. Luckily, with Photoshop 5.5 and ImageReady 2.0 it is fairly easy to compare the file sizes of GIF and JPEG images simultaneously with the **Save for Web** command.

WHICH FORMAT FOR WHICH IMAGE?

If you have any experience with Web design (or have read even one or two articles on the subject) you have surely come across the generalization that JPEGs are for photos and GIFs are for graphical images. While this is generally true, the answer might not be as simple if an image has both elements in it (like image B; a combination of a photo with graphics) in which case you might be better off with a GIF. This generalization is also only partially true for very small images. As you can see in the graph on page 187, photos below a certain dimension should be saved in the GIF format. All those things need to be taken into consideration before you choose one format. In the graph on the next page, you can get an overview of how different images fare under various formats and settings.

Once you have opted for JPEG, GIF, or PNG, the graphs and overviews in the chapters devoted to those formats will give you more detailed information. They will also compare visual quality, since the file's size isn't the only basis for your decision. A GIF saved with 3-Bit is always going to produce a smaller file than a JPEG, but if that image is a photo, the visual quality of 3-Bit (eight colors) just isn't enough.

USING SAVE AS OR SAVE FOR WEB WITH JPEGS

The new **Save for Web** command in Photoshop 5.5 brings up the question of whether it differs greatly from **Save As** in terms of quality and file size (as I explain in the JPEG chapter, there can be substantial differences between different JPEG encoders.) File size and quality depend on various factors; to get an idea of the difference between the two commands, I saved a sample image with various settings. Since Photoshop's **Save As** command has thirteen quality settings, and **Save for Web** in Photoshop and ImageReady lets you

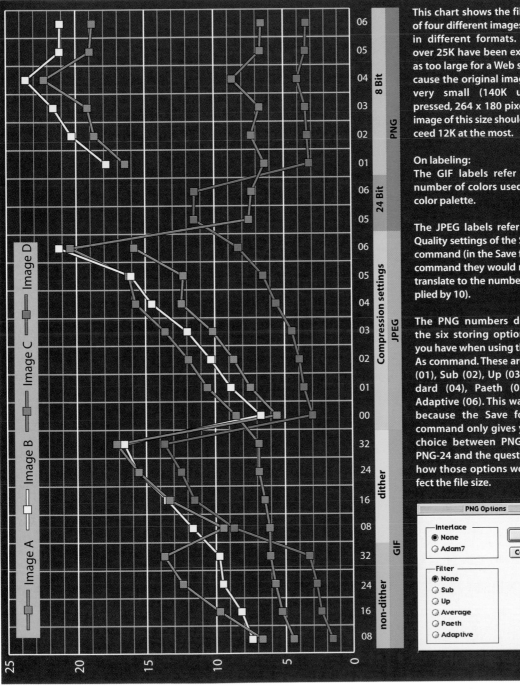

This chart shows the file sizes of four different images saved in different formats. Values over 25K have been excluded as too large for a Web site, because the original images are very small (140K uncompressed, 264 x 180 pixels). An image of this size shouldn't exceed 12K at the most.

On labeling:
The GIF labels refer to the number of colors used in the color palette.

The JPEG labels refer to the Quality settings of the Save As command (in the Save for Web command they would roughly translate to the number multiplied by 10).

The PNG numbers describe the six storing options that you have when using the Save As command. These are: None (01), Sub (02), Up (03), Standard (04), Paeth (05) and Adaptive (06). This was done because the Save for Web command only gives you the choice between PNG-8 and PNG-24 and the question was how those options would affect the file size.

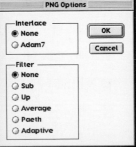

Save As	0	1	2	3	4	5	6	7	8	9	10	11	12
File Size	7.12	7.52	8.62	10.47	11.63	13.10	15.29	15.14	18.67	22.61	28.86	39.21	56.06
S. F. Web	0	9	17	25	33	42	50	58	66	75	83	91	100
File Size	3.55	4.40	4.97	6.97	7.96	9.40	11.25	13.95	16.62	21.24	27.03	36.35	50.98

▲ These are the results in file size of an image saved with the Save As command and the Save for Web command. Even though both commands use different quality settings (0-12; 0-100), which makes it difficult to compare, it is obvious that the Safe for Web command achieves the better compression.

choose a setting between zero and one hundred, I divided one hundred by twelve. (Note: I am dividing one hundred by twelve, not thirteen, to get the maximum setting for both commands to match.) So for each quality-step in **Save As** I used 8.33 increments in **Save for Web**. (I had to round the values to integers.) All other settings were similar, but I used the **Optimize** option in **Save for Web** since there is no point in not taking advantage of this option.

As you can see from the chart above, it is clear that you get better compression of JPEG files with the **Save for Web** command, especially if you use all the low-quality settings. This has to do with the **Optimize** option, but is probably also because **Save As** uses the standardized JPEG quantization table, while the **Save for Web** command uses an optimized quantization table. Whatever the reason, **Save for Web** produces better results in visual quality and file size for each setting and should always be used when saving images for the Web.

JPEG OR GIF FOR SMALL PHOTOGRAPHIC ELEMENTS?

For larger photographic images, you will definitely get better compression with JPEG. But the question remains, at what image size should you switch from GIF to JPEG? This question is particularly important when you are slicing an image into pieces or using small navigational elements like 3D buttons and so on. At what point will you get better compression using GIF instead of JPEG? To answer this question I cropped an image and saved it as both a GIF and a JPEG, with different quality settings.

▲ JPEG 0 saved with the Save for Web command (top) and in the Save As command (bottom). The subtle differences are difficult to reproduce in print—they are more apparent on screen—but it is clear that the Save for Web command produces a better visual result.

My results showed that large photo images should always be saved as JPEGs. Even with low-compression/high-quality settings you get a smaller file size than with a GIF—plus the JPEG image looks better. However, this doesn't hold true for images with an original file size of 10K- 25K (roughly 900 pixels in total) that require a color depth of eight to thirty-two colors. In such cases you'll get better results with a GIF than a JPEG.

Pixels/K	GIF (8)	GIF (16)	GIF (32)	GIF (256)	JPEG (3)	JPEG (6)	PNG-8	PNG-24
100x150/78.8	3.082	4.249	5.838	11.790	2.421	4.372	11.910	32.430
80x120/51.1	2.156	2.940	4.123	8.217	1.760	3.143	8.286	21.990
60x90/28.7	1.328	1.886	2.576	5.418	1.290	2.231	5.379	13.700
50x75/19.9	1.005	1.429	1.980	4.083	1.087	1.795	4.112	10.120
25x38/5.05	0.369	0.525	0.707	1.731	0.610	0.873	1.880	3.235
12x19/1.31	0.171	0.228	0.323	1.055	0.428	0.526	1.142	1.072

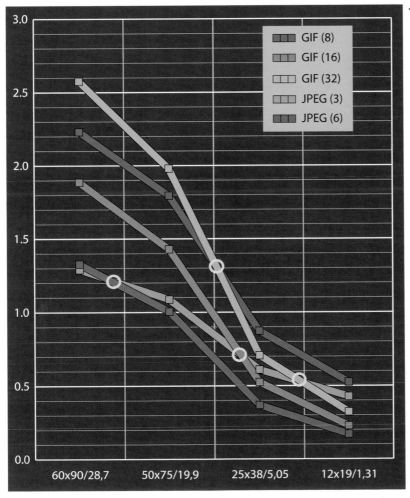

◄ FROM THE GRAPH, YOU CAN SEE THAT:
- For images smaller than 25K, a GIF (8 colors) is smaller than a JPEG (3).

- With images of 12K, a GIF (32 colors) is smaller than a JPEG (6).

- With images of around 7K, a GIF (16 colors) will produce a better result than a JPEG(3).

- With images of 3K, a GIF (32 colors) will be smaller than a JPEG(3).

▲ Wherever the red lines (GIF) crosses one of the blue lines (JPEG), the file-size saving with GIF surpasses that of JPEG.

Illustration: Michael Baumgardt

GIF

GIF—Graphical Interchange Format

GIF is the most flexible of all the image formats for the Web. It can display photos with a decent level of quality, does an excellent job when it comes to compressing graphics, and even offers animation. So it should come as no surprise that GIF gets such a large chapter. There is a lot to learn—and hopefully I'll be able to answer all your questions.

HOW DOES GIF COMPRESS?

GIF uses two techniques to compress images. One is called CLUT, which stands for Color Look-Up Table. The other is the LZW compression algorithm. Let's take a closer look at both of them, since together they explain why you get much better results with certain images than with others.

➤ CLUT—Color Look-Up Table

To understand why a CLUT is so useful for data compression it is helpful to understand how image formats work without it. For each pixel that your scanner creates when it digitizes a photo, twenty-four bits of color information are saved. For an image of 100 x 100 pixels, this requires 240,000 bits of color information. Since very few photos require a full spectrum of sixteen million colors (which is what twenty-four-bit color gives you), someone had the clever idea of limiting the total number of colors to 256 and saving those val-

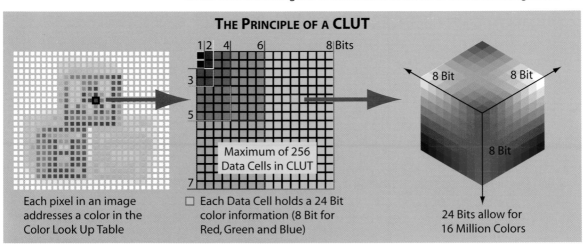

THE PRINCIPLE OF A CLUT

Each pixel in an image addresses a color in the Color Look Up Table

Maximum of 256 Data Cells in CLUT

☐ Each Data Cell holds a 24 Bit color information (8 Bit for Red, Green and Blue)

24 Bits allow for 16 Million Colors

▲ Every pixel in a GIF contains a CLUT value. The size of the CLUT depends upon the number of used bits: one bit can only address two values (0 and 1), two bits can hold four values and eight bits will store 256 values. Regardless of how many colors a CLUT holds, each color always has 24 bits, which means that GIF has a color range of more than 16 million colors.

ues in a table. Then, instead of saving a full twenty-four bits of information to define each pixel, all you have to do is reference a location in the table. To address 256 locations you need only eight bits per pixel, a two-thirds reduction in the amount of data. Instead of requiring 240,000 bits, the same 100 x 100-pixel image can be stored in 86,144 bits.

All the math whizzes will probably have realized by now that this is a little less than a two-thirds reduction. The reason is that the CLUT itself requires some data. In fact, a CLUT with 256 colors needs 256 x 24 bits, which equals 6,144 bits. Our 100 x 100-pixel image therefore will be down to 10,768 Bytes. (For all of you who are wondering about the difference between bits and bytes, a computer stores bits in chunks of eight, which are called bytes. That's why I had to divide 86,114 by eight.)

THE FILE SIZE OF A CLUT				
	Colors	**Bits**	**Bytes**	**kBytes**
1 Bit	2	48	6	0.006
2 Bits	4	96	12	0.012
3 Bits	8	192	24	0.024
4 Bits	16	384	48	0.048
5 Bits	32	768	96	0.096
6 Bits	64	1536	192	0.192
7 Bits	128	3072	384	0.384
8 Bits	256	6144	768	0.768

This technique of creating a Color Look-Up Table (CLUT), and referencing it, is called indexing. In Photoshop 5.0, in order to save a GIF you first had to switch from RGB mode to Indexed colors. Now, with the **Save for Web** command, you don't need to go through that tedious process any more.

But the more important reason to use **Save for Web** in Photoshop/ImageReady is that the command is intelligent enough to reduce the CLUT to the absolute minimum requirement. For example, if you have only two colors in your image, but you choose to save it in 256 colors, the **Save for Web** command realizes that the CLUT is much bigger than needed and reduces it accordingly. And the smaller your CLUT, the less memory your file requires.

Let's do some math here: How large would a 100 x 100-pixel image be if it had a CLUT with only two colors (black and white)? Since the image has to refer to only two color values, it only needs one bit per pixel to reference the

With photographic images, GIF compresses at a ratio of about 4:1. The advantage is that GIF compresses losslessly (aside from the limitation to 256 colors through indexing). Lossless means the image will look identical after decompression. Even repeated saving won't change it. JPEG behaves differently.

Color Depth in Bits	
Bits	Colors
1	2
2	4
3	8
4	16
5	32
6	64
7	128
8	256

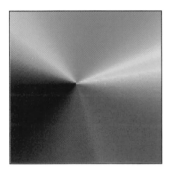

▲ This 100 x 100-pixel image was indexed with 256 colors and saved as a GIF with a file size of 6,664 bytes, although it should require 10,768 bytes. The difference is due to the LZW Compression algorithm.

CLUT. The CLUT itself has two colors, each with twenty-four bits of color information. The total then is 10,024 bits or 1,253 bytes. If you save the same image with a 256-color CLUT, you end up with 16,114 bits instead—an increase of almost sixty percent. Okay, I admit, this is an extreme example, but I want to illustrate the importance of using the **Save for Web** command. It makes your life a lot easier, and helps you create the smallest possible image files.

Coming back to our original example (the one with 100 x 100-pixel image and a two-color CLUT), if you save this image with the **Save for Web** command in either ImageReady or Photoshop, you will actually get an even smaller file size: 266 bytes instead of 1,253 bytes. That additional eighty percent saving comes from GIF's second compression technique: the LZW algorithm.

➤ The LZW Algorithm

CLUT is only part of the reason for GIF's great compression abilities. Lempel–Ziv and Welch are programmers who came up with a compression scheme they named LZW—the initials of their last names. This algorithm works with pattern recognition. Basically, it goes through the image file row by row, from left to right, from top to bottom, looking for adjacent pixels of the same color. Let's say, for example, that five pixels in a row are the same shade of red, the LZW algorithm would write down "Five x Red" instead of "Red, Red, Red, Red, Red." Although this is a pretty simplified explanation (for a more accurate and lengthier explanation see page 194), it shows why graphics with large areas of identical colors are perfect for GIF. If you want to create a Web site with a sidebar, and you need a background pattern, it should be apparent by now which format you should choose.

THE GIF COMPARISON CHART

When you decide to save an image in GIF format, your goal is usually to get the smallest possible file size along with the best quality. To achieve this, you may have to adjust the color depth of the CLUT relative to the LZW compression; the fewer colors the CLUT uses, the better the LZW gets. However, if the image loses too much of its quality and detail you may want to try dithering to get a better-looking image—although dithering can keep LZW compression from achieving its best results.

Luckily, the complex dance of adjusting these factors is a breeze with ImageReady or Photoshop 5.5. Both programs allow you to display as many as four different versions of your image at the same time. Each version can have

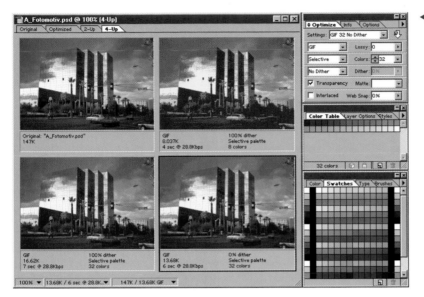

◀ ImageReady doesn't have the Save for Web command, but the commands and parameters of the Optimize Palette and the Color Table are identical to the Save for Web command (see bottom). So whenever I refer to the Save for Web command in the text, you can apply the same information to ImageReady. Some commands that are accessed in the Save for Web dialog box might only be available through the regular menu in ImageReady.

its own settings, which allows you to compare the differences in visual quality. This makes it much easier to optimize an image, but to get a feel for it, check out the comparison chart, which shows the results for three typical images: a photographic image, a graphic image, and a hybrid image that combines graphics and photograph. There is also a color spectrum, which is a

LZW PATTERN RECOGNITION

Are you (like me) hopelessly curious about why things are the way they are? Then this section is for you: an in-depth look at LZW compression. The fact is, the LZW algorithm works quite a bit like the Color Look-Up Table. The only difference is that LZW stores patterns it finds in the image and indexes them. One funny thing is that once the algorithm builds the look-up table it then throws it away—it is not stored along with the compressed data. But since there is a logic behind the indexing, the decoder can recreate the look-up table when needed.

Let's look at an example. Say we wanted to compress this chain of characters: ABACABA (imagine they represent colors). We know that we have four possible values (A, B, C, and D), so we could start by putting those four values in a table and calling them #0, #1, #2 and #3. As we look through the chains of pixels that make up the image, we will always be checking to see if the next two pixels match one of the four entries in the index table. If they do, we look to see if pixel three matches as well. We keep on checking and including the next pixel until we find one that doesn't match. Then we put this pattern in the index, give it an index number, and repeat the process until we're at the end of the image.

The first two characters are AB. Since this pattern is not in our table, we put it down and write 0 for the A that we found. The second character is a B and we check to see if this character and the previous one are already recorded in our table as a pattern. Since they are not, we give this pattern a new index (#4) and write down 1 for the next B. The character after that is the A again, so we check if the pattern BA is in the table. That is not the case so it is indexed as #5 and we note 0 for the next A. Since neither the next letter, C, nor the pattern AC is in the table, we put it down as #6 and write 2 for the next C. The next character is A and the combination CA gets indexed since it is not in the table, but (!) we realize now that the A and the following character already exist as a pattern, so we write down 4. For the last character, A, we can only write down 0 since there is nothing following, but not before we register the combination ABA as #8.

This example hasn't produced much of a saving—instead of seven characters we have now six numbers, but you can imagine that with larger images the LZW algorithm finds more and more patterns it has already indexed. Once the image is saved, the LZW doesn't require the index table any more, but to decompress the image, the browser regenerates the index table for each GIF, which takes some time and processor power.

ENCODING EXAMPLE	
ABACABA	**010240**
A	= 0
B	= 1
C	= 2
D	= 3
AB	= 4
BA	= 5
AC	= 6
CA	= 7
ABA	= 8

▲ This is an example of how the LZW-algorithm would index seven pixels (each letter in ABACABA represents a pixel with a color; same letter equals same color.) Each line in this table represents a position in the index table: in the first four position of the index are the basic colors (ABCD), followed by the various patterns that the algorithm finds. At the end the result is 010240, which is only a saving of one (instead of seven letters you have six numbers), but if the image was larger, the savings would be more substantial.

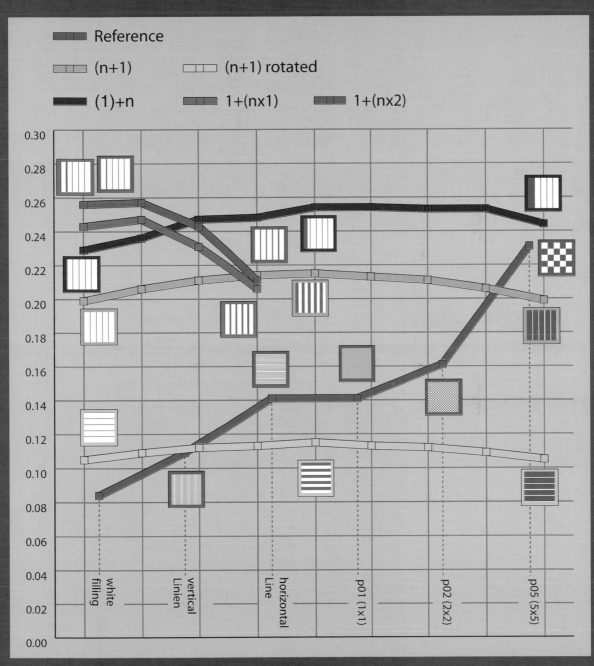

▲ To get a better feeling for the LZW algorithm, look at this comparison of a group of one-bit GIFs that all are variations on patterns. See next two pages for the individual graphs.

1+(nx1)	kByte
01+2x1	0.243
01+3x1	0.247
01+4x1	0.231
01+5x1	0.206

1+(nx2)	kByte
01+2x2	0.256
01+3x2	0.257
01+4x2	0.243
01+5x2	0.211

▲ The width of the five vertical lines was continuously increased by one pixel.

(1)+n	kByte
01+1	0.229
01+2	0.236
01+3	0.247
01+4	0.248
01+5	0.254
01+6	0.254
01+7	0.253
01+8	0.253
01+9	0.244

▲ For reference, only the first red line was widened by one pixel, until it measured 10 pixels in width.

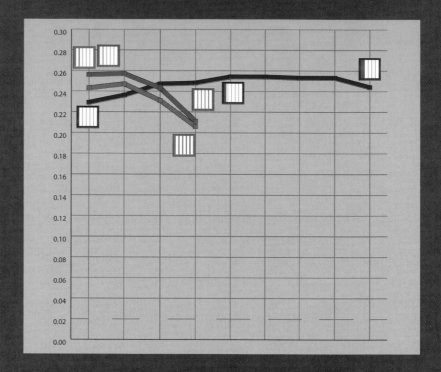

Now that we have gone through this lengthy explanation of LZW compression, can you see why an image with horizontal lines compresses better than one with vertical lines? Look at the comparison chart on page 197: The image with vertical lines requires more memory than its rotated version. This makes sense, since same-color runs create fewer patterns than if pixel colors alternate.

But there are exceptions to this rule. If you look at the chart on the top of page 197, you will see that a pattern with one-pixel vertical lines requires less than its rotated counterpart with horizontal lines. It's a bit confusing, but the reason is that after LZW has indexed the patterns and written all the index numbers, it compresses the resulting byte patterns. To simplify this, just imagine that while earlier we looked for horizontal patterns, now we are looking for vertical patterns. The image with the horizontal lines is much more complex in that respect, and it therefore carries more data.

What does all this mean to our work? Not much, really, since you don't want to design an image on the basis of how well it compresses. But it will help you to make a more educated choice when need to decide which format will yield the best results.

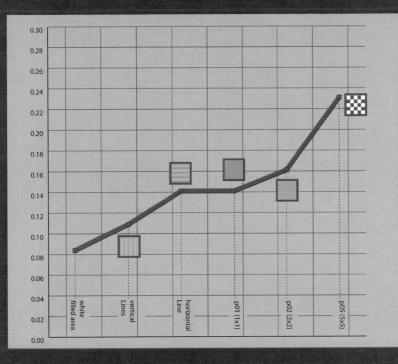

Reference	kBytes
white	0.084
vertical lines	0.109
p01 (1x1)	0.141
horizontal lines	0.141
p02 (2x2)	0.161
p05 (5x5)	0.231
Noise**	2.900*

*(-0.76 kByte for the CLUT)
** not shown in graph

▲ I created several files as references. As expected, the White file is the smallest, and the Noise file, created with the Add Noise filter is the largest (not shown on graph). Strangely enough, the file with vertical lines is smaller than that with horizontal lines—this has to do with final byte compression (see previous page)

	vert.	horiz.
01	0.199	0.105
02	0.206	0.109
03	0.211	0.112
04	0.214	0.113
05	0.215	0.115
06	0.213	0.113
07	0.211	0.112
08	0.206	0.109
09	0.199	0.105

▲ A red vertical line with a width of one pixel is repeated every 10 pixels. With every instance, the line is widened by one pixel. As expected, the file size decreases as soon as the line width surpasses 5 pixels. Rotating the files to make the lines horizontal decreases the file size.

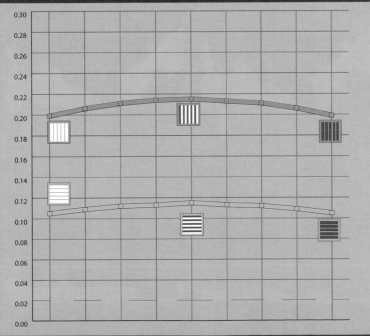

GIF COMPARISON TABLE

This table focuses on color depths of 3 bits (8 colors) through 5 bits (32 colors) which is usually the color depth used for saving photos as GIF. All images with less than 8 colors should always be saved as GIFs and all images that require more than 32 colors should always be stored as JPEGs.

8 COLORS (3 BITS), ADAPTIVE			
Dither	Q	Non-Dither	Q
IMAGE A			
9,451 Bytes	5.0	6,689 Bytes	4.0
IMAGE B			
11,643 Bytes	4.0	7,411 Bytes	2.0
IMAGE C			
7,739 Bytes	4.0	6,424 Bytes	7.0
REFERENCE			
8,695 Bytes	6.0	1,579 Bytes	1.0

16 COLORS (4 BITS), WEB/ADAPTIVE

Dither	Q	Non-Dither	Q

13,311 Bytes   7.0

9,736 Bytes   5.0

13,488 Bytes   6.0

8,189 Bytes   2.0

13,450 Bytes   9.0

9,769 Bytes   6.0

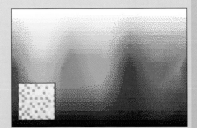

11,524 Bytes   6.5

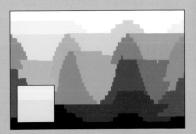

2,412 Bytes   1.5

▲ The JPEG comparison chart on page 238 uses this image as a graphic image (Image C), an image with which GIF would certainly produce the smallest file size with the best quality. For this comparison I used a less obvious image of two hands.

If you're interested, here are the results for the image above:

WITHOUT DITHERING	
Colors	**Size**
8	4,465
16	5,277
24	5,733
32	6,092

WITH DITHERING	
Colors	**Size**
8	6,127
16	6,463
24	6,875
32	6,875

All images measure 264 pixels (width) x 180 pixels (height). Uncompressed file size is 140 K.

32 Colors (5 Bits), Web/Adaptive			
Dithered	**Q**	**Not Dithered**	**Q**

| 17,182 Bytes | 9.0 | 13,752 Bytes | 6.0 |

| 16,609 Bytes | 8.0 | 9,754 Bytes | 3.0 |

| 16,975 Bytes | 9.0 | 10,005 Bytes | 6.0 |

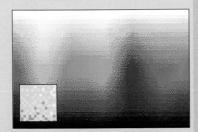 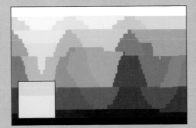

| 13,679 Bytes | 7.0 | 3,311 Bytes | 2.0 |

THE DITHERING COMPARISON CHART

The graph to the right shows the file size of the four images A, B, C and D, saved with dithering (line graph). For reference, the quality values are displayed as well (column graph).

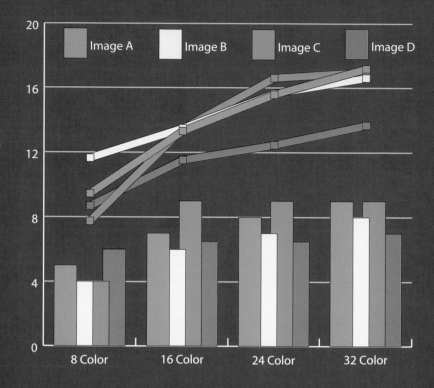

These graphs show how much the dithering affects the file size of each image. ▶

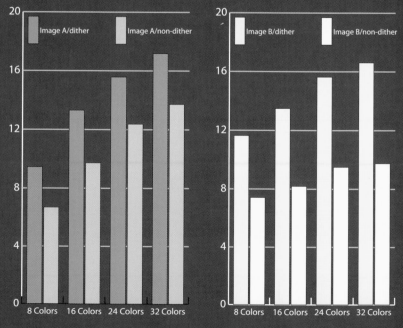

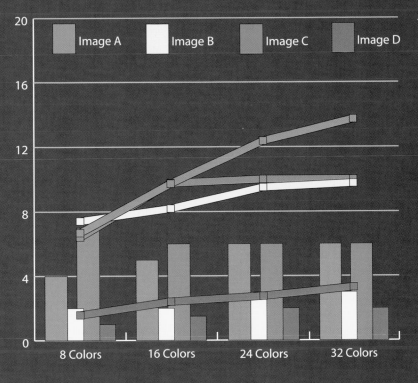

◀ This diagram shows the file sizes of the four images A, B, C and D, saved *without* dithering. They are significantly smaller than the dithered files on the previous page. For reference, the quality values are displayed as well (column graph).

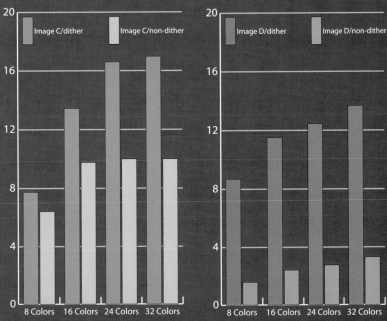

To interpret the graphs, look for dots that represent the same number of colors in each of the three files (they're connected with yellow lines). The vertical axis in each chart is the file size, and the horizontal axis represents the quality; dots in the lower-right corner of the charts indicate the best images.

Both the Save for Web command and the Optimize palette in ImageReady offer the Lossy option. This new option reduces file size by replacing pixels with already indexed patterns (as explained on page 194). The result can look either like a pixel storm, in the worst case, or like a dithered image, in the best case.

To get a better idea of the effects of Lossy on file size and image quality, I compressed a photo (Image A), a photo with graphics, (Image B), and a spectrum (Image C), with a Lossy setting of 30%, which is pretty much the upper limit if you want to obtain good results. I also used a regular GIF with an adaptive palette as a reference image. Since GIF quality falls between two and 256 colors, I assigned them quality values between zero and ten. First I looked at the quality of the images compressed with the 30% Lossy setting, then I looked at each of them again with a Dithering setting of 100% and a Lossy setting of zero.

I left out the graphic image used in the GIF comparison chart (Image C) because it consists mostly of areas of flat color; the Lossy option has no effect on the quality, and its file size stays pretty constant no matter what the Lossy setting is.

▲ The chart shows that with Image A, the photograph, Lossy achieves the best results between sixteen and sixty-four colors. With sixty-four colors, the Lossy GIF is 45% smaller than the regular GIF while maintaining the same image quality. The sixteen-color version shows 30% less quality with Lossy, but it's also 1K smaller than the regular GIF. These results suggest that a photographic image saved as a GIF can greatly benefit from the Lossy option.

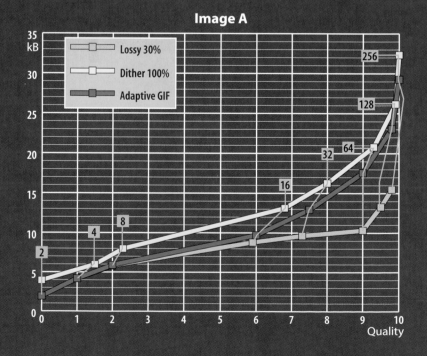

Image A

Image B

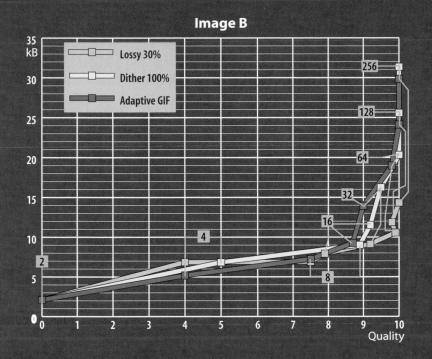

▲ Image B is a photograph with areas of graphics, which makes it easier for the LZW algorithm to compress. The results in the chart are similar to those of Image A; the difference is that the three GIFs are much closer to each other in file size and quality. The best ratio of file size reduction/image quality occurs between thirty-two and sixty-four colors.

Image C

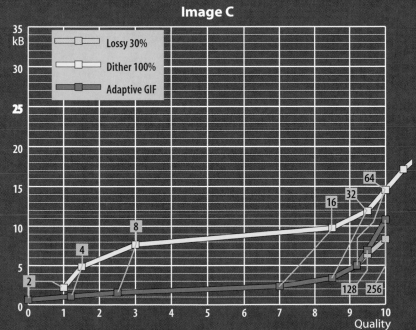

▲ Image C is the color spectrum, just about the worst kind of image for a GIF. Although the graph shows quite high marks for quality, keep in mind that these are just relative assessments; they're not meant to be compared with the quality of the other two images. Sixty-four colors is really the minimum number you can use to get a decent result with this image. Dithering improved the results quite a bit, which is why a couple of the results are actually better than ten.

Photo: Paul Ehrenreich

▲ This image was saved with the Adaptive palette setting, 8 bits and dithering.

▲ This image was saved with the Adaptive palette setting, 8 bits and no dithering.

very good reference, since almost every pixel has a different color value. This is almost a worst-case scenario for GIF, since the LZW algorithm can't find many patterns. At the same time it will give you a good idea of how the CLUT affects the image.

● **Adaptive Web Palette**

The photographic image was saved with an Adaptive palette; more Web designers use this than the Web-safe color palette, which doesn't work so well for photos. Using an Adaptive palette means that Web site visitors with a monitor card that enables thousands or millions of colors will get a much better result. It also means you will have to check those images in a browser with a monitor setting of 256 colors, but it's worth the effort.

● **To Dither or Not to Dither, That Is the Question**

For the graphic image I used the Web-safe color palette and different color depths. Since dithering is an important tool for simulating intermediate colors, the GIF comparison chart shows the image both with dithering and without. It's often said that you should avoid dithering a GIF because it has a negative impact on LZW compression. But while it's true that dithering always results in a decreased compression ratio, the file-size increase is not nearly as bad as you might think. And the image really improves with dithering, particularly if you choose **Noise Dithering** in the **Save for Web** dialog box. If you want the best of both worlds, you can consider partially dithering an image. I'll explain how to do that later in this chapter.

● **Quality**

The last important factor to consider when comparing GIFs is image quality. In a book it is difficult to see the subtle differences, due to the conversion of the indexed RGB color space to CMYK. Some colors that are displayable in the RGB color space just aren't available in print; also, dot gain and rasterizing cover up a lot of fine details. To give you a better idea of the quality differences, I evaluated the GIFs and included a quality value in the comparison chart. While this is definitely a subjective value, it may help as a point of reference to see where some quality leaps are.

CREATING GIFs

There are basically two ways to create a GIF in Photoshop. One is the "old" way, and the other is with the **Save for Web** command. If you want to use the old you have to change the mode from **RGB** to **Indexed** in the **Image: Mode** submenu. The Palettes offered in the **Indexed Color** dialog box are pretty much the same as with the **Save for Web** command (with some minor differences). But I don't want to encourage you to use the old way, because the **Save for Web** command offers more data reduction features. There are still a few occasions when it might make sense for you to use the old way of saving a GIF (using Index and Export) which I'll explain, but first, here is an overview over the modes offered for indexing your image.

➤ Color Reduction Algorithms

When indexing an image, you have to decide which colors to include in the Color Look-Up Table (CLUT). This is a difficult task, because each image is unique and requires its individual setting. Photoshop offers a series of Color Reduction Algorithms and CLUT templates that you can access either when you index an image in the **Image > Mode > Indexed** menu or in the **Save for Web** command (in the following section I listed them in order of importance for your work.)

● Adaptive
Next to **Selective**, this is the most important mode that you have. It allows you to reduce the size of the CLUT to thirty-two colors or less and still get the best result. As the name suggests, this mode adapts to the colors in the image, meaning it picks the most frequently occurring colors for the CLUT.

▲ This image was saved with the Web palette setting and dithering.

▲ This image was saved with the Web palette setting and pattern dithering.

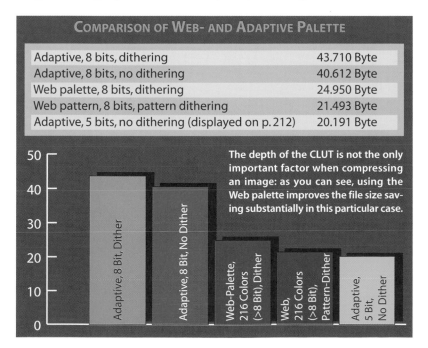

COMPARISON OF WEB- AND ADAPTIVE PALETTE	
Adaptive, 8 bits, dithering	43.710 Byte
Adaptive, 8 bits, no dithering	40.612 Byte
Web palette, 8 bits, dithering	24.950 Byte
Web pattern, 8 bits, pattern dithering	21.493 Byte
Adaptive, 5 bits, no dithering (displayed on p. 212)	20.191 Byte

The depth of the CLUT is not the only important factor when compressing an image: as you can see, using the Web palette improves the file size saving substantially in this particular case.

(Bar chart with y-axis values: 0, 10, 20, 30, 40, 50; bars labeled: Adaptive, 8 Bit, Dither; Adaptive, 8 Bit, No Dither; Web-Palette, 216 Colors (>8 Bit), Dither; Web, 216 Colors (>8 Bit), Pattern-Dither; Adaptive, 5 Bit, No Dither)

▲ This image was saved with the Adaptive palette setting, 5 bits and no dithering.

Since those colors are rarely in the Web-safe color palette, you will always have some additional dithering or color shifting when viewed on systems with 256 colors or less. The **Web Snap** slider in the **Save for Web** dialog box gives you back some control by allowing you to gradually shift your colors to the closest Web color (marked with a Diamond icon). According to Adobe, the Selective color reduction algorithm produces images with the greatest color integrity, but personally I favor the Adaptive color palette.

● **Selective & Perceptual**

Adobe thinks **Selective** is the best choice for Web design and therefore uses it as the default setting. The Selective color table is very similar to the Perceptual color table, but it favors broad areas of color and the preservation of Web colors. **Perceptual** gives priority to colors for which the human eye has greater sensitivity. You can check this out if you set the **Web Snap slider** to 25% and then switch between **Selective** and **Perceptual** or **Adaptive**. The **Selective** reduction algorithm will give you more Web colors in the color table than **Adaptive** or **Perceptual** (if this is not the case with your image, try another one. It could be the exception to the rule.) .

The best way to see what the different color algorithms do is to choose a color spectrum and save it as **Perceptual**, **Selective** and **Adaptive**—which is exactly what I did here. All the images have sixteen colors, and even though the differences are very subtle it's easy to see which color-reduction algo-

The Save for Web command is a little "smarter" then the Index command. If your CLUT is larger than needed , Save for Web will reduce the CLUT to only the required number of colors, which can save up to 500 Bytes. To test this, index an image with 16 colors, convert it back to RGB and save it once with Save for Web and Indexed (both times with 256 colors). When you check the file size, the Save for Web file will be smaller by exactly the amount that the CLUT takes up.

To get a better feel for the three color reduction algorithms, use the 4-Up option to display them while checking the Color Table.

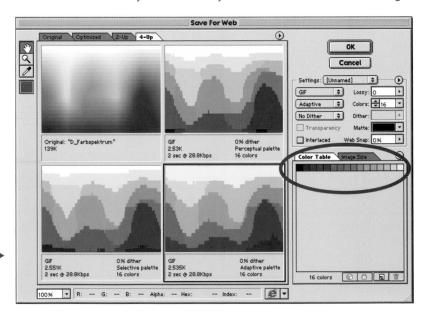

rithm will be best for your image. The point I want to make here is don't stick to the **Selective** color algorithm just because it's the default setting. Depending on your image, you might get a better result with an Adaptive or Perceptual palette.

> **Summary for Selective, Perceptual and Adaptive**
> For more detail in dark areas use Selective.
> For more detail in lighter colors use Perceptual or Selective.
> For more detail in the red spectrum use Adaptive.

● Web

The advantage of this table of 216 colors is that all the colors will be displayed on all platforms without major color shifts. (The different Gammas on each platform will still create slight shifts, but using this color table ensures that, for the most part, what you see really is what you get, with no additional dithering or color changes.) In real life, this color table is not used very often, because it means saving your image in the worst possible color mode just to be sure it will look good on 256-color displays.

There is another, slightly more labor intensive, way to do this that gives you better results on high-end computers. Use an adaptive color palette and a reduced CLUT (maximum five bits). Because the color table is adaptive, it will

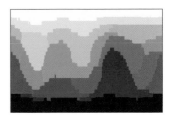

▲ PERCEPTUAL
The Perceptual palette is more detailed in the brighter parts of the image, so bright colors are differentiated more than in the Adaptive color palette. You will see that both Selective and Perceptual palettes emphasize the yellow part of the spectrum.

▲ SELECTIVE
The main difference between Perceptual and Selective is that Selective shows more detail in the dark areas.

▲ ADAPTIVE
In the spectrum saved with the Adaptive palette there is less differentiation in the bright and dark parts of the image, but you get more detail overall throughout the spectrum (for instance, look at the magenta).

▲ The Save for Web dialog box lets you display the image in the Browser. This is important when you don't use the Web safe color palette because Netscape and Explorer adjust the CLUT quite differently on monitors with 256 colors.

pick the colors that occur most frequently in the image, giving you the best possible display. The only drawback is that you have to view the image in each browser and on each platform, with a monitor display setting of 256 colors to be sure your image looks decent. Using **ImageReady**, you can get an idea how the image will look by selecting **Browser Dither** in the **View > Preview** menu, but that is just an approximation.

Even though using an adaptive CLUT requires more work, it is also more rewarding. You get the best looking image on high-quality displays while still looking good to low-end users. So use **Web** only on graphics that you have created, and that contain only Web-safe colors.

● Exact (Index command in Photoshop only)
This mode is only available if the image contains less than 256 colors. The CLUT is built of all the colors in the image, and it makes sense that the dithering option in the dialog box is deactivated.

● Macintosh and Windows Systems
You have the choice of either operating system, and you can save the image with a platform-specific color table. These two modes are most important for multimedia designers who might work on a project with Macromedia Director and want to optimize the images for specific computers. For Web design neither of them has much significance unless you really need to optimize your images for one specific platform.

● Custom
Custom allows you to create or import your own CLUT, which can be helpful if you want to use a common palette for all your images. There are two reasons why you might create and use your own palette. The first is that if you save every image on your page with its own **Adaptive** palette, you might run out of video memory on 256-color displays. For example, if you had ten images with thirty-two colors each, then the total number of colors would be 320—which means that sixty-four colors on your page would be shifted. (Don't worry too much about this. Since most of the images probably share many of the same colors anyway, it only can affect your page if you have a lot of different pictures.) To prevent unpredictable color shifts or dithering, you might consider using one custom palette for all your images.

The second reason for using a custom color table is if, for example, your page uses many different tones of yellow. If you optimize each image individually, you will end up with many different CLUTs, because the frequency of certain yellows might vary in each individual image. This could mean that the same color will be shifted differently in the individual images. In cases where the images are adjacent (for example, in an image table), this might become a problem.

● Previous (only with Indexed)

The Previous command does exactly what it says: It uses the last-used color table, which is a simple way to apply the color of a sample image to additional images without having to go through the process of saving the color table and re-importing it.

● Uniform

According to Adobe, this color palette is created by distributing the available colors evenly over the whole color spectrum. The effect can best be seen if you open a photo and index it with sixteen colors. This will shift all the colors in your image, with a result that looks like you used the Posterize filter. If you use 256 colors you end up with the Web-safe color palette. The only notable thing about this mode is that you are free to choose the numbers of colors in your image. To be honest, I haven't found one useful application for this.

➤ Dithering

In addition to the CLUT, you can also define the dithering in the **Indexed Colors** dialog box and the **Save for Web** dialog box. Dithering improves the visual quality by using two colors from the color table to make up for a missing intermediate color. In general, dithering makes GIF compress less well (that is, it

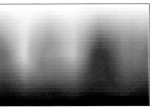

creates bigger files), but as compensation you can usually reduce the number of colors in the image when you increase the dithering percentage. Most of the time, reducing the number of colors is the ultimate key to producing smaller files. Therefore, you should reduce the number of colors to a point just before you can see a substantial drop in quality, then use the Dithering slider to improve the display, all the while keeping an eye on the file size. Check the chart on page 207 to see how variations in color palette and dithering can affect the image: there is virtually no visual difference in quality between the eight-bit image (on page 206) and the five-bit image (on page 208), but at the same time the file size of the five-bit image is only half of that of the eight-bit image. The reference image (adaptive palette, 8 Bit, without dithering) doesn't save that much in file size, because this image contains so many colors that it is hard for the LZW-algorithm to find any patterns (typically, this image would be saved in JPEG format.) This also explains why indexing the image with

▲ What dithering does can best be seen in the reference image: without dithering, the spectrum gets reduced to flat color areas, with dithering the colors blend gradually.

▲ Activate the Preserve Exact Colors option in the Indexed Color dialog box. This ensures that the colors in the image won't be dithered if Photoshop finds an exact match in the color table. Use this option when you have graphics containing fine lines and text that are created with colors from the Web-safe color palette, and you want to make sure that their colors don't shift.

the Web-safe color palette produces such a great result in this particular image: because the Web-safe color palette disregards all the subtle color changes, many adjacent pixels get flattened to the same color, which in return improves the pattern recognition.

In the **Save for Web** dialog box you can choose between three dithering options: **Diffusion**, **Pattern** and **Noise**. If you select **Pattern** the two colors will mix in a regular pattern that's easy to spot. Pattern dithering should generally be avoided for this reason; you get much better visual results using **Diffusion** or **Noise**, which use very similar algorithms. Most of the time **Noise** seems to deliver the best results, but **Diffusion** has the advantage of allowing you to set the amount of dithering you want by using a slider. Dithering will increase your file size, but in most cases the increase won't be too bad, and the improvement in image quality can be substantial. You can use the **Lossy** command to counteract the file-size increase that you get with dithering. How well this works varies quite a bit between different images.

➤ Lossy

This command works miracles with GIF files. As explained in detail on page 194, the LZW algorithm looks for patterns within the image and stores them in a compression table. The Lossy command makes use of this by reusing those patterns in the image, thus improving the compression. This command can be set from 1 to 100%. For more details see page 204.

➤ Transparency and Matte

The Save for Web command offers you a Transparency option. This option is greyed out when there are no transparent parts or layers in your image (in ImageReady's Optimize palette this option can be selected regardless.) This is completely different than the **Export** command, where you need only select a color in order to make it transparent—but there is a good reason for this "new" way. The **Matte** option (next to the **Transparency** option in the **Save for Web** dialog box) allows you to select a background color—by which I mean the background color of your Web page. As you may recall, if you place a transparent GIF on a page with a background color, you can get a halo ef-

In order to use the Transparency option in the Save for Web command, the background layer needs to be transparent. A transparent layer is displayed as a grey checker pattern.

▶

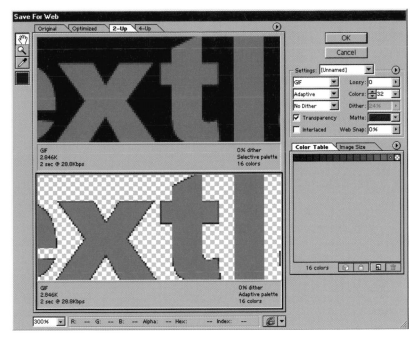

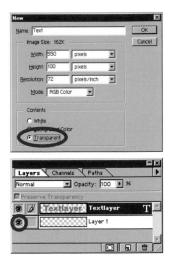

▲ As you can see, the edges of the text have a blue halo. Placed in the HTML document in front of the same color background, the text will blend seamlessly and best of all, if the background color changes, you have only to change the Matte color.

▲ You can either create a new document with a transparent layer or later hide the background layer before you call up the Save for Web dialog box. Activate the Transparency option in the Save for Web dialog box and select a Matte color.

fect unless you have placed your GIF in front of the same color background in Photoshop. In that case, the edges (which always create intermediate colors due to anti-aliasing) will blend nicely with the background color, eliminating the halo. Hence, **Matte** is a convenient way to get rid of halos.

To see this effect better, create a new layer with text (like a headline), make the background layer invisible by clicking on the eye icon in the **Layers** palette, and choose **Save for Web**. Click on **Transparency** and select a color in **Matte**, and as you will see your text will have a halo in the color you picked.

➤ Interlaced

This feature becomes very important if you have many images on your Web site. As you know, if you don't limit the number of images and the total file size, the page will take so long to come up in the browser you may lose visitors. (If you are lucky, they'll just get up and make coffee while they wait.) So what does interlacing do? Technically speaking, it rearranges the pixel rows when saving a GIF (or a JPEG). This means that the browser can display

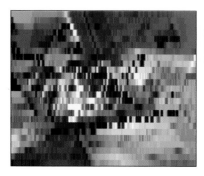  

▲ The Interlace option will encode an image in multiple passes. GIF uses always four passes—you can see how the first three passes are displayed in a browser. Some browsers, like Explorer, will display it line by line instead.

a low-resolution preview of the image while downloading the remaining data. (Some browsers, like Explorer, actually display interlaced GIFs line by line.) Gradually, the resolution of the image gets better and better until it is completely downloaded. On a subconscious level, the visitor has the impression that the download is faster; the reality is that an interlaced image actually takes longer to download (the time difference is usually unnoticeable).

GIF interlacing works by transmitting every eighth row of the image (one, nine, seventeen, and so on) in the first pass. The second pass sends every fourth row (five, thirteen, twenty-one, and so on), the third pass sends the remaining odd row numbers (three, seven, eleven, fifteen, and so on), and the final pass gets the leftover even-numbered rows (two, four, six, eight, and so on).

JPEG also has an Interlacing option which allows you to choose between three to five passes; GIF always uses four. Interlacing also affects the file size of the two formats differently: a GIF will gain a couple of percent, while JPEG generally ends up with smaller file sizes. The reason GIF gains some size has to do with the compression algorithm it uses: since the rows are scrambled, the likelihood of finding patterns decreases. Nevertheless, in spite of the slower download the visitor to your Web page will still have the feeling of increased speed.

Important: Never use Interlacing and Transparency at the same time, because in some browsers you can end up with unwanted pixels in the transparent areas. The reason is that in some browsers the first data pass is used to display a low-resolution preview that is basically the first pass rows stretched to the full size of the image. This can cause part of the image to appear in areas that will later become transparent, and since not all browsers refresh, those pixels may remain visible. You won't always encounter this problem, but check the browser (older browsers in particular) to be on the safe side.

➤ Web Snap

Not many designers like to use the Web-safe color palette for their images because it subjects everyone, both high-end and low-end viewers, to the worst display quality. Most designers prefer to use an Adaptive or Perceptual palette since it produces much better results on monitors with millions of colors but still looks OK on low-end displays. To ensure that the image looks good on a 256-color display you have to view the image in a browser with your display set to 256 colors.

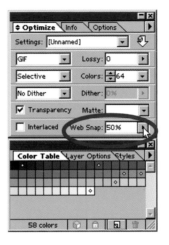

▲ Web Snap, shown here in the ImageReady Optimize palette.

Luckily, with Photoshop and ImageReady you can use the **Web Snap** option in the **Save for Web** dialog box. The slider allows you to shift the colors in the image to the closest Web-safe color. You can get an idea how the image is going to look on a 256-color display by choosing the **Browser Dither** option from the **Preview** menu in the top right corner of the image window. If you only need one color to be in the Web-safe color palette, you can use a different technique. Select the color in the image with the **Eyedropper** tool and the color will be highlighted in the color table. Click the Cube icon at the bottom of the color table to shift the selected color to the closest Web-safe color. A diamond appears in the square of color to indicate that it's Web safe.

OPTIMIZING A CLUT

Since optimizing the CLUT is an important task, let's take an in-depth look at several techniques to do it. I will show you both the old way and the new way, since the old way still can be useful in some cases. But most of the time, optimizing a CLUT with the **Save for Web** command in Photoshop/ImageReady is the way to go.

Optimizing a CLUT got a lot easier with Photoshop 5.5. Almost all operations—deleting unnecessary colors, shifting a color to the Web-safe color palette (or the opposite, preventing certain colors from shifting at all)—can

SAVING AND EXPORTING A GIF

There are several ways to save a GIF. One way—after you have indexed the image—is to save it using the **Save a Copy** command from Photoshop's **File** menu. A second way is to use the **GIF89a Export** command (also in the **File** menu). In the **Export** dialog box you will see the color table, and you can set the transparency color by selecting it with the **Eyedropper** tool. If you see a dialog box without the CLUT, you didn't index the image first. You can display the CLUT in a separate dialog box by clicking on the Preview button.

Although there are some instances in which using the Export or Save a Copy command might be useful, neither of these methods are as well optimized as the Save for Web command.

So now let's look at the **Save for Web** command in detail, to show you how you can get the best results with your image.

In the **Save for Web** dialog box you can view the image in the original quality or in an optimized view. The optimized view shows you how your image will look after compression. After you click on the **Optimized** tab in the upper left corner it will take Photoshop a moment to produce the result; a progress bar can be seen at the bottom of the window. Since it's always easier to make a decision if you can see the original and the compressed image simultaneously, you can also choose between **2-Up** and **4-Up**. These tabs will present either two or four views at the same time, and allow you to select compression settings independently for each view.

Use the Zoom tool to see more details and then move the image with the Hand tool. The Eyedropper tool is used to select a Matte color or to make changes to the CLUT.

If you decide to go with one of these two (or four) views, you may not be able to see the entire image at once, so use the **Hand** tool in the upper left corner to move to the part of the image that you want to see. You will also find the **Zoom** tool and the **Eyedropper tool** in the same corner of the screen. The **Zoom** tool allows you to magnify the view; the exact percentage can be seen in the lower left corner. The **Eyedropper tool** shows you the selected color within the color table, which is usually visible on the right side of the dialog box.

You can get Photoshop to assist you in optimizing the image. Click the triangle next to the **Settings** pop-up (in ImageReady use the Optimize palette menu); here you'll find one of the most helpful commands: **Optimize To File Size**. This command will let you designate a final file size, and Photoshop will then choose the appropriate settings automatically. You can even tell Photoshop to start out using your current settings (**Start With: Current Settings**) or select GIF/JPEG automatically. If you have to use a specific format, choose **Current Settings**. For example, suppose that you have to save an image as a GIF because you want to use transparency. Select GIF from the pop-up menu in the **Save for Web** dialog box, set all the other options like dithering and the color table mode, then activate **Optimize To File Size**, type in the desired size in Kilobytes, and choose the **Current Settings** option. Photoshop will automatically reduce the number of colors until it can match your file size. It does not "experiment" with the other settings, however,

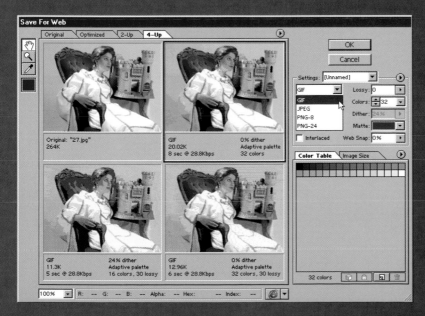

◀ **Activate the second view in the 4-Up and GIF in the Optimized File Format menu.**

▲ In the Color Table (of the Save for Web command in Photoshop, the optimized Palette in Image-Ready, seen here) the currently selected color of the Eyedropper tool will be outlined. The symbols at the bottom allow you to shift selected colors to the Web-safe color palette (Cube icon), lock a particular color to prevent any color shifts (Lock icon), insert a new color (Page icon) or delete a color (Trash icon).

Reduce the colors until there is a noticeable decrease in image quality, then use dithering to compensate for this effect. If this doesn't bring the desired improvement, increase the number of colors and reduce the dithering.

so don't rely on the **Optimize To File Size** command too much. It's helpful in some cases, but an experienced Web designer can get better results by adjusting the parameters manually.

Rather than explaining the different functions, let me run through a typical scenario for saving a GIF:

1. Choose 4-Up, and use the second view (upper right) to select the number of colors you think your image requires. A GIF should not use more than thirty-two colors; if you feel it requires more, you should probably save the image as JPEG (if you have a choice). Pick one of the Color Reduction Algorithms; the default is **Selective**, but when you later choose the number of colors for your CLUT, also try **Adaptive** or **Perceptual**.

2. Try reducing the number of colors even more using the arrows in the Colors box. You can also either choose a standard number (16, 32, 64, and so on) from the drop-down menu, or enter a number in the field. The fewer colors you need the better, but at some point you will notice a sudden drop in quality.

3. Now select a dithering method. Try **Noise** first, although it usually results in a much larger file size. (The exact file size is always shown at the bottom of each display.) Alternatively, use **Diffusion** dithering; the quality of the image will improve with dithering, and you can continue to decrease the number of colors until you see another sudden drop in quality.

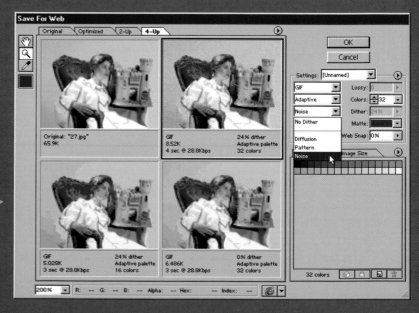

On the left you see the image with an Adaptive 16 color palette, on the right the same image with Lossy set to 50 %. Used moderately (10–20%), the effect looks a little bit like dithering, but when it's increased, the visual quality will go downhill.

4. Use the Lossy option if the current quality of the image is still good enough and you need to reduce the file size, though it is only accessible if Interlaced is deactivated. This option allows you to control how many color shifts occur in the image—it can be a big file-size saver! However, using the Lossy option too much creates an effect that looks like a pixelstorm: the pixels appear to have been blown from left to right across the image. To get a good idea on what the best settings are for the Lossy command, see the chart on page 204. This chart shows how the **Dithering** and **Lossy** commands affect the file size.

5. Finally, activate the Browser Dither option from the **Preview** pop-up menu (hidden behind a triangle on the top right corner of the view area). **Browser Dither** simulates how the image will look in the browser on 256 color monitors. However, this only gives you a very rough idea, because Navigator and Explorer use different dithering techniques and you still have to check the image in both browsers. Use the **Browser Preview** button in the lower right corner of the **Save for Web** dialog box (in ImageReady use **File > Preview In**). Set the color depth of your monitor to 256 colors and then compare the image in both browsers at the same time. You will then clearly see the difference.

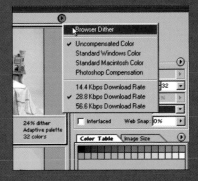

▲ The Browser Dither option gives you a very rough idea of how the GIF will look in browsers and monitors when they are set to 256 colors, but remember, it is only an approximation.

By now you should have a version of the image that looks decent and still boasts a small file size. Use the other two views in 4-Up to create variations of those settings and compare them.

▲ The Color Table has its own menu that can be accessed by clicking on the triangle in the upper right corner.

be done in the **Save for Web** dialog box. To access the commands, you have to click on the **Color Table** tab. At the bottom, you will see four icons:

Snaps selected colors to Web palette
Locks selected colors to prohibit being dropped
Adds Eyedropper Colors to palette
Deletes selected colors.

The name of the game is to reduce the numbers of colors and still achieve the best-looking image. Start by sorting all the colors by popularity, a command you'll find the in the **Color Table** palette drop-down menu (click the triangle next to the tabs). Look for colors in the CLUT that are very similar to each other; chances are you can delete one. **Sort by Popularity** puts the most frequently used color at the upper left corner, so it's usually safest to delete the rightmost color. Just click on the color and then on the Trash can icon, but keep in mind that you can't undo this command—so if you make a mistake you'll have to start over again by holding down the **Option** or **Alt** key and clicking on the **Reset** button, which appears in place of the **Cancel** button.

Another way to reduce the number of colors is by increasing the **Web Snap** factor; if want to keep certain colors from shifting, you can lock them prior to this action. Click on the color to be locked, and then on the Lock icon to prevent this color from being dropped. A small square icon in the color square indicates that a color is locked

If you've done a lot of Web design, especially with Photoshop 5.0, you probably know the trick of using a selection to force certain colors into the CLUT (I'll be describing it later). However, if you're using the Save for Web command you don't do this with a selection, you do it with the Eyedropper tool.

Here's one of the most important tricks you can learn: how to include colors that would otherwise get dropped. Usually when you choose a color-reduction algorithm, you have very little control over how that algorithm makes its color choices. It tries to analyze the histogram to select the most common colors, but since it can't see the image, you may lose colors in an important detail.

To include a color that got dropped in optimization, start by getting into **2-Up** or **4-Up** mode so you can see the original image. For example, in the image on the following page you see that the yellow of the traffic light has been dropped, along with the red brake lights on the cars. To include those colors in the CLUT, select them in the original image with the **Eyedropper** tool, activate the **Optimized** preview, and then click on the **New Color** command (Adds Eyedropper Color to palette). You should now see the color included in the palette, and most likely your image will also change because one of the more frequently used colors was dropped instead. If that is the case, you may have to reset the CLUT, start with more colors, include the new color, and then decrease the number of colors in your CLUT.

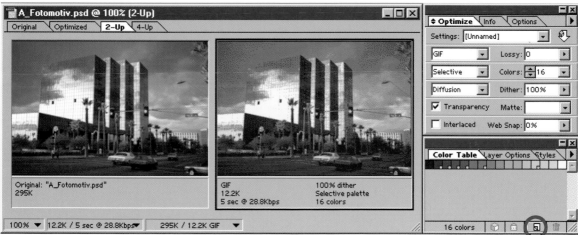

CONVERTING SEVERAL IMAGES WITH BATCH PROCESSING

As good as the **Save for Web** command is, the old way of optimizing a color table still has its uses, especially if you need to batch-process many images but still want to retain some control over the CLUT. A neat feature of the old way is that you can force a color into the CLUT by selecting it. This allows you to create an action with a built-in stop, so you can draw your selection and then continue with the indexing. This can make your life a lot easier if you need to convert hundreds of GIFs. Before I get into detail about how to set up the action, let me explain how you use a selection to control your CLUT.

▲ When you choose a color reduction algorithm, many of colors in your image get dropped, like the yellow of the traffic light for example. To force this color back into the Color Table, select the color with the Eyedropper Tool in the Original view, click on the Optimized view and the Page icon. The color will be inserted and locked (marked with a dot in the lower right corner.)

▲ I created two versions of the image above: one was indexed without a selection, one with a selection. See the results in magnification to the right.

▲ The left image was indexed without a selection, the right image was indexed with a selection. As you can see in the color table, the right image includes many more greens and yellows than the left one.

As with the Save for Web command, you can manually delete colors from the CLUT. All you need to do is to open the color table (Image > Mode > Color Table) and hold down the Command/Ctrl key while clicking on the color that you want to delete. If you delete more than you intended to, hold down the Option/Alt key and the Reset button will appear in place of the Cancel button. You can even choose the transparency color while holding the Option/Alt key: just click on the color you want to assign for transparency (the Eyedropper tool in this Color Table dialog does the same thing). Click on a color in the color table to change it in the color picker.

Basically, you use the **Lasso** tool to select elements whose colors you want to be included in the color table before you switch to Indexed Colors (**Image > Mode**). Look at the example with the flowers above. I chose a three-bit color palette (eight colors) for the flower image, and it's no wonder that this has had a dire impact on the image quality—particularly on the yellow petals, which have lost their color depth, making the whole image look flat. When you look at the color table (**Image > Mode > Color Table**) it becomes apparent that Photoshop has emphasized the color blue. Since blue isn't as important in this image as the different shades of yellow in the flower petals, draw a selection around the petals before switching to indexed color mode.

Since the left image was indexed ▶ without selection, only *one* shade of red is contained in the palette—not enough to show the various shades of the scarf. In the image on the right side, the selection forced more shades of red into the CLUT.

In the second example, the effect is just as easy to spot: The image of the woman at the beach was converted the first time without a selection, and the second time with a selection. In the image without a selection, the scarf has become a monochrome area in which all depth is lost. The second time I drew a selection around her scarf, and the difference can be seen easily. This time the CLUT contains many more shades of red.

If you want several different areas to be included in the color table, just hold down the **Shift** button and select additional areas with the **Lasso** tool. To subtract an area from a currently active selection, hold the **Option/Alt** Button while selecting that area with the **Lasso**.

1. Load your image, open the **Action** palette and create a new action by clicking on the Page icon. Convert the image to indexed color mode with **Image > Mode > Indexed Colors**. Stop the recording of the action.

▲ Actions can include stops, which will display a dialog box to inform the user what to do. In this example the stop is used to create a selection before the image is indexed.

◄ The inserted Stop command needs to be moved up in the Actions palette by dragging it to the right position.

2. Open the action by clicking on the triangle next to the action name. All the individual steps should be visible. Choose **Insert Stop** from the Palette menu and type in a reminder message. Because not every image will need you to make a selection, select the **Allow Continue** option. This option allows you to continue batching by hitting the **Return** key. Since you inserted the Stop after the currently selected step, you have to grab it with the mouse and move it to the first position.

3. Now you can set up batch processing with **File > Automate > Batch**. In the **Batch** dialog box, select the action that you just recorded, as well as the source and destination folder. (Please refer to the manual if you are unclear on how to do this. It is also explained in this book in the chapter titled "Optimizing Photoshop".)

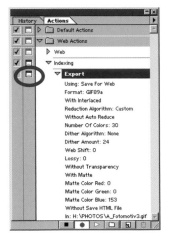

▲ If you create an action with the Save for Web command, you have to switch the Toggle Dialog on/off button.

If you want to batch process a series of banner ads with a customized palette you have to create a super palette. ▼

4. When you start batch processing, you will see a dialog box with the reminder message each time an image is loaded. Click **Stop** if you need to make a selection; click **Continue** if you don't. To continue after you stop an action, click the **Play** button in the **Action** palette.

You can also create an action automating the use of the **Save for Web** command, but instead of inserting a stop, you will have to use **Toggle dialog on/off** button in the **Action** palette next to the Export step. (The **Save for Web** command is considered an Export command.) However, if you have to optimize many images you will find that it's much faster to use the old way (forcing colors into the CLUT by using a selection) in an action. Because you can make multiple selections in the same image, this one step gives you a lot of control over the result.

CREATING A SUPER PALETTE

Now that you know how to optimize a CLUT for one image, you are ready to learn the secret method of creating an optimized CLUT for several images. DeBabelizer, by Equilibrium, is well known for its batch processing features, but also for its ability to create what we'll call a super palette—a CLUT that is optimized for all the images you are batch processing. DeBabelizer creates it by simply opening every file, doing a statistical analysis, and selecting the most common colors.

One situation in which you might need a super palette is when batch processing several banner ads. Banner ads usually include a company or product logo, and it is generally very important that the colors in the logo don't shift. This could be difficult to manage if the action you've set up converts all the

ads with a **Perceptual** or **Adaptive** sixteen-color palette. Since the logo may not always be dominant in the color scheme of the banner, it's quite possible that its color will be dropped—in which case you may end up with differently colored logos in each banner.

This is not desirable (to put it mildly), and the only way to avoid it is to create a custom palette that includes the logo color. You have to make sure that the customized palette will yield good results with most of your ads. To do this, pick a couple of the most important ads, index them, and save their color tables. Then combine those color tables into one, delete duplicated or unwanted colors, and save it. Finally, choose this customized palette during batch processing to get a consistent look for all your images. The following step-by-step procedure demonstrates this technique:

1. Open a banner ad and optimize the CLUT in the **Save for Web** dialog box. You have two choices: either use the CLUT of one banner ad as the master, and add a few colors from the other banner ads, or you can index several banner ads and combine them. In the latter case, the fewer colors you choose, the better. If you would typically use sixteen colors, you might try going with only eight. But there is no one right way; it all depends on the situation. To save a color table, use the **Color Palette** menu in the **Save for Web** dialog box; click the arrow in the upper-right corner of the Color Table area.

2. Now that you have saved several CLUTs, you need to combine them—and since the **Color Palette** menu doesn't offer this option, you have to find another way to do it. Open the **Swatches** palette (**Window > Show Swatches**). You can store frequently used colors in this palette, but it also allows you to combine several color tables simply by loading them; select **Load Swatches** from the Palette menu. (Note: While **Load Color Table** in the **Save for Web** command replaces the current table, in the **Swatches** palette it actually appends the new colors to the bottom of the palette.) To delete colors, press the **Command/Ctrl** key to bring up the scissors icon, then click on one of the swatches to make it disappear. Inserting new colors manually is just as easy; move the mouse over a free spot in the palette and a **Paint Bucket** tool will appear that lets you fill the swatch with the current foreground color.

3. Save the super palette via the Palette menu and then create your action. You will have to load the color table via the Color Table menu; the color reduction algorithm then switches automatically to **Custom**. After you have recorded your action, you can set up batch processing via **File > Automate > Batch**. For more details on the **Action** palette and batch processing, refer to the Photoshop manual or read the "Optimizing Photoshop" chapter.

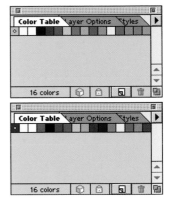

▲ These are the color palettes of the banner ads on the previous page.

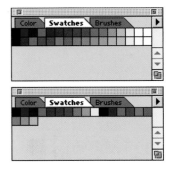

▲ To combine the color palettes from the top two images, you have to use the Swatches palette. Click on the colors while holding the Command/Ctrl key to delete redundant colors.

The essential information here is that you can combine color palettes in the Swatches palette. The way you optimize a CLUT for batch processing depends on the images itself, so this step-by-step guide might not work for other scenarios. If I had a series of banner ads to optimize, each with a photo and some solid colors, I would optimize a CLUT for the photos, one for the solid colors and then combine them.

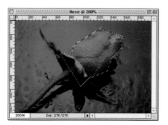

▲ To obtain the best result, a dithered image was combined with a non-dithered image.

IMAGES WITH PARTIAL DITHER

It's great that Photoshop's **Save for Web** dialog box makes it so convenient to choose the amount of dithering, but sometimes you are still trapped: the image saved with no dithering doesn't look good enough in some areas, but the dithered image gains too much in file size—and may not look as good in some areas as the non-dithered image. Wouldn't it be wonderful if you could exercise precise control over where and how much dithering you want in an image? Well, that's exactly what I'm going to show you how to do.

1. First, save two copies of your image—one dithered, and one without dithering. Both must use the same color reduction algorithm, otherwise you will end up with different color tables.

2. Load both images, and convert the dithered image back to RGB. This is important, because we will now select everything in the non-dithered image (**Select All**) and copy it into the clipboard (**Command-C/Ctrl-C**). Now, select the dithered image that we converted to RGB and paste in the non-dithered image from the clipboard.

3. You have two options: Either use a layer mask to hide some areas in the topmost image layer, or (the method I prefer) just use the **Eraser** tool. Double-click the **Eraser** tool in the **Tool** palette to bring up the **Tool settings**. Choose **Paintbrush** for your **Eraser mode**, and select an appropriate brush size from the **Brushes** palette.

Since the non-dithered image is in the top layer, it is very easy to determine where you want to smooth the colors—which is exactly where you use the Eraser tool. If you click on the Eye icon (for the top layer) in the **Layers** palette to hide the layer, you can see how the entire dithered image is going to look. In the end, you have to go through the **Save for Web** command again to get the final image. Don't forget that you must use the same settings you used before. In most cases you will now have a great looking GIF with a smaller file size.

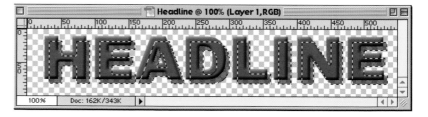

▲ With the selection being in the background layer, fill it with the transparent shadow.

A GIF WITH SEVERAL LEVELS OF TRANSPARENCY

The GIF format has only one level of transparency, nothing like the 256-level alpha channel available in PNG format. Still, it is possible to simulate a multi-level transparency with GIF. The trick is to use a transparent pattern; to demonstrate, I'll create a headline with a transparent drop shadow.

1. In Photoshop, create a new 2 x 2-pixel file with a transparent background (**File > New**). This new file will be our transparent fill pattern. Depending on how much transparency you want, you might need to start with a larger pattern. A 2 x 2-pixel pattern lets you create either a 25%, 50%, or 75% transparency, whereas a 3 x 3-pixel pattern allow increments of 11%, and so on. (The rule of thumb is that the percentage equals one hundred divided by the number of pixels, but this is just a guideline. Not all combinations are useful, or will give you the desired effect, so there is a limit on how many levels of transparency you can achieve.)

2. Magnify your pixels as large as you can and use the **Pencil** tool to draw a pattern like the one in the example (see top picture). The color black is going to dim the underlying background, so leave the other pixels transparent. Select the entire pattern with **Select > All**, and then choose **Edit > Define Pattern**.

3. Create another new image with a transparent background, and on a new layer, place all the elements for which you want to create drop shadows. Activate this layer in the **Layer** palette, and click with the **Magic Wand** tool in the transparent area. The selection should include all transparent areas. Invert the selection via **Select > Inverse**. Add or subtract any areas that didn't get selected—hold down the **Shift** key to add to a selection, or hold the **Option/Alt** key to subtract from a selection while working with the **Magic Wand** tool.

4. If you did everything correctly you should now have a selection around the objects and elements you placed on the new layer. To create the drop shadow, select the layer beneath the current layer. Use one of the Marquee tools (or the arrow keys on your keyboard) to move the selection to the desired position, then fill it by choosing **Edit > Fill** (**Contents: Use: Pattern**).

5. Now call up the Save for Web command and select the **Transparency** option and **Matte: None**. Save the GIF and import it into GoLive. If you have a background image, you will see how this drop shadow seems to blend with the background; if the black pixels in the transparency pattern are too apparent try using a different color than black. For a bright background you might want to use a combination of the background color and black.

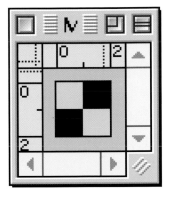

▲ This is the Shadow fill pattern, a temporary 2 x2-pixel file.

▲ When saved as a GIF with Transparency, the image can be combined in the browser with different backgrounds. If the pixels of the shadow don't blend well enough, try using a color of the background (mixed with black) as your shadow color.

▲ I developed this 50% Transparency trick for the Eye2Eye Web site, in order to have the CD blend with the background.

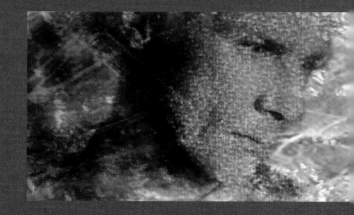

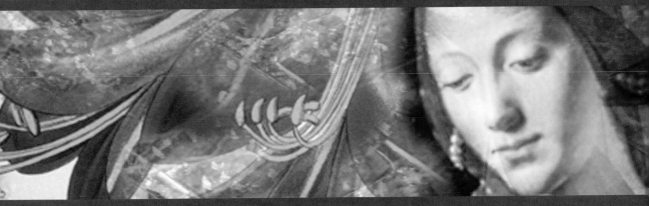

Illustration: Michael Baumgardt

JPEG

JPEG—Joint Photographic Expert Group

For digital movies, MPEG is equivalent to JPEG. JPEG is used for stills only.

JPEG is currently the single most important format for photos and images requiring more than 256 colors. In the future, we may see JPEG losing ground to PNG, which offers some advantages (like lossless compression and Alpha channels for transparency). But for now, and certainly for the next few years, JPEG will remain an extremely popular and important format.

➤ DCT Compression

JPEG uses a compression technique called DCT, which stands for Discrete Cosine Transform. DCT compression is based on the fact that the human eye is less sensitive to changes in color than to variations in brightness. While most image formats for the Web save the RGB color value for every pixel, JPEG actually splits color and brightness information and compresses each individually. The JPEG algorithm works on a group of 8x8 pixels at a time: first it calculates the DCT, which is then quantified, and finally, a Variable Length Code Compression scheme is used on it.

Text in an image is pretty much the worst thing for JPEG; if you place text in front of a background and compress it with a very low setting, you can see the effect very clearly.

Fortunately, you don't have to understand this to work with JPEG images, but it does explain why JPEG works so badly for images with extreme color changes: DCT tries to interpret the image as the sum of frequencies, and while this works pretty well for smooth color changes, such as gradients, if an image includes abrupt changes and high contrast it can be a serious stumbling block for the algorithm. The DCT technique is also the reason why blurring a photo improves the ratio of the compression: blurring smoothes color changes in the image.

➤ Transparency

Unlike the GIF image format, there is no transparency feature in JPEG—which makes sense, since JPEG is not lossless. Every time you save a JPEG image it makes changes to the image, and shifts colors (which made it impossible for the JPEG developer to use the croma-key color technique.)

➤ JPEG is not Lossless

When I said JPEG makes changes to the image and shifts colors every time you save it, I really meant it. Every time. So even if you open a JPEG image, make no changes whatsoever, and save it again, it will lose quality. You can limit this effect if you use the same settings under which the image was initially saved, but the difference is marginal.

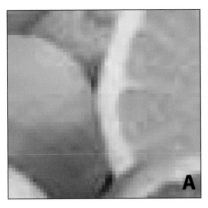 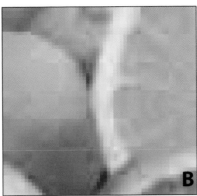 

At one point there was an initiative to create a lossless version of JPEG called JPEG-LS, but it never succeeded because its compression rate was only 2:1. And by now, PNG is the preferred solution.

➤ Progressive JPEG

The JPEG standard has seen one important improvement over the years: because of the growing popularity of the Web, you can now save your JPEG in progressive format—which works pretty much the same way as GIF's interlaced format. With progressive JPEG, the image starts to appear in the browser while it is still downloading. At first it's a blurry preview of the image, then it gets more detailed as the stream of data comes in. While GIF is limited to four passes, you can choose between three and five passes for a progressive JPEG image.

HOW WELL DOES JPEG COMPRESS IMAGES?

You're probably wondering how much space you can save with JPEG compression—compared with other methods it is actually quite impressive. The best lossless compression methods can reduce the amount of data for a 24-bit image by about half, or 2:1. By comparison, JPEG can compress the same image between 10:1 and 20:1 (high quality) without visible loss, which is why most stock photos on CD-ROMs are saved as JPEG images. After all, it means that you can store a 20 MB high-resolution image in only 2 MB of disk space.

At a compression rate of 30:1 to 50:1 (medium quality), you will start seeing some visible shifts, which are generally quite tolerable. Only with the maximum (low quality) setting will you end up with a serious loss in visual quality, but the benefit is a whopping 100:1 compression rate.

▲ The image above was saved ten times as JPEG in order to test the cumulative effect that the JPEG compression algorithm has on the image: to the far left (A) you see the result when setting 2 (in the Save a Copy command) is used. The image suffered a visible quality loss compared to the original image. The right example (B) was saved also ten times, but the compression settings were changed each time (four times with a setting of 2, three times with 3, three times with 4 in the Save a Copy command) to test any differences. It would be logical to make the assumption that image B should have the better visual quality, because it was saved with higher quality settings most of the time, but that is not the case. As a matter of fact, in image B you can see a slight decrease in quality, even though the difference is admittedly very small.

In conclusion: save your image as a JPEG as a final step *after* all editing is done. This will maintain image quality.

THE JPEG FILE STANDARD

For a long time JPEG didn't even have a file standard; it was simply a series of compression algorithms. The JPEG committee wanted to develop a global file standard, but because of internal disagreement in the International Standardizing Organization, it was a long time before they agreed on the SPIFF standard. Because it's impossible to exchange images without a common file standard, programmers initially created their own format; consequently, the JPEGs of many programs back then were incompatible. Thanks to the efforts of the programmers at C-Cube Microsystems a quasi-standard emerged. These standards are:

● **JFIF (JPEG File Interchange Format)**
This is a simple format that only saves the pixels without much additional information.

● **TIFF/JPEG, also known as TIFF 6.0**
An extension to the Aldus TIFF format; it stores all additional information with the image.

JFIF became the pseudo-standard for the Internet, because of the need for files to be as small as possible. The TIFF 6.0 definition, designed to be integrated with JPEGs, did not succeed, because it suffered from a few significant weaknesses.

For color photos there's no question that JPEG is the way to go. With grayscale images, however, GIF may yield better results. That's because JPEG does most of its compression on colors, not on luminance (brightness) information.

How noticeable are the differences in quality between different compression settings? To answer this, I saved three images (a regular photo, a photo with text, and a graphic) in nine different compression settings in the Photoshop Save As dialog box. Then I viewed all the JPEGs and compared the quality. Of course this is a subjective process—it wouldn't help much to show the images here, as a lot of the subtle differences in quality are lost in printing JPEGs—but giving you my assessment is one way to evaluate these differences.

JPEG is really excellent for use on the Web. It produces astonishingly small files, and while you will see slight losses in quality they are really quite acceptable. In the worst case, quality might decrease by 20 percent. In the graph on page 238, you can see that the compression rate is most effective with a setting of zero to four with the Save a Copy command and with zero to forty with the Save for Web command.

Personally, I always use a setting of 20–30 with the Save for Web command (or three with the Save a Copy command), because it seems to offer the best compromise between quality and file size. Images still look great, without major distortion, and the file sizes are usually small enough for my purposes.

THE CORRELATION OF COMPRESSION AND 8X8-PIXEL BLOCKS

As already mentioned, JPEG's compression algorithm divides the image into blocks of 8 x 8 pixels. But what if the dimensions of the image are not exactly divisible by eight? Does this have an impact on the file size? And does the algorithm create additional overhead? To find the answer to this question, I

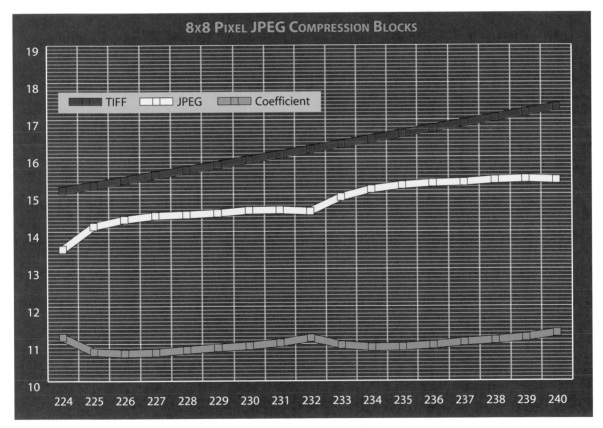

▲ The JPEG format compresses in 8 x 8 pixel blocks. To test for a correlation between file size and these blocks, an image was gradually cropped by one pixel at a time and saved as TIFF and JPEG. This graph shows the pixels on the X-axis and the file size on the Y-axis (TIFF values were divided by ten to be able to display them closer to the JPEG file size.) Apparently the compression blocks create an overhead, suggests that, if possible, the image dimensions should be divisible by eight.

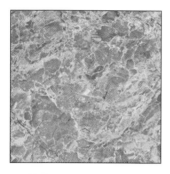

Meas.	TIFF	JPEG	Coeff.
224	151.087	13.525	11.17
225	152.435	14.139	10.78
226	153.787	14.320	10.74
227	155.147	14.418	10.76
228	156.511	14.448	10.83
229	157.883	14.491	10.89
230	159.259	14.564	10.94
231	160.643	14.573	11.02
232	162.031	14.536	11.15
233	163.427	14.918	10.96
234	164.827	15.126	10.90
235	166.235	15.233	10.91
236	167.647	15.290	10.96
237	169.067	15.314	11.04
238	170.491	15.375	11.09
239	171.923	15.402	11.16
240	173.359	15.372	11.28

▲ This image was cropped gradually by 1 pixel and saved as JPEG and TIFF (uncompressed) to find out whether the 8x8 blocks of JPEG had an impact on the compression.

cropped a 240 x 240-pixel image gradually by one pixel each time. I saved the same image as JPEG and as TIFF (without LZW compression). The TIFF was my reference to ensure that potential variations in the file size weren't caused by the motif itself.

As you can see from the graph on the previous page, there is indeed a correlation between the 8 x 8 blocks and compression. In the graph you can clearly see a notch at every eighth pixel in the JPEG curve (yellow line), while the TIFF curve (red line) is linear. (Note: The file size of the TIFF was divided by ten in order to display both lines closer together).

The notches also appear in the coefficient that was derived from both values (blue line). As you can see, the possible savings in file size are between two and four percent, really not that big a deal. Still it is useful to know, especially for images that you use as background in the browser. Keep their dimensions to a factor of eight to optimize the file size.

How a JPEG is Encoded

For all you technophile readers, here's a rough summary of how a JPEG encoder works. This will give you some understanding of the complex process that goes on behind the scenes.

1. Separation of Brightness/Color

The JPEG Baseline Compression algorithm works in several steps. For the first step it is irrelevant which color model is used (RGB or CMYK), although a CMYK JPEG is larger than its RGB counterpart (for use on the Internet the image should, of course, be saved in RGB mode). You can make JPEGs from grayscale images, but since the algorithm mainly compresses the color information, the compression factor in grayscale images is significantly less.

2. Reduction of the Color Space

When saving, the encoder has the option of reducing the color space by a horizontal and vertical factor of 2:1. Another option for an encoder is to scale only the color information on the horizontal axis and leave the vertical unchanged (1:1). Both options leave the brightness information, with its resolution and measurements, untouched. This compression step is only used by few programs.

3. Compilation in 8x8 Blocks

The pixels in the image are divided into 8x8-pixel blocks and then analyzed with a Discrete Cosine Transform (DCT) algorithm, which is closely related to the Fourier Analysis. In the process, the higher color frequencies are simply deleted, while lower frequencies, containing the significant color changes, are retained.

4. Quantization of Color Frequencies
In every block, each of the remaining 64 frequency components is divided by an individual Quantization Coefficient, and then rounded to the next integer.

This step creates the biggest data losses. The higher the Quantization Coefficient the more data will be truncated. Even the lowest possible Quantization Coefficient, 1 (equals quality setting 100 in Photoshop's Save for Web command), will change the color information, because the DCT doesn't generate integers.

In addition, due to the larger coefficient, higher frequencies are quantized less accurately than lower ones—it's okay, though, because the eye can't perceive those subtle differences anyway. Brightness information (luminosity), however, is quantized with a much higher level of accuracy (64 possible values) than the color information (Chroma). The quantization table can be set by the JPEG Encoder, but most encoders only use the simple, linear scaling, which is set by the JPEG standard. The Quality Level that the user sets in the encoder defines the scaling factor of this table.

This quantization table is responsible for the different qualities between some of the JPEG encoders, because JPEG's Standard quantization table only works well with medium image-quality settings, not so well for high or low compression levels. So you can get a smaller file size with an encoder optimized for low-quality settings, as is necessary for the Web (this explains the differences between the Save a Copy and the Save for Web commands).

5. Arithmetic or Huffman Encoding of Coefficients
This step is loss-free. Although arithmetic encoding generates a 10 percent better compression, its Q Encoding is patented. Therefore, Huffman Encoding is usually used instead.

6. Inserting the Correct Header and Saving the File
All compression parameters are saved with the image, so the decoder can reverse the process accordingly. These parameters contain the quantization table and the Huffman Encoding table, for example. The specification also allows you to omit this information, which saves several hundred bytes. However, the image can then only be decoded if the decoder contains the required tables itself.

Quality Differences with Different JPEG Decoders

You may never have considered it, but the way a JPEG image looks will vary in quality from one program to another. A good JPEG decoder will try to adjust and smooth the edges of the 8x8 blocks to make them less visible. This is totally dependent on the program; it is not built into the JPEG standard.

Another trick a JPEG decoder uses is saving processor power by doing a "fast" decompression, which basically involves rounding values; similar tricks exist for color mode conversion. (This is not really applicable to Web design, but if, for example, you want to save your JPEG image in CMYK mode, the browser would have to convert it to RGB in order to display it. How accurately this conversion is performed depends on the decoder.)

All this means that you ought to view your JPEGs in both browsers to get an idea of how they are really going to look. Don't rely on Photoshop or ImageReady, since they use their own decoders, which differ from the ones in your browsers.

▲ This is the original image (290 x 470 pixels, 400 K) that was treated with the Gaussian Blur filter and Despeckle to examine their impact on compression.

▲ This image was treated with the Despeckle filter before it was saved as a JPEG.

How Much Does Blurring Improve Compression?

One of the best-known tricks for reducing the file size of a compressed JPEG image is to apply Photoshop's **Gaussian Blur** filter before you save the image. You can read this in pretty much every book on Web design, but no one tells you how much blur buys you how much file-size savings. Also, none of the books tell you whether there are alternatives, and how much they might gain you. To find the answer to these questions I applied **Gaussian Blur** (with values ranging between 0.3 to 1.2 pixels) and the **Despeckle** filter in the **Filter > Noise** menu (applied between one and four times), each to a copy of the same image.

As you can see in the graph, it does makes a significant difference whether you apply **Gaussian Blur** or **Despeckle** to the image, but more filtering is not necessarily better. You get the biggest improvement with a value of 0.3

for **Gaussian Blur**, or when you apply **De-speckle** once. It is interesting to note that an increase in the **Gaussian Blur** value (from 0.6 to 1.2) or multiple applications of **Despeckle** (from two to four times), don't result in proportional improvements. At the same time, quality drops substantially: For 1.2 blur value the decrease is 50 percent, and for four applications of Despeckle it's around 30 percent. Bottom line: You can get smaller image files if you use **Gaussian Blur** or **Despeckle** before you save a JPEG image, but don't make the mistake of using too much. If you use as little as possible, you'll get the most compression for the smallest loss of quality.

◀ This image was treated with the Gaussian Blur filter before it was saved as JPEG.

	Original	D1	GB 0.3	D2	GB 0.6	D3	GB 0.9	D4	GB 1.2
JPEG 70	51.057	41.778	42.979	38.346	38.058	36.156	33.372	34.597	29.527
JPEG 30	24.143	20.354	20.589	18.695	18.429	17.665	16.358	16.934	14.565
JPEG 0	12.185	10.974	10.924	10.362	10.152	9.916	9.359	9.620	8.706

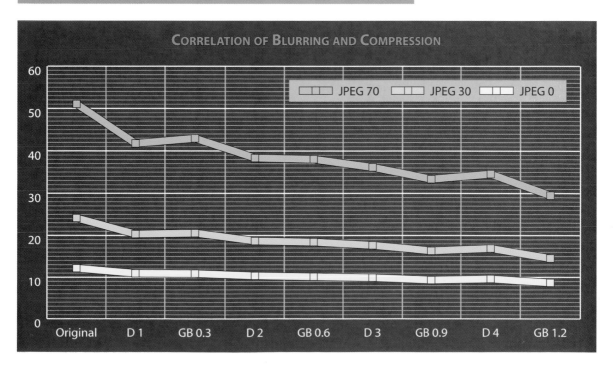

THE JPEG COMPARISON CHART

This chart compares the file size of three typical images: a photograph, a photograph with text and a graphic file (image D is a color spectrum, which is almost a best-case scenario for JPEG compression and therefore can be used as reference.) All images measure 256 x 180 pixels, require 140K uncompressed, and were saved at various quality levels. The **Save for Web** command offers 0–100, but as settings above 80 are never used in Web design, I excluded it to save space. In reality, only the first five levels in the **Save a Copy** command and the levels 0-40 in the **Save for Web** command are ever used, because the JPEG algorithm delivers excellent and sufficient results even at the lowest quality settings. Because the fine differences between the individual levels are so hard to discern in print, each image was assigned a visual quality factor (Q) of 1 through 10 (see small graph)—this should only be used as a ref-

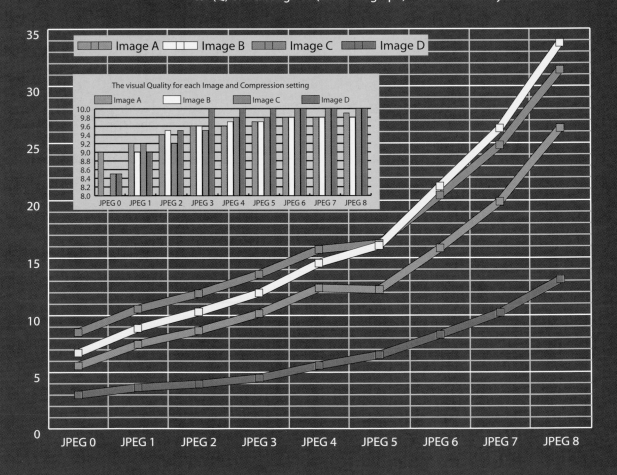

erence since it is just my personal judgement. The differences aren't so dramatic anyway—especially compared to GIF—so the quality factor can almost be disregarded. Generally, only the lowest quality levels 0–10 introduce a deterioration in quality. Aside from that, the differences can not be discerned without an side-by-side comparison.

As you can see from the graphs, the **Save for Web** command (right graph) achieves better file size savings then the **Save a Copy** command (left graph.) Interesting to note is the little bend in the curve between 4 and 5 with the **Save a Copy** command. This indicates that the command uses the standard JPEG Quantization Table while the **Save for Web** command apparently works with a special Quantization Table that is more suited for JPEGs on the the Web. Always use the **Save for Web** command to save your JPEGs; it also gives you the option of blurring and optimizing.

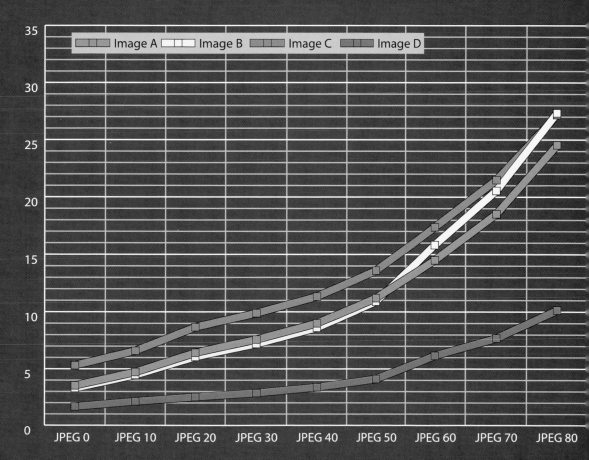

Illustration: Michael Baumgardt

PNG

PNG—Portable Network Graphic Format

PNG images are the next step of image formats on the Web. This format was developed to bring the best of two worlds together: it has all the pluses of JPEG and GIF, but transcends some of their limitations.

PNG allows lossless compression with 24-bit color depth (which yields over 16 million colors). In addition, it provides 256 levels of transparency, which enables you, for example, to create a transparent drop shadow that blends with the background. Another nice feature is that PNG eliminates the halo effect you sometimes get with GIF. Matting backgrounds can be problematic with GIF, because most images are anti-aliased at the edges to give a smoother appearance. A image with transparency that looks fine on one background may show a halo in front of a differently colored background. With PNG this isn't an issue, since 256 levels of transparency allow edges to blend seamlessly with the background.

That's not all. PNG saves a Gamma curve along with the image. Because Macintosh uses a different Gamma than Windows, images that are optimized for a Mac will appear darker on PCs, while images created on a PC look too bright on Macs. PNG has solved this problem by correcting the Gamma: Regardless of which computer the image was created on, it will look the same on both platforms. (By the way, ImageReady allows you to see how your images will look under different Gamma settings by switching between Macintosh Gamma and Windows Gamma in **View > Preview**.)

Does this mean that JPEG and GIF are obsolete formats, and PNG is about to take over the world? Not really—or at least not soon. For one thing, a PNG image file is bigger then the same image saved as GIF or JPEG. And for an-

PNG is based on compression technology that is also known as Deflation. The technology was developed by Jean-Loup Gailly and is also used for ZIP file compression.

The PC versions of Microsoft Internet Explorer 4.0 and Netscape Navigator 4.04 both support basic features of PNG. Navigator 4.04 doesn't support the PNG alpha channel and Explorer 4.0's capabilities are limited as well. Macintosh versions of Internet Explorer 4.5 and Netscape Navigator 4.08 do *not* support PNG directly. Basic PNG support is implemented in the QuickTime plugin, but there is no alpha or Gamma support.

The best way to experience PNG is in GoLive. Here you see an image with a drop shadow, placed in a layer that slowly moves in from the left: the drop shadow always blends together with the background.

other, PNG doesn't have GIF's animation capabilities. Yes, PNG may eventually become the most common image format, but who knows how long it might take. Only the latest browsers on the Windows side (versions 4.0 and up) can display PNG without a special plugin. There is *no* direct PNG support in Macintosh Internet Explorer 4.5 and Netscape Navigator 4.08 and Apple's QuickTime plugin (version 4.03) only provides basic PNG support (no 256 levels of transparency.) Because of these downfalls in PNG support, it is currently inadvisable to use it unless your Web site really requires that you do so.

SAVING A **PNG** IMAGE WITH SAVE A COPY

1. From the Window menu, choose the **Channel** palette. Because PNG uses Alpha Channels to store transparency information, you should delete any unwanted Alpha Channels. To do this, select the channels that you want to delete from the Channel palette and choose **Delete** from the palette menu. If you have only one Alpha Channel you can select the **Exclude Alpha Channels** option in the **Save a Copy** dialog box.

2. In the File menu, select **Save a Copy** to save the image in PNG format. The first option in the PNG dialog box is **Interlacing**. As with GIF and JPEG, selecting this option means that the image will appear as low resolution before it has completely downloaded, and will gradually improve in quality as more information arrives. PNG uses seven passes, which is why it's called **Adam 7**. Its method is much better then the one GIF uses, because it starts displaying the image after only 1/64th of the data has been received; GIF needs at least 1/8th of the data before it can begin displaying anything. You'll see several other options that relate to PNG's "zlib" compression methods:

● **None:** No filter will be used, which is best for an indexed image or a 1-bit bitmap.

● **Sub:** Use this compression method if your image has a lot of horizontal pixel rows with the same color.

● **Up:** Use this filter if the color areas or patterns run more along the vertical axis. This demonstrates another difference between GIF and PNG: GIF's compression algorithms only work on horizontal pattern recognition, while PNG can switch between horizontal and vertical axes.

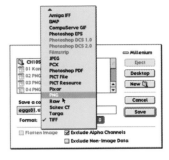

▲ Select the PNG format from the Save a Copy dialog box. Use the Exclude Alpha Channels option to minimize file size if you are not intending to use Transparency. To create an indexed PNG, you will need to change its mode via Image > Mode > Indexed Color prior to saving it.

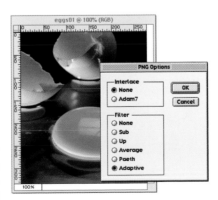

◀ Finally, choose a compression filter from the PNG dialog. See the comparison chart to see how these filters affect file size.

Since the Save for Web command produces the smallest file size 95% of the times, you should stick with it. Only in special cases will you get better results with the Save a Copy command.

● **Standard:** This filter compensates for some noise within the image. It works by calculating the interpolated color value of adjacent pixels.

● **Paeth:** If the image has some noise, Paeth (which is similar to Standard) can be quite useful. The difference is that instead of interpolating two adjacent pixels and their color values, Paeth looks at all the color values used in the image and interpolates between similar color values. This reduces the number of colors in your image, which increases compression opportunities for the pattern recognition algorithm.

● **Adaptive:** Don't confuse this mode with the Adaptive or Flexible options in the GIF dialog box. Here, Adaptive is sort of an autopilot: PNG analyzes the image and chooses the most effective filter for you. This is useful if you are undecided about which filter to apply.

SAVING A PNG IMAGE WITH SAVE FOR WEB

1. Selecting Save for Web from the **File** menu gives you better preview control (only relevant really for PNG-8, which is always larger then a GIF and therefore shouldn't be used). In the upper right corner of the dialog box you'll find the settings to save a PNG image. Select either PNG-8 for an indexed, GIF-like image or PNG-24 for images requiring more than 256 colors.

For a PNG with 256 levels of Transparency, you need to select PNG-24. Like GIF, PNG-8 only has one Transparency level. ▶

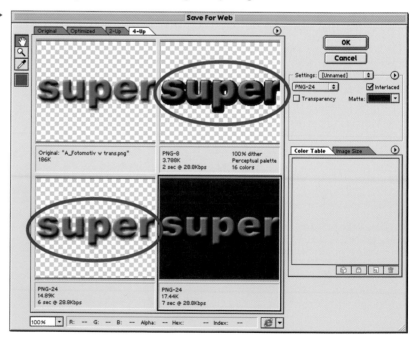

2. If you use PNG-8 you'll have to work with the image like a GIF: select a color palette (**Perceptual**, **Adaptive**, and so on), pick the number of colors you want to use, and choose a Dithering method. Picking **Diffusion** dither brings up a slider that allows you to set the percentage of dithering you want; the other two modes (**Pattern** and **Noise**) don't offer that feature. When you want to use Transparency, you need to have a transparent background layer, but again, the PNG-8 mode will give you only 1 level of transparency.

3. If you use PNG-24, you can only set the **Interlaced** and **Transparency** option plus the **Matte** color. The Matte command has no effect when using Transparency with a PNG-24, because of the 256 Transparency levels. This command has only an effect if the Transparency option is deactivated: the background will then be filled with the Matte color.

THE PNG COMPARISON CHART

To get a better idea of exactly how PNG compresses, I created the chart that you can see on the following two pages, using the same four types of images as in the JPEG chart in the previous chapter. You can see the file size, but I left out the images themselves; because PNG-24 is lossless, and images saved in the 8-bit mode are identical to GIF. However, I compared the Save a Copy and the Save for Web commands and as you can see, in almost every case, the Save for Web command works better. The PNG-8 images were saved with a 32 CLUT (color look-up table; 5-bit) to make this chart comparable with the GIF chart.

	Image A	Image B	Image C	Image D
Ph/8/01	16.470	17.842	6.378	3.175
Ph/8/02	18.692	20.314	7.337	3.319
Ph/8/03	19.170	21.600	6.720	3.445
Ph/8/04	22.265	23.582	8.691	4.018
Ph/8/05	18.996	21.139	6.662	3.431
Ph/8/06	18.824	21.109	6.571	3.369
Ph&IR/PNG-8	15.960	16.970	5.100	2.320
Ph/24/01	129.529	106.125	7.703	33.270
Ph/24/02	105.354	91.102	8.598	10.575
Ph/24/03	101.481	91.708	7.383	9.177
Ph/24/04	99.973	89.401	11.488	17.637
Ph/24/05	94.344	87.687	7.530	11.461
Ph/24/06	94.180	86.989	7.331	11.429
Ph&IR/PNG-24	90.670	81.320	8.870	16.920

THE PNG COMPARISON CHART

If you use Photoshop's **Save for Web** command, you have very few options when saving a PNG-24. Basically, all you can do is select **Interlaced**, which adds roughly 20% to 30% to the file size. The **Matte** option is only necessary if you are working with transparency; it has no direct effect on the compression.

This comparison chart clearly shows that for the near future PNG will only be suitable when you need multiple levels of transparency (like an Alpha channel for a drop shadow) or if you work with small images. When comparing the compression results of Photoshop's **Save a Copy** command and **Save for Web** command, you can see that **Save for Web** operates sometimes better and sometimes worse than the regular **Save a Copy** command (which offers more options for compression).

This diagram shows the values of the PNG files saved in 24-bit mode. ▼

The graph on this page shows the values of the PNG files saved in 24-bit mode. The file sizes are so large that the graph had to be split, which makes

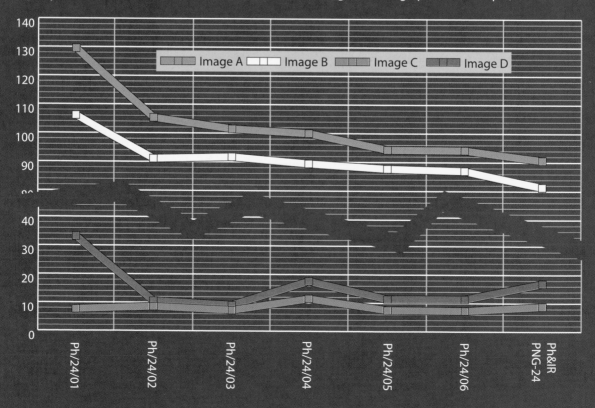

one wonder whether PNG will ever be useful for large images. The values to the left represent an uncompressed PNG image (Filter: None), but even with the Adaptive Filter (Ph/24/06) the results for Image A and B are unsatisfactory. Oddly enough, PNG yields acceptable results for graphics in 24-bit mode.

The results with 8-bit PNGs (see graph on this page) aren't much more encouraging. These compression rates are no more sufficient than the others; amazingly, the smallest file sizes for Image A and B result from using no filter at all (Ph/8/01, on the left side in the graph).

It's important to remember that if you're using **Save a Copy**, the transparency information must be in an Alpha channel (this isn't necessary for **Save for Web**, which can be a little confusing). Also, the effect of the transparency channel is best seen in GoLive, but don't get your hopes up; a lot of browsers won't yield the desired effect (Macintosh versions are lacking the support.)

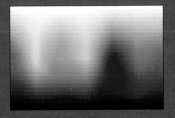

▲ These are images A, B (see previous page), C and D that were used for this comparison chart.

This diagram shows the values of the PNG files saved in 8-bit mode (5 Bit/32 colors.) ▼

Labeling: for example Ph/8/02

Ph =	Photoshop	8 =	8 Bit (5 Bit)	None = 01	Standard = 04
IR =	ImageReady	24 =	24 Bit	Sub = 02	Paeth = 05
				Up = 03	Adaptive = 06

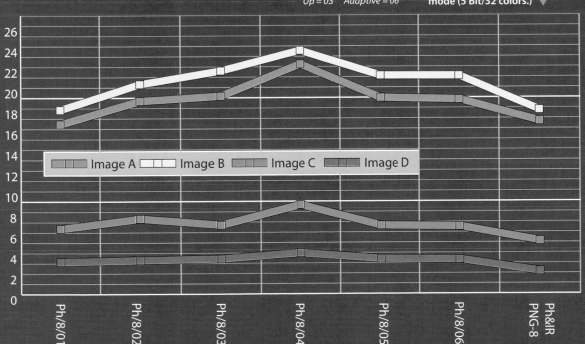

Legend: Image A | Image B | Image C | Image D

X-axis labels: Ph/8/01, Ph/8/02, Ph/8/03, Ph/8/04, Ph/8/05, Ph/8/06, Ph&IR PNG-8

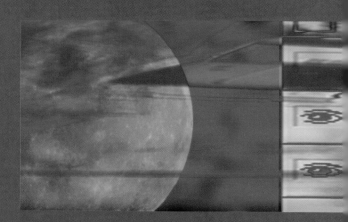

Illustration: Michael Baumgardt

THE WEB-SAFE COLOR PALETTE

The Color Cube

Color is an essential element of most designs. While using color in print media is relatively easy and uncomplicated, this unfortunately doesn't hold true for Web design. There are numerous pitfalls in using color online: for instance, you have to be prepared to compensate for different color depths on different monitors, and color shifts between different browsers and different platforms. Problems like these make it a real challenge to get your Web site to look as fantastic as you intended. Knowing why color doesn't always equal color, and how you can fix the most common problems is essential to achieving consistently great-looking designs.

COLOR DEPTH

As I've already mentioned several times, the most common color problems occur because different monitors offer different color depths. But what does "color depth" actually mean? To answer this question, it helps to look at how a computer stores images in memory.

Binary Code	Hexadecimal Code
0000	0
0001	1
0010	2
0011	3
0100	4
0101	5
0110	6
0111	7
1000	8
1001	9
1010	A
1011	B
1100	C
1101	D
1110	E
1111	F

➤ How Computers Store Information

All computers save information as bits. A bit is the smallest unit of data that a computer recognizes; it means either On or Off (or the mathematical equivalent: 1 or 0) All the information on your computer, from software to photographic images, is saved on the hard drive or stored in memory (RAM) in the form of bits. Because you can't do much with just one instance of on or off, a number of bits are combined to form a byte. Eight bits equal one byte, which is able to represent—in different combinations of one and zero—up to sixteen numbers. This hexadecimal system is represented by numbers zero to nine and letters A-F.

➤ Color Depth of an Image

In order to save an image, you have to store the vertical and horizontal position of the pixels as well as their color value. Most image formats use a color depth of 24 bits (or hexadecimal FFFFFF), which allows you to represent 16,777,216 color values (256 levels for each color channel).

Not every monitor or graphics card can display so many different colors, so color values may be rounded up or down (when necessary) to the closest equivalent. This causes the color displayed on the monitor to shift. Many graphics software packages try to compensate for this error by using a technique called "dithering" (see Chapter 8, on GIF). But dithering can't change the fact that an image that looked great on your monitor may look really bad on someone else's. Luckily monitor dithering has no permanent effect on the image; the information in the file is still stored with 24 bits of color information, and as soon as you view the image with a graphic card that is capable of displaying all those colors, you'll see the photo in its original quality.

WEB-SAFE COLOR PALETTE

The Web-safe color palette is a collection of colors that look the same on any monitor that's capable of displaying 256 colors—basically on every computer monitor. There was a time when 16-color monitors were considered the latest in technology, but don't worry—most of those machines are safely tucked away in museums. Even so, while the latest surveys show that most home-computer users now have monitors and video boards capable of displaying at least 16-bit (which equals 65,536 colors), quite a few monitors in the corporate world are still limited to 256 colors. If you expect most viewers

MONITOR COLOR DEPTH

Physically, a computer monitor can display far more than 16 million colors; it's simply a question of how much VRAM (Video RAM) is installed in the graphics card—it also depends on the video card's ability to handle more than 24-bit display. Since the human eye can't distinguish this kind of subtlety anyway, 32-bit video cards use the additional 8 bits to address a transparency channel, also known as Alpha channel.

Bits	Colors
1 Bit	2
2 Bit	4
4 Bit	16
8 Bit	256
16 Bit	65,536
24 Bit	16,777,216
32 Bit	4,294,967,296

of your Web site to be home users, you can build images using thousands of colors—but if you expect some users to access your site from work, you should use as many colors as possible from the Web-safe color palette.

The Web-safe color palette actually uses only 216 colors; the remaining 40 are reserved for the Operating system (Windows). Those 216 colors are evenly divided, and assigned to different shades and intensities of red, green and blue. In addition, the palette uses a linear system, in which every color value is increased or decreased by twenty percent; this was done largely for con-

The MiB Color Chart basically un-wraps the color cube. In the first chart you see the shell of the cube and the second and third ta-bles display the next deeper lev-els of the cube. To find a "related" color, simply flip the page and find the color at the same posi-tion. Next to the hexadecimal values, each color field also shows the RGB value and color number. For print, all shades of gray were created using CMY values as well as a K screening (black).

venience, since the resulting hexadecimal values (00, 33, 66, 99, CC and FF) are easy for programmers to remember. So if you want to create an element in GoLive using a Web-safe color, just use these hexidecimal values and you are sure to get a Web-safe color that won't dither on 256-color monitors.

The linear division of the color space means that the Web-safe color palette doesn't give you much choice if you want to create, for example, brown or skin-tones. The palette would have been much more useful if it had been modeled after the color perception of the human eye; there's no reason not to include different color values, but unfortunately this wasn't considered im-portant enough at the time the palette was devised.

THE WEB-SAFE COLOR PALETTE SEEN AS A CUBE

You often see the Web-safe color palette presented as a cube in which red, green and blue are placed at three opposite corners, cyan, magenta and yel-low are dropped in between those colors, and white and black take up the re-maining two corners. Most books show the cube in six slices, which, in my opinion, isn't very helpful, because it's very difficult to see the relation of the colors. If you pick a color, and want to find a related color, you have to locate it in another slice. Even though this isn't very difficult, it isn't natural either, and it takes up a lot of your time.

Other authors have tried different ways of presenting the color cube, but while some of them are helpful, none of them real-ly satisfy me. I wanted to find a way of showing the rela-tionship that each color has to its neighbor, as well as making it easy to find colors with the same quality (light, dark, pastel, and so on). While searching for this new color organization, I realized that the best solu-tion was to basically dismantle the color cube rather then slice it. This solution has many advantages: for one, it shows you the whole spectrum with all the colors and their relationships. And for another, it is sorted by brightness and luminance, which makes it a breeze to pick, for instance, two pastel colors with the same quality.

▲ The Web color table, shown as a cube. The eight corners of the cube are occupied as follows: Three corners show the basic colors Red, Green and Blue. Their complementary colors Cyan, Magenta and Yellow are placed on opposite corners. Black and White occupy the remaining two corners.

00 FF 00	33 FF 00	66 FF 00	99 FF 00	CC FF 00	FF FF 00
00 CC 00	33 CC 00	66 CC 00	99 CC 00	CC CC 00	FF CC 00
00 99 00	33 99 00	66 99 00	99 99 00	CC 99 00	FF 99 00
00 66 00	33 66 00	66 66 00	99 66 00	CC 66 00	FF 66 00
00 33 00	33 33 00	66 33 00	99 33 00	CC 33 00	FF 33 00
00 00 00	33 00 00	66 00 00	99 00 00	CC 00 00	FF 00 00
00 FF 33	33 FF 33	66 FF 33	99 FF 33	CC FF 33	FF FF 33
00 CC 33	33 CC 33	66 CC 33	99 CC 33	CC CC 33	FF CC 33
00 99 33	33 99 33	66 99 33	99 99 33	CC 99 33	FF 99 33
00 66 33	33 66 33	66 66 33	99 66 33	CC 66 33	FF 66 33
00 33 33	33 33 33	66 33 33	99 33 33	CC 33 33	FF 33 33
00 00 33	33 00 33	66 00 33	99 00 33	CC 00 33	FF 00 33

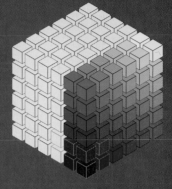

THE WEB COLOR CUBE SHOWN IN SLICES

Choose the colors for your design from this table and enter the color values into the program. In Photoshop, you can now select the Only Web Colors option in the Color Picker. If the software you're working with doesn't give you an HTML color picker, use the following table to convert the values accordingly:

Hexadecimal		in %	in RGB
00	=	0%	0
33	=	20%	51
66	=	40%	102
99	=	60%	153
CC	=	80%	204
FF	=	100%	255

The hexadecimal color value "CC FF 33" translates to Red = 80%, Green = 100% and Blue = 20%. In an RGB color picker, values are divided into 256 steps, so accordingly, you would need to enter Red = 204, Green = 255 and Blue = 51.

The color fields in this table with white outlines represent shades of gray.

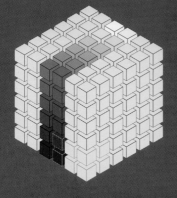

00 FF 66	33 FF 66	66 FF 66	99 FF 66	CC FF 66	FF FF 66
00 CC 66	33 CC 66	66 CC 66	99 CC 66	CC CC 66	FF CC 66
00 99 66	33 99 66	66 99 66	99 99 66	CC 99 66	FF 99 66
00 66 66	33 66 66	66 66 66	99 66 66	CC 66 66	FF 66 66
00 33 66	33 33 66	66 33 66	99 33 66	CC 33 66	FF 33 66
00 00 66	33 00 66	66 00 66	99 00 66	CC 00 66	FF 00 66
00 FF 99	33 FF 99	66 FF 99	99 FF 99	CC FF 99	FF FF 99
00 CC 99	33 CC 99	66 CC 99	99 CC 99	CC CC 99	FF CC 99
00 99 99	33 99 99	66 99 99	99 99 99	CC 99 99	FF 99 99
00 66 99	33 66 99	66 66 99	99 66 99	CC 66 99	FF 66 99
00 33 99	33 33 99	66 33 99	99 33 99	CC 33 99	FF 33 99
00 00 99	33 00 99	66 00 99	99 00 99	CC 00 99	FF 00 99

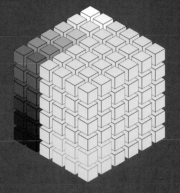

00 FF CC	33 FF CC	66 FF CC	99 FF CC	CC FF CC	FF FF CC
00 CC CC	33 CC CC	66 CC CC	99 CC CC	CC CC CC	FF CC CC
00 99 CC	33 99 CC	66 99 CC	99 99 CC	CC 99 CC	FF 99 CC
00 66 CC	33 66 CC	66 66 CC	99 66 CC	CC 66 CC	FF 66 CC
00 33 CC	33 33 CC	66 33 CC	99 33 CC	CC 33 CC	FF 33 CC
00 00 CC	33 00 CC	66 00 CC	99 00 CC	CC 00 CC	FF 00 CC
00 FF FF	33 FF FF	66 FF FF	99 FF FF	CC FF FF	FF FF FF
00 CC FF	33 CC FF	66 CC FF	99 CC FF	CC CC FF	FF CC FF
00 99 FF	33 99 FF	66 99 FF	99 99 FF	CC 99 FF	FF 99 FF
00 66 FF	33 66 FF	66 66 FF	99 66 FF	CC 66 FF	FF 66 FF
00 33 FF	33 33 FF	66 33 FF	99 33 FF	CC 33 FF	FF 33 FF
00 00 FF	33 00 FF	66 00 FF	99 00 FF	CC 00 FF	FF 00 FF

THE MiB COLOR CHART

The MiB Color Chart unwraps the color cube. In the first chart you see the mantle of the cube.

FF FF FF				FF 00 33					00 00 00			
0				215					0			
FF CC CC				FF FF CC					CC FF CC			
7				1					37			
FF 99 99			FF CC 99	FF FF 99	CC FF 99				99 FF 99			99 FF CC
14			8	2	38				74			73
FF 66 66		FF 99 66	FF CC 66	FF FF 66	CC FF 66	99 FF 66			66 FF 66		66 FF 99	66 FF CC
21		15	9	3	39	75			111		110	109
FF 33 33		FF 66 33	FF 99 33	FF CC 33	FF FF 33	CC FF 33	99 FF 33	66 FF 33	33 FF 33		33 FF 66	33 FF 99	33 FF CC
28		22	16	10	4	40	76	112	148		147	146	145
FF 00 00	FF 33 00	FF 66 00	FF 99 00	FF CC 00	FF FF 00	CC FF 00	99 FF 00	66 FF 00	33 FF 00	00 FF 00	00 FF 33	00 FF 66	00 FF 99	00 FF CC
35	29	23	17	11	5	41	77	113	149	185	184	183	182	181
CC 00 00		CC 33 00	CC 66 00	FF0033	CC CC 00	99 CC 00	66 CC 00	33 CC 00		00 CC 00		00 CC 33	00 CC 66	00 CC 99
71		65	59	53	47	83	119	155		191		190	189	188
99 00 00			99 33 00	FF0033	99 99 00	66 99 00	33 99 00			00 99 00			00 99 33	00 99 66
107			101	95	89	125	161			197			196	195
66 00 00				66 33 00	66 66 00	33 66 00				00 66 00				00 66 33
143				137	131	167				203				202
33 00 00				33 33 00					00 33 00			
179				173					209			
00 00 00				00 00 00					00 00 00			
215				215					215			

Conversion Table

Hex	in %	R/G/B	R=MY	G=CY	B=CM
FF	100	255	100%	100%	100%
CC	80	204	80%	80%	80%
99	60	153	60%	60%	60%
66	40	102	40%	40%	40%
33	20	51	20%	20%	20%
00	00	0	00%	00%	00%

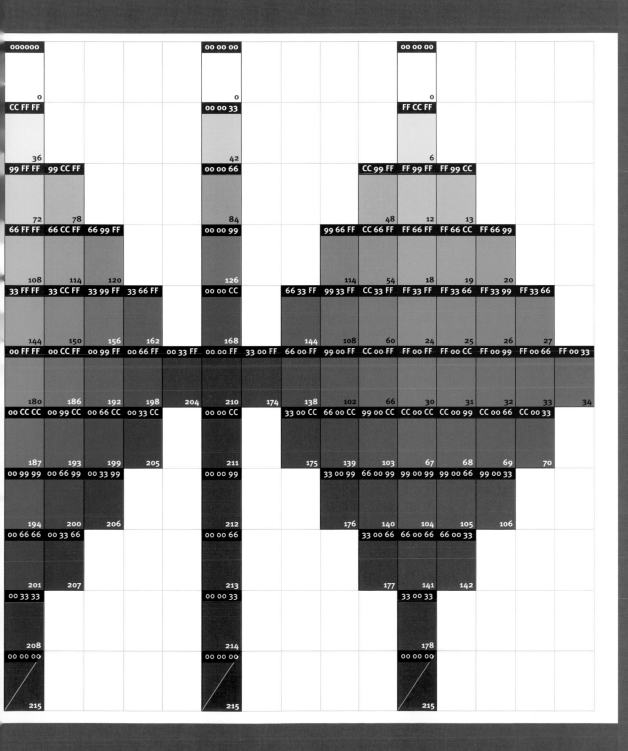

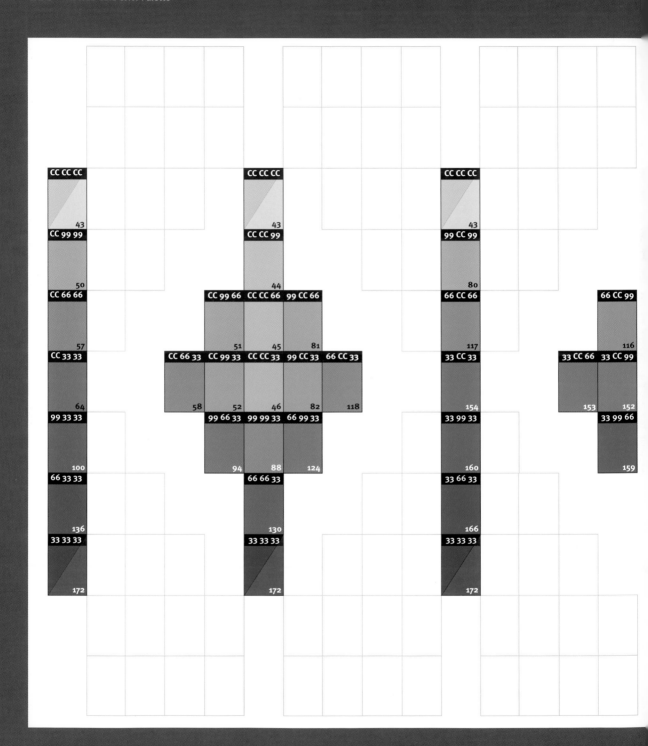

CC CC CC
43

CC 99 99
50

CC 66 66
57

CC 33 33
64

99 33 33
100

66 33 33
136

33 33 33
172

CC CC CC
43

CC CC 99
44

CC 99 66   CC CC 66   99 CC 66
51   45   81

CC 66 33   CC 99 33   CC CC 33   99 CC 33   66 CC 33
58   52   46   82   118

99 66 33   99 99 33   66 99 33
94   88   124

66 66 33
130

33 33 33
172

CC CC CC
43

99 CC 99
80

66 CC 66
117

33 CC 33
154

33 99 33
160

33 66 33
166

33 33 33
172

66 CC 99
116

33 CC 66   33 CC 99
153   152

33 99 66
159

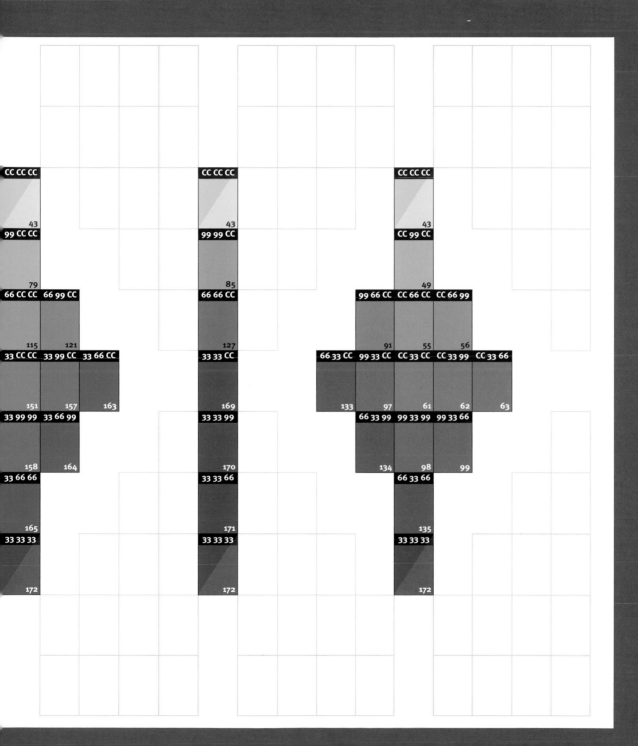

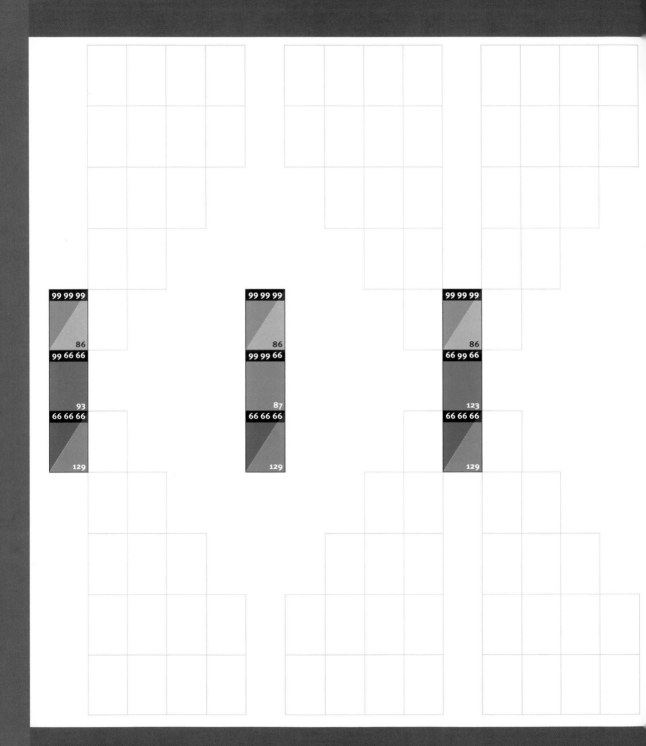

99 99 99
86

99 66 66
93

66 66 66
129

99 99 99
86

99 99 66
87

66 66 66
129

99 99 99
86

66 99 66
123

66 66 66
129

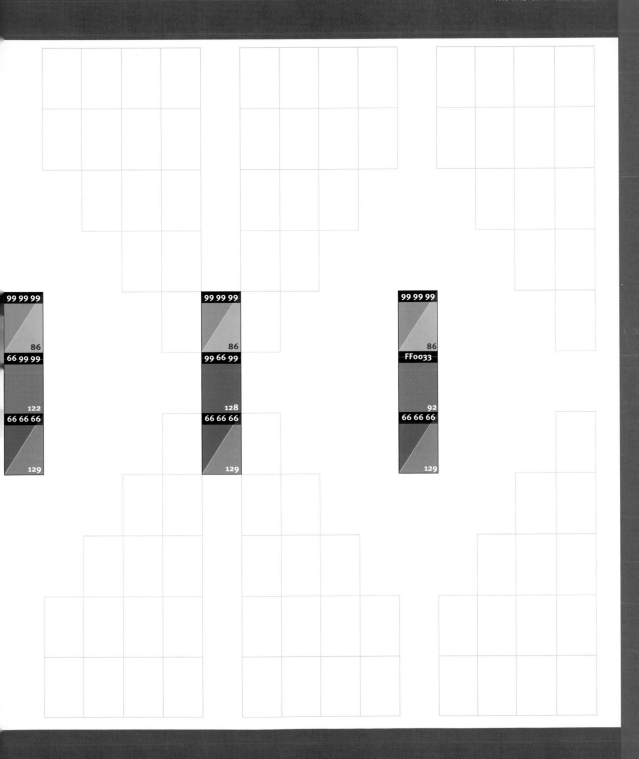

Illustration: Michael Baumgardt

GOLIVE BASICS

GoLive Basics

After you have designed your Web site in Photoshop or ImageReady (or both) it is time for you to move it into GoLive and re-create the Web site as HTML documents.

If you have some knowledge of HTML and maybe even GoLive, this chapter will help you to work efficiently and understand how all the pieces come together. I will lead you through a step-by-step examination of how a transition from Photoshop/ImageReady to GoLive can be done. I won't, however, explain all the design features of GoLive in detail in this chapter.

UNDERSTANDING THE CONCEPT OF STATIONERY AND COMPONENTS

Before we get into how you start a Web site in GoLive, it is important to understand the concept of stationery and components, since these features are the key to working efficiently.

The term "stationery" refers to a predefined page that you can drag and drop into your site structure. If you have worked with layout programs like Adobe PageMaker or InDesign before, you probably are already familiar with this concept (other programs might use the terms "master pages" or "templates"). However, the pages that you create in GoLive are not linked to the stationery, so if you make changes on a stationery page, they won't automatically show up on the body pages in your site (this is quite different from the way it is handled in a layout program). The stationery in GoLive is really nothing more than a copy of a page; if you need to create elements that are dynamically updated on every page that they are used, you can create a component.

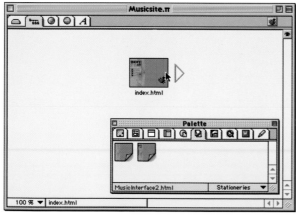

A component is an element on a page that will be updated to reflect changes in the original. Since components can be placed on stationery, you can make GoLive mimic the way master pages are handled in a layout program.

▲ Stationery will allow you to easily create the structure of the Web site.

OVERVIEW: BRINGING YOUR PHOTOSHOP DESIGN INTO GOLIVE

Before I walk you step-by-step through an example, I want to give you an overview. Let's assume that you and your client have finalized the main page and the concept for all the following body pages. You have also already exported all the images and elements that you need. The next step is then to create a new site in GoLive.

Instead of designing the Web site page by page, you want to take advantage of GoLive's ability to automate. This requires the creation of a site (project), which is essentially a bunch of folders and a database that keeps track of what you are doing. Once the site is created, GoLive presents you with an empty "index.html" page as starting point. On this

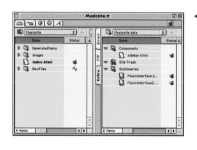

◀ The Site window lets you manage the mirror site as well as all other aspects of the Web site.

page, you should define every common element for the site, such as the background color and pattern, text and link colors, a layout grid, a logo, and fonts. Save the page in the Stationery folder. Documents saved here or in the Components folder will appear in GoLive's Palette under the **Site Extra**s tab. This tab has two subcategories: stationery and components. Switch between the two by using the pop-up menu at bottom right.

You can use components to create more complex versions of your stationery page. It is important that you develop components for navigation, for example. Typical navigation tools are text links in a sidebar (vertical arrangement) and the same links at the bottom (and even the top) of a page. Since you might not yet know how many links your page

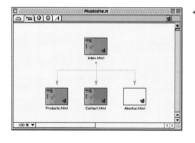

◀ Using stationary pages makes it easy to create the site structure in the Site tab of the Site manager window.

will contain, just put some text or placeholders where the links will be. Components are automatically updated when the original is changed, so you can finish them later.

When you've designed your stationery pages, switch to Site view and drag the stationery pages from the Palette into the appropriate positions to create the site structure.

Once the whole architecture is designed it's time to update the navigational components: double-click on them in the open document and they will open automatically. The text or images are defined as links and can then conveniently be connected to the pages using GoLive's **Point and Shoot** tool.

▲ A new site always includes a home page (index.html) in the File Manager of the Site window. Click on the tab in the upper right corner to reveal the Extra, FTP and Errors tab.

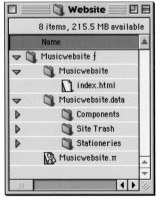

▲ On the Desktop, you will find a folder with the name of your site with an added "ƒ". Inside this folder is the Site Manager and two subfolders. One is for the mirror site and one is for data like Components and Stationery.

The pages are now ready to be filled with content. The last step is to organize the files in folders (which is done directly in the **Files** tab of GoLive's Site window, before the site is uploaded to the server via FTP.

A Case Study

Creating a Web site is as easy following the description above. The only tricky part is memorizing where all the features are hidden, but that will become much clearer to you after going through this example.

➤ Setting up a new site

Choose File > New Site > Blank to create a new site. In the file selector dialog box, choose the folder (or hard drive) in which you want to place your project folder, name the site and check the Create Folder option. This option will create a project folder with the name of the site plus "ƒ" (in Windows it will have the addition "folder".) In this folder GoLive puts the site management document ("Testsite.π", for example on Macintosh; "Test-site.site" on Windows) and two subfolders. The folder with the extension ".data" holds three subfolders called **Components**, **Site Trash** and **Stationeries**. The other folder in the project folder has the site name without any extension; it represents your actual site. It is the local copy of the site which will later be uploaded to the server. You can create folders inside it that reflect how you want your files to be organized. While you can create any subfolders directly in the Finder/Desktop, you should get into the habit of using the GoLive **Site window** for this. GoLive keeps track of all the files and folders in the local site folder in its internal database; if you place any documents or folders in your mirror site via the desktop, GoLive won't have a record of them. This can be confusing for new GoLive users, since a folder or document that was created using the operating system commands is not visible in GoLive's Site window. It's easy to fix using the **Site > Rescan** command, but you won't have to do this if you only create files and folders within GoLive.

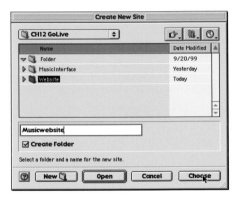

▲ Select the folder into which you want to place the Web site. If Create Folder is activated, everything gets placed into a subfolder with the same name as the site.

Personally, I use both the Finder/Desktop commands and the GoLive **Site window** to create the folder structure of my mirror site, but you should do this only if you have a clear understanding of what's going on behind the scenes; otherwise, you run the risk of corrupting the GoLive database.

➤ Creating the first stationery

In the **Site window**, double-click the index.html page to open it. An empty gray page will appear. Change the page title from "Welcome to Adobe GoLive 4" to your desired title. Because most search engines put a lot of weight on the title when indexing a document, be sure to use descriptive keywords. If your site is about music, for instance, you may want to include keywords like Music, CDs, MP3, or Songs in the title.

➤ Setting up the main page

The second step is to set the colors and background for your page. Click on the page icon next to the title of your page, and all the page-related parameters will appear in the **Inspector Palette** (the inspector switches to Page Inspector). Open the **Color Palette** via **Window > Color Palette (View > Color Palette** on Windows**)**, choose the **Text, Link, Active Link** and **Visited Link** and drag your chosen colors to the appropriate color fields in the **Page Inspector.** GoLive will automatically activate them (the check boxes will be marked).

▲ To give the document a title, click on the text next to the page icon.

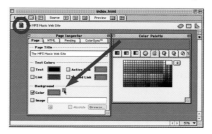

◄ Clicking on the page icon will change the Inspector to the Page Inspector, in which the colors for the Links and the background can be set by dragging them from the Color Palette.

You can also choose a background image for your page by activating the **Image** option, which introduces you to one of GoLive's most unique features: the **Point and Shoot** tool. This is the little spiral icon beneath the Image field in the **Page Inspector**. Click it and drag to bring up a pointer with which you can select the background image from the list in the **Site window**. Since this window may be obscured by your document, how do you point to anything in it? Drag the **Point and Shoot** line to the **Site window** icon in the toolbar, and it will come to the front. If necessary, select the **File** tab. Once there, select the background image file and then release the mouse button (if the image file is in a folder, first select the folder, and it will pop open). Although it may seem like a complicated process at first, it will eventually become second nature. However, if you are not comfortable with **Point and Shoot**, you can use the **Browse** button in the **Page Inspector** instead.

▲ If you have a folder with all your images, drag it from the Desktop into the Site Window and GoLive will insert a copy of that folder.

▲ Sometimes the Site window is hidden behind the page. Bring the Point and Shoot Tool over the Site window Icon in the Toolbar and it will come to front. Without releasing the mouse button bring the Point and Shoot tool over the file that you want to load.

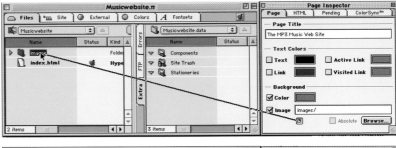

▲ When the mouse is over a folder it will open up automatically. To move up a folder bring the Point and Shoot tool over the arrow button.

One more thing: If you are using a background image, always pick a background color that comes close to the overall color of the image. Then, if the background image can't be loaded (due to a network error for example), the page will at least look as close as possible to what it is supposed to look like.

➤ Creating a layout grid

The next step is to place a layout grid on your home page. It is essentially just a table, but with some specific settings that allow GoLive to position elements on it more precisely. The layout grid is the first element in the Palette (**Window > Palette**). When you place the grid in your document, the Inspector changes to the **Layout Grid Inspector**, in which you can set the dimensions of the grid. The default setting of 16 pixels for the horizontal and vertical spacing can be changed to a more useful value of 5 pixels. Place on the grid all the elements that will be standard on each and every page. Usually this comes down to a logo and a main container for the content. Place the logo by dragging an image object from the Palette onto the grid (select the file with the **Point and Shoot** tool or the **Browse** command). The main content container can either be another table or a layout text box, which is just a table cell. Don't place links on this page yet unless they are never going to change. Dynamic elements should be placed as components.

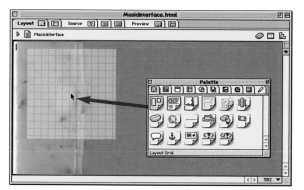

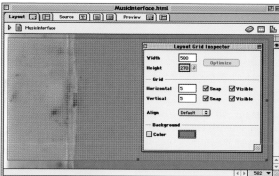

OVERVIEW OF THE GOLIVE LAYOUT GRID

The Layout Grid feature in GoLive automatically builds HTML tables in your documents. This table is optimized to display as consistently as possible in version 3.0 and later of Netscape Navigator and Microsoft Internet Explorer Web browsers. The table includes an invisible control row and control column, which tell browsers how wide and how tall the table is; this helps minimize display differences between Navigator and Internet Explorer.

Each time you place or move objects on a Layout Grid, GoLive generates a new table to contain the objects. This table contains the fewest table cells that your grid's layout will allow. When objects in a Layout Grid are not aligned with each other vertically and horizontally, GoLive creates a more complex table than if the objects were aligned. This is because the table cells define each object's location both within the table and in relation to other objects; aligned objects require fewer table cells to refer to them than do unaligned objects. Documents that contain complex tables may not look as expected in Web browsers and will have slightly larger file sizes. Internet Explorer may be unable to correctly display Layout Grid tables that contain unaligned objects; it may overestimate the table's width and display a horizontal scroll bar when it isn't needed.

You may want to use a plain table instead of the Layout Grid for some objects (for example, objects that won't be the same size in all browsers or operating systems). And you should always use a table when creating forms—different browsers display form elements, such as text boxes and pop-up menus, at different sizes. When your document's design requires that paragraphs of text stay aligned with an image, you should put the text and image in a table. That way they'll always line up, even if the text is different sizes in different browsers and operating systems.

▲ Drag the Layout Grid from the Palette and adjust its size. The Grid size can be adjusted in the Layout Grid Inspector as well as the background color.

Tables are one of the most important elements for designers, because it gives them some control over what a page looks like. Because tables can contain text, images and multimedia files, and the width and visibility of borders can be precisely controlled, HTML authoring tools use tables for layout purposes. GoLive's layout grid or text box is nothing more than a specialized version of a table. When I say specialized, I mean that GoLive adds certain attributes to those tables that contain some information for GoLive exclusively. Browsers will ignore these attributes, but there could be a problem if several people using different tools work on an HTML document. I had such an unpleasant experience with someone using Microsoft FrontPage, which resulted in a completely destroyed HTML document that would look good only on Microsoft Internet Explorer for Windows.

HOW TO PLACE TABLES WITH GOLIVE
Placing a regular table in GoLive
is as simple as dragging the
Table icon from the palette to
the document. By default,
GoLive always will give you a
table with three columns and
three rows, but you can click the
top or left edge of the table to
change this. Enter the desired
number of rows and columns in
the Table Inspector. GoLive
measures the width in pixels, but
you can also use Percent or Auto
to set the dimensions of a table.
One very nice feature of GoLive
is the ability to import tab-
separated text files into tables
with the "Import Tab-Text"
button, which can save you a lot
of time.

You can actually convert the Layout Grid to a table to see how it's built.
This trick can help you to make sure all your objects are in alignment. Don't
try this on your only copy of a page, though; if you make a mistake, you can
damage the page and will have to recreate it (in the best-case scenario
you'll just have to reload the last version.)

First select Source view and remove the COOL table attribute from the
Table tag. This is a flag that tells GoLive to display the table with the Layout
Grid interface. Switch to the Layout Editor to see the table. Don't modify
it—you could very easily ruin the page. Without making any changes, return to Source view and replace the COOL attribute. When you go to Layout view again, the Layout Grid should be in place. Then you can make any
necessary adjustments.

➤ **Setting up the fonts**

As you know by now, fonts are a major issue when it comes to designing for
the Web. In the early versions of HTML, you had no choice whatsoever in
defining fonts. Later the FONT tag was introduced, which allowed you to at
least designate a font, but with the major restriction that this font had to be
installed on the user's system. So it's almost impossible to use anything exotic; it literally comes down to using Arial, Helvetica (sans serif) or Palatino,
Times (serif) combinations, since these are the only fonts that come standard
on both Windows and Mac systems. You now also have the option of using
Dynamic Fonts, which is a format that embeds the PostScript information of
a font in a special PFR file that is stored on the server. But since older browsers
won't be able to interpret Dynamic Fonts, you should use the FONT feature of
HTML as an alternative.

▲ If the Stationery page contains
text that should always be for-
matted in a special font, place
some sample text on your Stationery page and assign a Font Set
to it. Doing this on the Stationery
page will later on help you to
work more efficiently.

Another option is Cascading Style Sheets (CSS). CSS was created in an at-
tempt to go beyond the FONT feature, but unfortunately it was implemented halfheartedly by Netscape and Microsoft into their browsers. So most of
the cool things that you can do with font and style definition can't be used
unless you don't mind your pages looking very different on each browser.

For these reasons, I like to use just a little bit of each. First I specify the
FONT tag by using **Style > Font > Edit Font Sets**, which brings up the **Font
Set Editor**. Click the **New** button to insert an Empty Font Set. In the Font
Names column, choose the font from the **New** pop-up menu or just enter
the name of the font in the text field. It's customary to pick a couple of sans

SOME TIPS ON USING DYNAMIC FONTS

In order to use Dynamic Fonts, you need to download Internet Explorer 4 (or higher) for Windows, or Netscape 4.03 (or higher) for Windows, Unix, or Macintosh. If you are using Internet Explorer for Windows, you should also download the Microsoft Font Smoother. Font Smoother is included with Windows NT 4.0, and is a free download for Windows 95/98 users. Microsoft Internet Explorer for Macs has not been developed as completely as the Windows version, which means that Dynamic Fonts will not work in IE for Macs.

Before you can even use Dynamic Fonts, you have to declare the PFR MIME Type "application/font-tdpfr" for the browser. Also make sure that the font files have the extension ".pfr". More important, talk to your ISP's system administrator, because the Web servers must also be set up to recognize the PFR MIME type.

It is possible to use Dynamic Fonts that are located on a different server. You can for example use fonts from "www.truedoc.com" which at least ensures that the fonts and server are set up correctly. If the Dynamic Fonts do not seem to be loading, make sure you allow enough time for the fonts to download to your browser. Download times vary, depending on the size of the Dynamic Font and the speed of your connection to the Internet.

Dynamic Fonts is a way to download a font that you defined in the Font tag. This requires you to save the font in a special file format.

serif fonts, so choose Arial, then click the **New** button and select Helvetica. You can pick additional sans serif fonts, but it is a good idea to just keep it down to two or three fonts, since this information is embedded every time you assign the FONT tag to text. The order in which you put fonts into your font set does make a difference: If Arial is your first font, then the browser will use Helvetica only if Arial is not installed. To have Helvetica be selected, it must be your first choice in the font set.

To assign your newly created Font Set to text, select the text and choose the set in **Style > Font**. It will save you some time if you format some text on your page before you set it up as stationery; then you can just select the text later and overwrite it.

◀ Click on Font Sets New button and then on the New button to insert a font.

BACKGROUND COLOR AND IMAGES
Microsoft implemented some very useful extensions to the table tag in Internet Explorer 3.0, such as the ability to color the background of a table cell or use a background image for cells that Netscape Communicator 4.0 and higher can interpret. The same principle applies to the BACKGROUND="name.gif" attribute, that loads an image and places it either in all the cells or only in a single one. To assign a background image to a table in GoLive, use the HTML Outline Editor of GoLive. Look for the Table tag and select "background" from the pop-up menu. After this attribute has been inserted, you can click on the arrow next to the attribute to open a file selector dialog box in which you choose your background image. To see the result, you have to view the page in one of the browsers; GoLive won't display background images for tables.

▲ The best way to use Cascading Style Sheets is as an external document. This way it is referenced in all documents.

CASCADING STYLE SHEETS

The major problem of HTML is that you cannot control the font or the font size, at least not to the degree that DTP designers are used to. The only way to specify a font in HTML is the FONT tag, which allows you to set a list of fonts as your preference. The Cascading Style Sheets extension was incorporated into the HTML standard as a possible solution. With Cascading Style Sheets Level 1 (CSS1) you can set the fonts, colors or white space of your text and redefine the built-in HTML styles. This means that you can still use the regular structural tags like <H1> or <P> (Heading or Paragraph), but include formatting information for these tags in a style sheet. If the browser doesn't understand CSS, it will at least interpret the structural tags as usual. This was actually one intention of the creators of CSS: instead of creating more HTML tags for the display, they wanted to ensure that HTML would remain a structural language.

Implementing a CSS into your Web site is very easy, because you can place the specification in an external reference file and link to this file in every page of your Web site. The advantage of this is that any changes to the CSS file will change the appearance of the whole Web site.

There are actually three ways you can implement a style sheet: besides the linked style already mentioned, there are inline styles and embedded styles. A linked style sheet can be combined with embedded or inline style sheets. The styles that are included within an HTML tag (inline styles) have the highest priority, followed by embedded styles and then linked styles. This cascading affect allows the child styles to modify the display of the parent, very much like it is in a layout, where you can format a paragraph, but then still give individual words a different appearance. For example, marking a paragraph like <P STYLE="background: #660033">Top Ten</P> gives this particular header the appearance of highlighted text without affecting any of the other formatting. You can find more on Cascading Style Sheets in the GoLive manual or on the Web Site of the World Wide Web Consortium (www.w3c.org).

Using CSS to set up your font definitions allows you to define the alignment of text or specify the line height, among other things. For more information, read the GoLive manual or the online documentation at the World Wide Web Consortium Web site at www.w3c.org. The most important thing that you need to know for now is that CSS can be implemented in three different ways: as an external document, page-specific, or locally for as little as one line of text. Using an external CSS document is best, since all pages will reference this document and you can literally change the appearance of your whole Web site by changing the settings in the external CSS document.

To create an external CSS document, choose **File > New Special > New Stylesheet** Document. The untitled.ccs window that appears contains Classes, Tags, IDs, Imports and Font Faces. For now, we'll focus on the tags, because CSS allows us to redefine the formatting of the standard HTML tags. Click on the **New Tag** button in the **Tool Bar** to insert a tag in the CSS document. Enter the HTML tag (H1 in our case) in the CSS Selector Inspector, and then use the various tabs to set the values that you want to assign to this HTML tag. The possibilities range from text color to having a border and a background color for text—don't go overboard. Since support for some of the features varies between the browsers, always double check to make sure the targeted browser displays it correctly.

▲ To redefine an HTML tag, it needs to be inserted by clicking on the New Tag button.

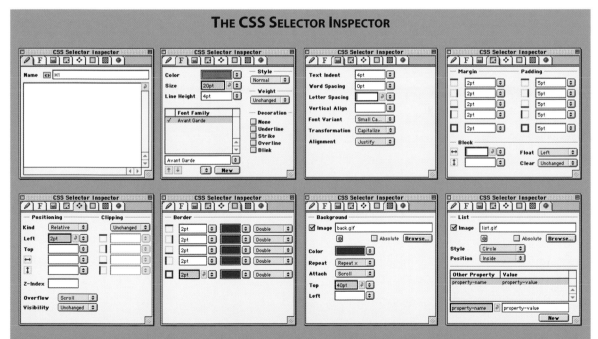

THE CSS SELECTOR INSPECTOR

The Cascading Style Sheet specification is very complex. In order to set them all, the CSS Selector Inspector Palette has many tabs (from left to right): After typing in the HTML tag, the font size and style are set. In the third tab, paragraph formatting like Alignment or Text Indent are set. Fourth and fifth tabs allow you to define the appearance and position of the box that surrounds each elements. In the seventh tab the background can be determined, including how often the background should be repeated. Because the background can be set for every tag, it is even possible to give a headline a textured background. In the last tab are the properties for lists and for all unsupported properties.

To link the CSS document to the Web page, the External tab needs to be clicked and a New Item inserted. The Inspector then allows you to link to the file. ▶

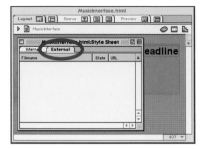

Since the Cascading Style Sheet document is external, it needs to be linked to the HTML page. Bring the index.html page to the front and click the stair-shaped icon in the upper-right corner. The CSS window for this page will open. Click the **External tab** and then the **New Item** button in the Tool bar to insert an "Empty Reference" in the window. This reference must be linked to the saved CSS document with the Point and Shoot tool or the Browse button. GoLive will display the CSS settings even in Layout mode, but again, to avoid surprises, check your document in all the targeted browsers.

➤ Creating a component

To create a component, you have to create an empty HTML document via **File > New**. Let's use this document to create a sidebar for our stationery page: in this example (see picture) I used five lines of text.

You don't have to convert the text into links yet, this can be done later. All you need to do is to save this page in the **Component folder** of your site data folder. The **Save dialog** box has a shortcut to this folder: click on the icon in the lower right corner to pick the **Components**, **Site Trash** or **Components** folder. Name and save the document in the Components folder, and then you are ready to place the component on your Index/Stationery page (don't delete the ".html" extension of the filename, otherwise it won't show up).

▲ A document with navigational elements for the sidebar is saved in the Components folder, which can be found by clicking in the lower right of the Save As dialog box.

Activate the **Site Extra** tab of the Palette, and select **Components** in the lower right corner. When you drag the sidebar onto the layout grid, you may even notice that the colors of the sidebar switch automatically to match those of the stationery page. If you don't drag a component onto a layout grid it will be placed inside a frame that can't be resized; you should usually use a layout grid when dealing with components.

After you have set up all the components that you need for your stationery, save your home page (index.html) with the **Save** command, then use the **Save As** command to save a copy into the Stationery folder. Since the stationery page can't be assigned later to an already existing page, this is the best way to ensure that home page and the rest of the site match. Alternatively you can open the stationary page and use the **Save As** command to overwrite the "index.html" file in the site folder.

➤ Setting up the colors

Before creating the site structure with this stationery page, it's a good idea to set up the colors you want to use throughout your site. Select the **Color tab** in the **Site window** and choose **Site > Get Colors Used** to import all the colors used so far. Since we haven't yet defined many colors, you'll probably get just the colors that you used for the text, links, and background. Name them appropriately to make sure you know when you are using a link color for something else; I recommend using the link colors sparingly. It is certainly not a good idea to color regular text with the link colors, since this can be very confusing to the visitor.

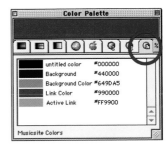

◄ All the colors that are used in the Web site up to this point can easily be gathered by using the "Get Colors Used" command. They will then appear in the last color tab of the Color Palette.

You can drag additional colors into the Colors tab, and you'll also find these colors, that are in the Color tab of the Site Window, in the rightmost tab of the Color Palette.

➤ Creating the site structure

The last step before filling your site with content is to create the site structure. Activate the Site tab of the Site window and drag the Stationery document over from the Palette. As the page icon comes beneath the index.html page icon, a blue arrow indicates that GoLive is ready to insert the page beneath the home page. If this arrow isn't visible, it probably means that the Link Hierarchy option is selected in the **Site View Controller**. To verify this, click on the Eye icon in the upper right corner of the **Site window** to call up the **Site View Controller**, then switch to **Navigation Hierarchy**. While you are there, let's make some other changes: in the Display tab select **Show items as Thumbnails**—this will display a preview of the page. The previews will only appear once you make changes to the page and save them. It's also useful to

EXPORTING ELEMENTS FROM IMAGEREADY TO GOLIVE

As mentioned before in this book, it's most efficient to design your web site in Photoshop/ImageReady and bring it over into GoLive after the final design has been approved. There are a couple of things to know that will make this process easier, especially if you are using interactive elements like rollover buttons. To illustrate the process, I'll go through a typical example:

1. This is a mock-up of a music web site done entirely in Photoshop. I click the Jump to default **Graphics Editor** command on the bottom of the **Tool Palette**, and the file is saved and opened directly in ImageReady.

▲ On the left side is the complete mock-up of the Web site in Photoshop. This is brought over into ImageReady to create the rollover buttons and to slice the composition into its individual elements, which are then saved with the HTML file and imported into GoLive.

There are two good reasons to do rollovers and the image export in ImageReady. For one, it is easier to test the result with ImageReady's Preview command (**File > Preview**), which switches to a Browser. Also, it's very convenient to optimize several images at once. In Photoshop the export process needs to be done for each piece of the image individually, while in ImageReady the slices can all have different optimize settings.

2. As complex as this design looks, it often comes down to exporting the logo, a couple of buttons and maybe an image here and there. The first step in bringing the elements over to GoLive is selecting the individual elements with the Slice Tool. Once all the elements are sliced, I open the **Optimize palette** (**Window > Show Optimize**), select a particular slice and set the Optimize settings. It is best to open the **Optimize tab** in the document window for this process so you can see the results directly. You can activate several slices at once and change the settings for them together, although this works only for the slices that you created. The original main slice will always behave like one entity, even though it is automatically sliced each time you use the Slice tool. You can easily spot the original slice by its label in the upper left corner.

3. Most of the elements in this mock-up will later be re-created in HTML, so all the text, all the table cells and all the banner ads need to be hidden by clicking on the eye icon in the Layer Palette. This holds also true for the background on the background layer. ImageReady's HTML Background command in the File menu lets you choose a background color and image, which will later appear in the HTML document, but will not be displayed in ImageReady. The reason you need to hide the background layer even before you start creating the rollover buttons is that otherwise you end up with the background image being sliced up and saved/exported.

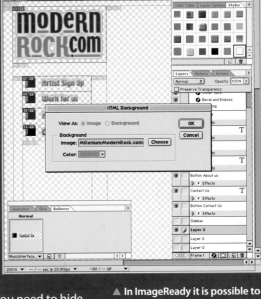

▲ In ImageReady it is possible to define a HTML background that is later also used when the page is exported.

4. From the Windows menu, select the **Rollover Palette** and also the **Style Palette**. Select a slice and click on the Page Icon at the bottom of the Palette to insert a new Rollover State in the Rollover Palette. All the changes on any of the layers will be recorded, so the design should be finalized. As you can see, the color of the square and the text was changed. To avoid having to change those settings manually every time for each button, drag the effect settings from the **Layers Palette** and insert them in the **Styles Palette**. Activate another slice and create a new **Rollover State**, then drag the two Styles onto the button element. You don't even have to activate the layer they are on, which makes this a very fast way of creating the design for all the buttons.

5. Preview the page in one of the browsers; if everything seems to work as it's supposed to, use **File > Save Optimized As** to save a copy of the HTML page. Only the **Save**

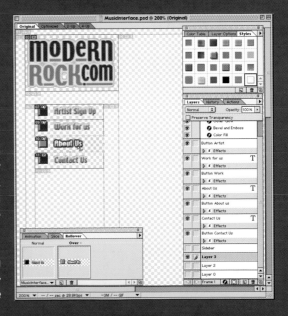

After the HTML page is imported it can be broken up into stationary and components. ▶

Optimized As command has the Save HTML File, **Save Images** and **Save Selected Slices Only** options. Click on the HTML Options to display another dialog box that lets you change, for example, the JavaScript Code to GoLive, which you have to do to ensure compatibility with GoLive. It is important to decide how the empty cells should be generated; in this example, **NoWrap, TD W&H** basically leaves the cells empty but puts the Width and Height attribute in the table cells. If **GIF, TD W&H** is selected, the cell will be filled with a transparent GIF image.

At the very end, everything is exported at once as HTML files along with the individual elements. To get the best result in the HTML authoring program, ImageReady offers many HTML specific features. It even allows you to export an optimized code for GoLive. ▶

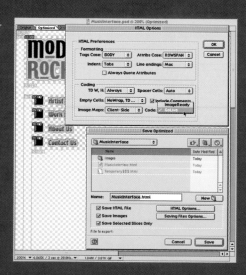

6. Since the **Save Selected Slices Only** option was activated, the HTML document will only include a small table with the navigational buttons and the logo. That's better than having everything be part of a large table, because it allows you to drag a Layout Grid into the document on which the smaller table can then be placed. At this point, you can save the page as stationery.

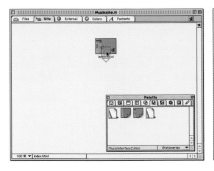 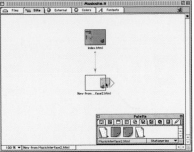

◀ To insert a page, drag a page from the stationary folder and bring it over the index page in the Site view. When a blue arrow appears, the page is ready to be inserted.

have the file name be used for the item label (instead of using the title of the page). This also allows you to edit a file name directly in the Site window by clicking on the name.

To insert additional pages on the same hierarchical level, just bring the Stationery page icon close to one side of an already placed page and drop it there. Pages can even be moved around by dragging them to the new location, or deleted by pressing the Delete button.

 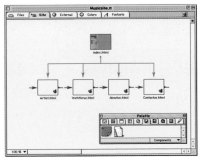

▲ The documents can be renamed and dragged to a new folder.

◀ Once the Sidebar Component with all the links is set up correctly and updated, the connections between the pages in the Site view will turn solid to indicate that the pages are linked.

After renaming your documents in the **Site tab** of the **Site Window** by clicking on the name once, it is time to switch back to the **Files tab**. All the pages that you created are in one folder named "NewFiles;" since this probably doesn't reflect your desired folder structure, use the **Site > New > Group** command to create an empty folder. Rename this folder and drag into it all the HTML files that you want here from the NewFiles-Folder. A **Move Files dialog box** will ask you to confirm which files and links need to be updated.

➤ Updating components

The sidebar that we created above needs to be updated to make the site navigable. To edit the component, locate it in the Site window and double-

After renaming and moving the pages, GoLive lists all the pages that needs to be updated. If you want to exclude some pages from being updated, click on the button next to the file name. ▶

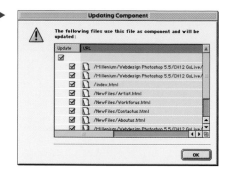

click the file. Locating the Component requires you to activate the split-view by clicking on the tab in the upper right corner and then selecting **Extra**.

After the component is opened, make the necessary changes and save the document again. GoLive will again display an **Updating Component dialog box**, which you need to confirm. As for our sidebar, I selected the text and converted it into a hyperlink using **Special > New Link** and then using the **Point and Shoot tool** to target the HTML document in the File or Site tab of the Site window.

➤ The last word

After you've set up the entire navigational structure and the hyperlinks, the pages displayed on the Site tab will be connected by solid lines rather then dotted ones. This ensures that you have a Web site with a complete functional navigation. Now you can easily fill the site with content—just double-click a document in the **Site tab**. To preview your Web site in the browser click the **Show in Browser** button on the tool bar.

UPLOADING THE SITE

The "almost" last step in the Web design process is the uploading of the Web site. First you must set up the FTP connection. Choose **Site > Settings**, then select FTP and enter server, username and password. After closing the Settings, open an Internet connection and click on **Site > Connect to server**.

Username, password and Server need to be entered in the FTP Set up in order to upload the Web site to the server. ▶

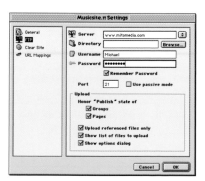

The server directory is only visible if you click the tab on the upper right, which splits the window in two (select the FTP tab). To upload, you can manually drag the folder and files from the left to the right window, but GoLive automatically synchronizes the directory of the server with your mirror site when you click on the **Upload to Server** button in the **Toolbar**.

APPLE WEBOBJECTS

If you have toyed around with the GoLive preferences, you might have tripped over the Modules folder and maybe even activated the WebObjects module. You would find that the GoLive palette then displayed an additional tab with a plethora of new objects. Unfortunately, you won't find much information on WebObjects itself in the GoLive manual (there is complete documentation on the Installation CD-ROM). WebObjects support has been available in GoLive since Version 3.0 and companies like Adobe use it to manage human resources information on their Intranet. Also, Apple's award-winning online store is based entirely on WebObjects.

Allen Denison, the marketing manager for WebObjects at Apple, explains: "The idea behind WebObjects is to allow the creation of Web-based GUIs. This market came alive when companies realized that they could run their applications through a browser, and that they needed a tool where it was possible to have the GUI in the browser interacting with the application on the server."

WebObjects resides on the server near where you typically put your CGI, "but instead of a CGI script that usually does only one task, you create the whole application to handle all the pages and the interaction for the whole Web site. So whatever you would do, like … a credit card transaction or a database query, all this is taken through the browser to the application that runs on the server. WebObjects provides all the information and mechanisms to access the database and to feed the information back to the browser as HTML pages," says Denison.

Instead of having the HTML templates included in the application, they reside on the server like a regular Web site; since the functionality is not spread out over several independent CGI scripts, everything becomes more maintainable. "And the separation is very clean: you can have your designers do the layout while your developers write the code to fill in that specific piece of the HTML," explains Denison.

ColdFusion, which is also a very popular Web developer tool, is more suited to a database-driven Web site, while WebObjects' scalability and integration with existing information systems makes it more flexible. "WebObjects is not designed to be an e-commerce out-of-the-box solution," says Denison, because it requires programmers with Java or C++ experience. But it is likely that "third-party developers will build e-commerce solutions on the basis of WebObjects."

▲ The WebObjects Palette features objects similar to those on the regular HTML Palette. Additional objects can be found in the palette's pop-up menu.

▲ Because WebObjects are basically just modified HTML tags, the Inspector for each object is very similar to the regular HTML counterpart.

WebObjects is usually not a solution for a one or two person Web design firm. Its use requires significant programming and database skills. It is a powerful tool that is most frequently used in universities and large corporations.

Illustration: Michael Baumgardt

VIDEO AND AUDIO

Video and Audio

If you are a designer working with GoLive, you should really spend some time with the QuickTime features of GoLive. The possibilities for enhancing your Web site are tremendous and QuickTime is widely installed.

With more and more people having 56K modems or even DSL connections, we will definitely see more Web sites utilizing video and audio. Luckily GoLive makes it easy to create real multimedia Web sites because it comes with extensive QuickTime features that make it easy to integrate QuickTime into your Web site. This chapter will give you all the information you need to spice up your Site.

CAPTURING FORMATS

Although Web video doesn't yet allow for high-bandwidth real-time video, it's a good idea to capture your media in high quality anyway. There are several reasons for this:

- Highly pre-compressed video can not be compressed again, or at least you won't get the result that you want. It might not be clear why this is such a big issue, but you can now use compression algorithms—Sorenson II, for example—that produce stunning quality even for Web use. But these algorithms won't work well on already compressed images, and the image quality will significantly deteriorate.

- Aside from Web publishing, you might want to use your videos for CD-ROMs, high-resolution screen shots or even your own movie edits that go back to video.

- You can always scale down a movie file, but you can't scale it back up without a loss in quality. This is especially important if you want to create several smaller clips designed for different connection speeds (a feature that comes with QuickTime and RealMedia SureStream G2 standard). Scaling means that a visitor on your Web site with a 28K connection will see a movie with 160 x 120 resolution while 56K modems will see one with 240 x 180 resolution.

- Not all compression algorithms work equally well for all purposes. Even with some experience you might still need to test the different output options (algorithms) for your particular project.

CREATING A TWO-FRAME POSTER MOVIE IN QUICKTIME PLAYER PRO

One of the problems with embedding QuickTime movies into your page is that they will immediately start downloading, even if a visitor doesn't want to

▲ These are the two images for the poster movie.

▲ Instead of using QuickTime or RealAudio Player, movies can be embedded into the HTML page. To avoid having movies download immediately to the browser cache, you can use poster movies that link to the real movies.

watch them. To avoid this, you either have to get your ISP to install the Quick-Time Server Software, or you use a poster movie. Technically a poster movie can be anything from a single image to a movie trailer that acts like a place-holder. Of course, it makes sense to keep the poster movie as small as possi-ble; I'll show you how to create a poster movie with two frames (two frames ensure that there is some animation in the movie itself).

First, create two images with the same resolution as the movie file for which the poster movie will be used (in this example, 160x120 pixels). Quick-Time has some movie controllers always displayed at the bottom of the screen; if you want to hide the movie controller, add an additional 16 pixels to compensate. This is important, because later on you will position the poster movie in GoLive and if it doesn't have the exact same measurements as the movie itself, you will end up with a squeezed movie. You could display the controller for the poster movie, but visitors may be confused about where to click. In order for a poster movie to load the real movie, users have to click in-side the poster movie. I recommend including a message like "Click here to start the movie" in your poster movie, as in the example above.

▲ Save the movie and click on Options to set the Codec.

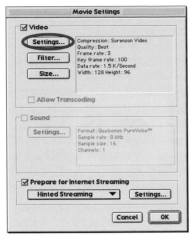

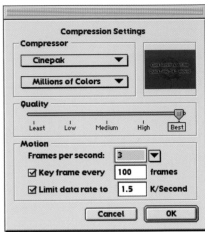

▲ In the Options dialog box click on Settings to get to the Compression Settings. For a Poster movie use Cinepak and select a Frame rate. In this example the two frames will flash in intervals of 0.66 seconds because the frame rate is set to 3 frames per second.

▲ In QuickTime Player Pro, the images can be imported as PICT sequences and then saved as a movie.

For this example I created two images in Photoshop using the Outer Glow layer effect to achieve the effect of flashing text. The two images were saved in a separate folder as TIFFs with the sequential names poster1.tif and poster2.tif. It's important to name files sequentially, because when you choose **Open Image Sequence** from the **File** menu, QuickTime Player Pro will load all the images in the folder in the order that they're listed. Choose one frame per second as the frame rate, and the frame will flash in one second intervals. To preview the flashing movie, select **Movie>Loop** and hit **Play**.

To use this as a poster movie, choose **File>Export**; in the dialog box that appears, click **Options** to select a compression method. Cinepak yields the smallest file size, but shows visible degradation. The Animation codec will yield good results, but generates higher file sizes; since this is really an issue in Web design, I suggest you stick with Cinepak. This example ended up using 20K, which is quite a lot, but still better than having an entire movie embedded.

Given GoLive's ability to create sprite tracks in QuickTime movies, poster movies can be divided into different sections, pretty much like image maps, to provide several links or other actions. This feature lets you provide several options: clicking one section of the poster movie could open the movie in a new window, clicking another would open it in the original spot. A third area could open the movie in QuickTime Player and a fourth section could open a universally compatible version of the movie that runs on all systems. All options can be made accessible from one poster movie.

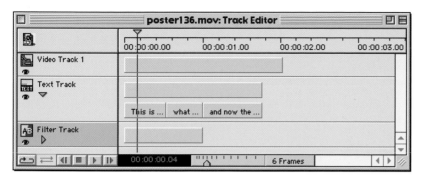

▲ The Track Editor lets you edit QuickTime's Special Features. Here, for example, I added a text track that will show up as closed captions.

▲ A double click on an embedded movie in GoLive will open the movie in its own window. The Track Editor can be opened by clicking on the button in the upper left corner. In this example you can see the generic Fire effects filter in action.

COMPRESSING AND EMBEDDING MOVIES FOR THE WEB

Compressing your movie for publishing on the Web is the last significant step of media preparation. Although there are a couple of formats, the two most popular compression codecs for Web video are certainly Apple QuickTime and RealSystems RealVideo. While RealSystems' Web standard has been around a little longer, Apple's inclusion of live Web streaming with free server software has boosted its popularity.

Apple offers QuickTime Player Pro and FinalCut Pro for compression. RealSystems offers several versions of RealProducer with different feature sets (RealProducer, RealProducer Plus, RealProducer Pro).

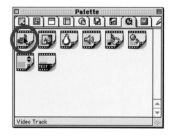

▲ The QuickTime Palette contains all the objects and modules for the Track Editor. To insert a new Video Track just drag the element into the Track Editor.

Although both of these products are inexpensive, consider buying Terran Media Cleaner Pro if you plan on using video more frequently on your Web sites. Media Cleaner Pro is a dream for everyone who has to work with video or audio encoding. It does cost quite a lot more, but is worth its price tag. It supports the highest-quality compression codecs, such as Sorenson Developer Edition, Qdesign2 Professional Edition, Real G2 and original source MP3. Those formats are all becoming increasingly important on the Web; if you've ever seen the amazing results that you can get with Sorenson II, you'll understand why. And since Me-

◄ This is RealAudio Player, which opens automatically when the sound or video file is just linked. It can be downloaded from www.real.com.

▲ In the left column Media Cleaner Pro lists all the available codecs and settings.

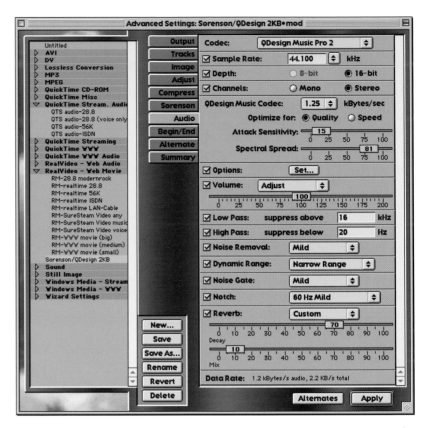

▲ Media Cleaner Pro offers an incredible variety of formats, commands and options for saving files. Here's an example of the Audio settings of a Sorenson QuickTime video.

▲ For novices, the Media Cleaner offers a Wizard that walks the user through the settings step by step and even gives visual examples when necessary. Here, for example, it shows how the Sorenson video compares to a regular version.

dia Cleaner Pro also does batch processing, you can set up a computer to do the time-consuming encoding task at night. This alone could justify the investment, but there is so much more.

The visual control and support throughout the program is excellent. It gives you a number of settings to edit the source material without having to leave the program: audio and video fades, several audio filters and several video filters like brightness, hue and saturation, adaptive noise and removal. Some special codec features can only be accessed from Media Cleaner Pro; for example, the Disable saving from WWW option prevents visitors from storing published QuickTime movies to their hard drives, thus providing copy protection of your media. This method works more reliably than the HTML QuickTime attribute that is supposed to do the same thing.

Working with Media Cleaner Pro is very simple. A settings wizard will guide you through a multiple-choice sequence to pick the right compression setting for your situation and chances are that if you're looking for a feature, Media Cleaner Pro has it. At this point, it's certainly the unchallenged powerhouse of media preparation.

➤ Which video codec should you use?

When deciding to use video on your Web site, you have to choose a compression standard. Since RealVideo entered the streaming media market before Apple, it's likely that more users will have RealPlayer installed (although most new content is delivered in the G2 standard, which requires a new player that some users may not have). If you're trying to decide between RealVideo and QuickTime, here are some facts to think about:

Generally, QuickTime creates less CPU overhead, is more responsive and will therefore work even on slow systems without breakups. With the QDesign Music 2 codec it also sports better audio quality (16 Bit, 44.1 kHz stereo at 3 K/s) and the data rate can be adjusted in finer increments. Video playback also works smoothly on slow systems.

RealVideo creates an impressive image quality that is sharp and crisp but yields sluggish response on slow systems due to high demands on the CPU when decompressing images. This may result in low frame rates (one image or less per second) and net congestion errors even at local playback.

If you have Media Cleaner Pro and the Sorenson II codec (which costs almost as much as Media Cleaner Pro itself), you do get the best of both worlds. QuickTime's Sorenson Professional codec offers a variable bit rate (VBR) for encoding, and the video image quality will be equal to (or even better than) RealVideo. If you can't make a clear decision for one or the other, you probably will end up having to have both.

➤ How to embed video in HTML

Finally, it's time to embed your prepared media into your Web pages. GoLive is the best tool to do this, as it supports QuickTime and RealMedia attributes. Make sure you install the appropriate plugins that come with the GoLive Installation CD, otherwise it will be much harder to preview the media (GoLive will also not provide all the HTML features for the media type.)

▲ Media Cleaner Pro shows a Preview of the movie while converting. It is even possible to split the screen and show before and after simultaneously.

▲ Sorenson II offers the best video and audio quality available to date for QuickTime. It is amazing how much Sorenson is able to compress a video/audio file. It's a must-have for anyone who wants to deliver high-quality video on the Web.

▲ **Many of the QuickTime attributes like Loop and Autoplay can be set in the QuickTime tab of the Plug-In Inspector. For a complete list of all the attributes, you need to switch the the Attribs tab. More exotic attributes can be entered here by entering the attribute and its value manually.**

The simplest way to integrate video on your Web page is to just create a link to the file. When the user clicks on the link, the file will be opened externally in either QuickTime or RealPlayer. That might do the job, but personally I find it much more appealing to have the movie actually embedded in the page. In order to have movies play directly in your Web browsers, you should know at least a few attributes of the different Plugin standards. Keep in mind that since Plugins are updated continuously, the authoring software may not supply all current attributes. Below you will find several QuickTime and Real-Media attributes and descriptions of their practical use.

▶ QuickTime attributes

Before you embed your QuickTime movies into your Web page, make sure that their file names end in ".mov." QuickTime movies also need to be flattened (their headers need to be removed) before they are put on the Web (QuickTime Player Pro and Media Cleaner Pro will do this automatically).

To place the QuickTime movie, just drag it into the document window or choose the **Plug-In object** from the **Palette** and hit the **Browse** button in the **Plug-in Inspector**. Then set the following parameters:

● **AUTOPLAY=true** to have the movie start automatically after the page has loaded

● **LOOP=true:** This will loop the movie after it's ended

● **CACHE=true:** will cache or temporarily store the movie on the visitor's hard drive

● **HREF=true.mov:** With reference to the QuickTime poster movie mentioned earlier, the HREF attribute can be used to load another movie when the visitor clicks on the movie. HREF defines a URL that can be absolute or relative. Use the Target attribute to define where the HREF movie should play. Setting it to "_self" or "myself" will open it in the original place of the SRC movie.

● **CONTROLLER=false:** Set this attribute if you want to hide the controller for the SRC movie. This attribute does not apply to the HREF movie. To avoid placement anomalies of the two movies, the SRC movie from the example should have a height of 136 pixels without the controller and the HREF movie should measure 136 pixels with controller (120 without).

All of the above attributes can easily be set in the QuickTime tab of the **Plug-in Inspector** by clicking on the appropriate options (the most important attributes can be activated this way, but for more exotic attributes you have to use the **Attribs** tab in the **Plug-in Inspector**). As mentioned earlier, the QuickTime plug-in needs to be placed in GoLive's Plug-in folder in order for the QuickTime Inspector to appear. There are many more QuickTime attributes than are currently available in GoLive; to enter these attributes click on the **Attribs** tab of the **Plug-in Inspector** and click **New**. Enter the attribute name in the left field and the attribute value (without quotation marks) in the right field. Press **Enter** on the keyboard to finish.

The following example will display the flashing poster movie from the earlier example in a loop and without controller until the visitor clicks on it to load the target movie. The poster movie has a height of 136 pixels without controller and the target movie has height of 120 pixels. Note that the order of the attributes has no relevance:

```
<EMBED SRC="poster.mov" WIDTH="160" HEIGHT="136" AUTO-
PLAY="true" LOOP="true" CONTROLLER="false" HREF="target.mov"
TARGET="myself" TARGETCACHE="false">
```

These are just a few examples of the many attributes available in Quick-Time. If you would like to find out more, point your browser to www.apple.com/quicktime/.

RealProducer Plus and Pro allow you to encode videos in the RealVideo format. RealProducer is available at www.real.com. ▼

➤ Embedding RealMedia

Embedding RealMedia content into Web pages is a little more complicated but still not very difficult. First of all, it's important to know that you need to create a Metafile if you want to use Web-based streaming without a server. A Metafile is a simple text file that contains the URL of the media file to be streamed. You can use a simple text editor to create such a file, or in GoLive, choose **File > New Special > New Text Document**.

The information inside the Metafile consists basically of a single text line with the absolute URL of the audio/video file. It could look like this: http://www.mysite.com/media/movie.rm

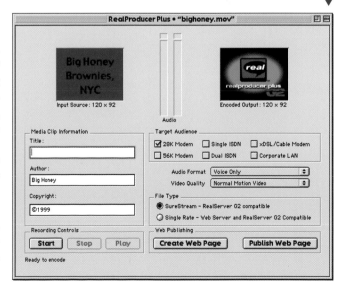

▲ The before and after is display-ed when the movie is being converted.

▲ After the conversion is com-plete, RealProducer gives detailed information in the Statistics window.

▲ In order to have the RealVideo stream, the link in the browser must address a text file (Meta file) with the URL of the video.

Again, the URL needs to be absolute in order to work, which makes it a bit more tedious to preview your work locally before uploading to the server. If you'd like to preview the result in your browser locally, the path needs to start with "file://" and must include the complete path to the destination: file://harddisk/documents/Web sites/mysite/media/movie.rm

If you create a local path, don't forget to change it to a URL before up-loading, or your link will not work. Actually, it will still work on your comput-er but not on anybody else's, and you might not even realize it.

Another very important thing is that the name of this Meta-Text file needs to have the extension ".ram" or ".rpm." A ".rpm" file will commonly be used to play movie or audio content inside the Web page and a ".ram" file will play a movie or audio in the RealPlayer application. All you need to do to play the ".ram" file is create a hyperlink to it in the Web page. If the plug-in is installed on the visitor's browser, the associated MIME type will direct the file to Re-alPlayer automatically.

To display the video (or the audio) in the Web page, you need a few at-tributes; just like QuickTime media, RealMedia is embedded in the page using the Plug-In object from the Palette. One major difference between RealMedia and QuickTime is that QuickTime displays its controllers as part of the video window, RealMedia doesn't. The way RealMedia works is that you place in-stances of the movie in the Web page and use the CONTROLS attribute to define what the SRC window should contain. It could be the video itself or just the controller for it. This gives you the flexibility to display, for example, only a Start and Stop button or also show a progress bar. Among the values available for this attribute are ImageWindow (displays movie content), Play-Button, StopButton, PositionSlider and VolumeSlider.

You might decide to use the CONSOLE attribute to have the Position Slid-er control the movie. Here is an example of a movie file measuring 160 x 120 pixels with associated Play, Stop and Position controls.

```
<EMBED SRC="movie.rpm" WIDTH="160" HEIGHT="120"
CONTROLS="ImageWindow" CONSOLE="movie">
<EMBED SRC="movie.rpm"WIDTH="44" HEIGHT="26"
CONTROLS="PlayButton" CONSOLE="movie">
<EMBED SRC="movie.rpm" WIDTH="26" HEIGHT="26"
CONTROLS="StopButton" CONSOLE="movie">
<EMBED SRC="movie.rpm" WIDTH="90" HEIGHT="26"
CONTROLS="PositionSlider" CONSOLE="movie">
```

Note that the width and height values for Play and Stop buttons can't actually vary much from the ones given in this example. This limits your placement and design choices and quite frankly, speaking from a design point of view, I don't find the controllers all that appealing. Hopefully, RealMedia will come up with something nicer one day.

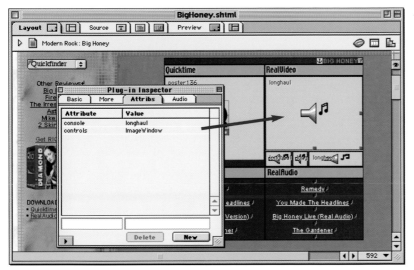

◀ To have a RealVideo embedded in a Web site along with its controls, it is necessary to create several instances of the video and use the Controls attribute to specify the function. For example, "Controls=ImageWindow" will display the actual movie.

▲ Switch to Preview to check that everything works correctly.

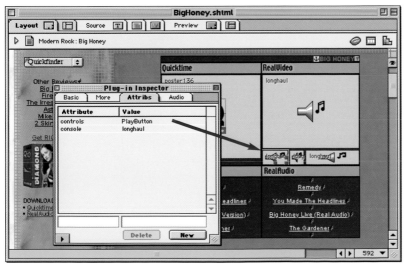

◀ To insert a Play button, I placed an instance of the movie in GoLive and used the attribute "Controller=PlayButton." "Console=Name" is required so that this Play button only starts the movie with this name (in this example the name is "longhaul").

▲ Most attributes for sound can be set in the Audio tab of the Plug-Inspector. Only the more exotic attributes need to be set manually by switching to the Attribs tab.

WAV (.wav): This format is the standard audio format on an IBM-compatible computer running Microsoft Windows.

AIFF (.aiff): This is the standard audio format on Mac OS computers and is good for music and high-quality sound.

AU (.au): Developed by Sun, this has a poor sound quality, but a small file size.

MIDI (.mid): If you are a musician, you are probably familiar with this format, because it is used to record music with a sequencer or hook up two keyboards. Because MIDI is not an audio format, it requires an installed sound card on a PC or an installed QuickTime Music system extension.

MUSIC AND AUDIO

With MP3 becoming so popular and bandwidth increasing, we will probably see more Web sites using sound to enhance the online experience. There are basically two methods for delivering audio over the Web: files that have to be downloaded before playback and audio that plays during download, which is called streaming audio.

In general, the first scenario gives you better control over the sound quality and doesn't require any plug-in. Both Internet Explorer and Netscape Navigator can play these files directly. The problem is that the download of a long audio file takes awhile. Streaming audio has the advantage that the sound starts playing even before the file has completely loaded.

➤ Implementing a sound file

There are several ways of implementing sound into your Web page, but the most commonly used is the <EMBED> tag, which both browsers understand and which can play WAV, AIFF, AU, and MIDI files. The Embed tag is automatically placed when you drag the Plug-In object from the Palette in GoLive and link it to a sound file.

```
<EMBED SRC="music_file.mid" AUTOSTART="true"
WIDTH="144" HEIGHT="60" LOOP="1">
```

Here's an example of a sound file placed with an EMBED tag. Depending on the file type, you need to use the right attributes. In this example a MIDI file is loaded and the attribute AUTOSTART="true" automatically plays the sound after it is completely downloaded. If this attribute is set to "false," the sound will only play when the user hits the play button in the control panel.

The LOOP attribute tells the browser how many times you want the sound to be played, and it can be an integer or true/false. "True" means that the browser will continue playing the sound until the stop button on the console is clicked.

➤ MP3 audio format

MP3, or MPEG Audio Layer-3, is a very advanced audio format that provides almost CD-quality sound with reasonable file sizes. The compression ratio is up to 12:1. The resulting files are bigger than RealAudio files in best quality mode (17:1), but also superior in sound. MP3 compresses sounds by remov-

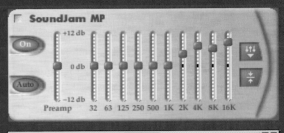

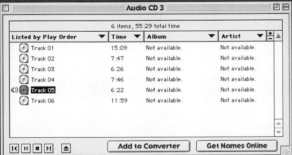

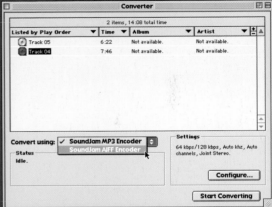

ing parts that are inaudible, while retaining the full frequency and dynamic spectrum. Streaming of MP3 files is incorporated in the file format, but requires high-bandwidth connections, such as ISDN.

If you are looking for a great MP3 player software, I strongly recommend SoundJam from Casady & Greene. This software has great features, from the ability to change the design of the user interface to nice visual effects to batch encoding of MP3 from a CD.

➤ RealAudio

Thanks to streaming technology, this popular file format allows almost instant access to very long sound files, such as songs, interviews or even live transmissions. The RealAudio algorithm uses high compression rates ranging from about 17:1 to 170:1, which are based on CD-quality audio. A three-minute song can be reduced to as little as 180K, compared to about 30 MB in CD quality. There is a definite deterioration in sound quality when using these high compression ratios with slower modems. However, the resulting low data rate necessary for those files provides real-time audio access for modems as slow as 14.4 kbps.

▲ SoundJam is one of the best MP3 Players available. It comes with several interfaces (skins), but most important, it offers batch conversion of music directly from CD. Other converters copy the original sound files to the hard drive first, which might be a problem.

▲ The Eclipse is a spectral display that makes it fun to view the music.

INDEX

To have the Web Safe Color Palette close to your computer, cut the three following pages out and glue them together

THE MiB COLOR CHART

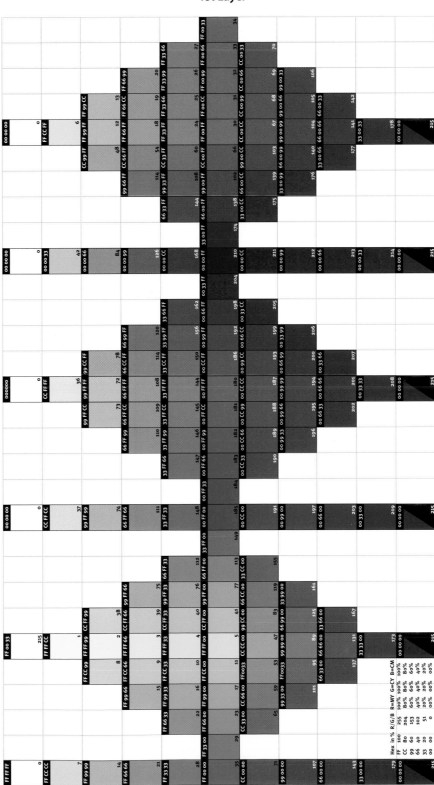

2nd Layer

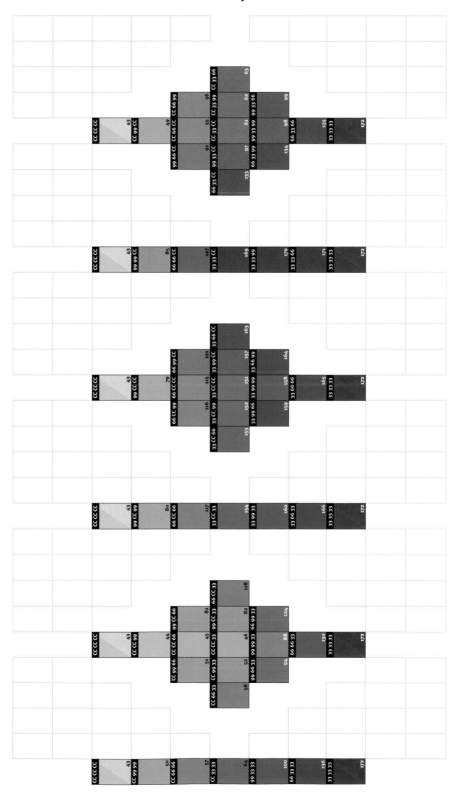

3rd Layer

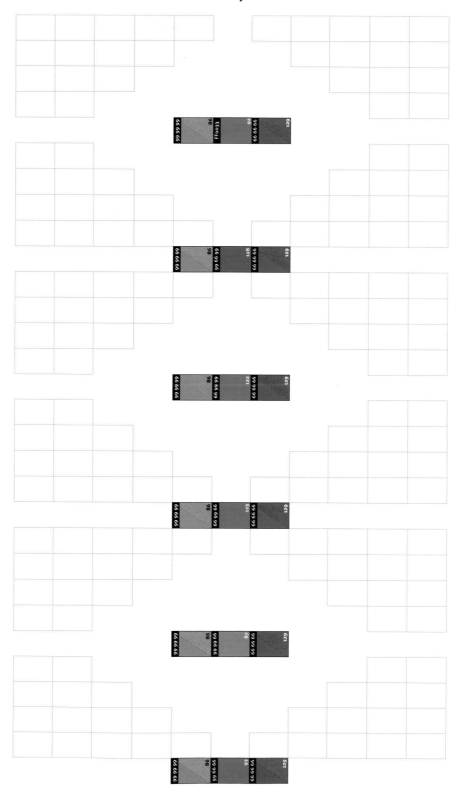